BAWDY LANGUAGE

Everything you always
wanted to do
but were afraid to say

BAWDY LANGUAGE

Everything you always
wanted to do
but were afraid to say

Lawrence Paros

KVETCH PRESS

Published by Kvetch Press, a division of Neurobics,Inc.
Copyright ©2003 by Lawrence Paros
Library of Congress Control Number: 2003092291
ISBN 0-9672005-3-9

The artwork used in the book is primarily in the public domain; including the works of Aubrey Beardsley secured primarily thought the agency of Raganarok Press and the Scriptorium of Austin Texas and Dover Books; the Van Maele works, through original sources comprising his "Satyrical Drawings," and the Rops through original sources and a variety of internet sites. The right to reproduce André Masson's "Erotic Land" was graciously granted through © 2003, Artists' Rights Society (ARS), New York/ADAGP, Paris. Every effort was made to identify and contact all individual copyright holders; any omissions are unintentional.

Parts of this book appeared in an earlier edition as *The Erotic Tongue*, published by Henry Holt and Co. (1988) and Madrona Publishers (1984).

Kvetch books are available at special quantity discounts for bulk purchases for sales promotions, premiums, fund raising, or educational use. Special books or book excerpts can also be created to fit specific needs. For detail, write or telephone Kvetch Press, 11230 Champagne Pt. Lane, N.E., Kirkland, WA 98034, (425) 821-4968. Our website is www.bawdylanguage.com.

Printed in the United States of America

Cover design: Elizabeth Watson

Mea Culpa

To prevent any charge of immorality being brought against this work, the editor begs to observe, that when an indelicate or immodest word has obtruded itself for explanation, he has endeavoured to get rid of it in the most decent manner possible; and none have been admitted but such as either could not be left out, without rendering the work incomplete, or in some measure, compensate by their wit, for the trespass committed on decorum. Indeed respecting this matter, he can with great truth make the same defence that Falstaff ludicrously urges in behalf of one engaged in rebellion, viz, that he did not seek them, but like rebellion in the case instanced, they lay in his way, and he found them.

—Jon Badcok, writing as Jon Bee, *A Dictionary of the Turf, the Ring, the Chase*, 1823

Contents

Book II
Haste Makes Waste: The Book of the Toilette

Preface

Give us your tired, your poor, your much maligned phrases; your shop-worn clichés, and scabrous puns; your huddled masses of vile and ill tempered expressions; your blasphemies, obscenities, and profanities. They have a home here. Here we celebrate the outcasts and the misfits of the literary world. We take them off the street, putting them to creative use that all may see the beauty and magic in them.

The book is a significant advance on earlier efforts. Free of all the restrictive asterisks, the words finally appear as they were meant to be. Events and personalities of the 21st century have been incorporated in the telling, fully reflecting the changes in our language, attitudes, and mores. Dozens of quotations have been added from the contemporary media. There is a comprehensive bibliography and a dual index to assist the reader in locating cited individuals or works. A new layout and design punctuates the text with selective illustrations, opening the book up visually, complementing the printed word, for your enjoyment and use.

I would like to express my appreciation to my sources, especially the late Eric Partridge, the word-master who provided an indispensable series of guides to the language. It was the estimable Partridge who first introduced me to Dr. John S. Farmer and W.E. Henley and their seven-volume *Slang and its Analogues*; Captain Bee (John Babcock) and his *Dictionary of the Turf etc.*; as well as the irascible Francis Grose and his *Classical Dictionary of the Vulgar Tongue*, all of which I have drawn upon quite heavily. A special tip of the cap to various unique websites: Harry Finley's *Museum of Menstrual History and Woman's Health*; Carl Forget's compilation of film quotations at *Sex-Lexis*; and Sidney Noble's *Simple Dictionary for Gay Slang*.

The art work which graces this book draws heavily on the classic works of Aubrey Beardsley, the "satytrical" drawings of Martin van Maele, and the illustrations of Félicien Rops, all now in the public domain. It also includes individual pieces by André Masson, Eugène Le Poitevin, Aristide Maillol, and René Magritte as well as original art by Michelle Couture and Elliott Negin.

Special thanks to Dr. Reinhold Aman for his personal support and encouragement as well as to his precious *Maledicta, The International Journal of Verbal Aggression*—a treasure-house of profanity and for the yeoman job he did in the first round of editing the new edition. Of course, the boys on the street corner and in locker rooms everywhere—without whom this never would have been possible.

The final product owes much to Barbara Noble's typing, the kibitzing of Charlie McCusker, and the stellar work of Joe Wahman, who was responsible for the second round of editing and the initial layout and design; and to Margarite Hargrave who completed the design of the book and readied it for the printer. Special thanks to Dan Levant who first recognized this work and JMP who helped bring it to fruition Ultimately, any errors of commission or omission are solely my own. A special tribute to Anne Depue who represented the new book unsuccessfully to major publishers, receiving nothing for her efforts but dozens of rave reviews and an equal number of rejections.

This book is dedicated to my favorite gadflies: Reinhold Aman, George Carlin, Lenny Bruce, Jon Stewart, and Kinky Friedman, as well as other unnamed free spirits presently in hiding—for their creative imagination, the courage of their vision, and the wonderfully funny mirror they hold up to us. There is no more precious freedom than that of personal expression; thanks to them and others of their ilk, they not only pushed the envelope but reduced it to tatters.

THE EROTIC TONGUE

Words to the Wise

elcome to *Bawdy Language*—everything you wanted to do but were afraid to say. Most people are only slightly familiar with the argot, primarily through a small group of words which polite society considers taboo. These words often evoke a hysterical response; they are symbols of a deeper, darker side of ourselves that we'd rather not acknowledge.

The Moral Majority considers them obscene. Feminists point out their aggressive character and the contempt they show toward women. Children love them, however, finding them useful for dramatic effect, for capturing the attention of the adult world and making it more responsive to their presence. Adults also find occasion to deploy these words as a declaration of independence, an editorial statement against the forces of restraint and convention, or as one commentator described their use, "an oral fart of sorts."

But there is much more to the lexicon than the four-letter words and their friends. We also have technical and scientific words, as well as those that are refined and even border on the poetic.

Euphemisms (from the Greek "to sound well") make up a good part of *Bawdy Language*. They are neat little rhetorical devices by which we cloak otherwise naked thoughts.

We take a taboo word and rephrase it with sufficient taste and delicacy as to make it acceptable. There are many ways to euphemize a word: We can render it somewhat abstract; we can make up words that are longer and more complex, bigger being better; we can understate, use indirection, or simply substitute a foreign word. Euphemisms, however, are not without their problems. They can be uninspiring, unimaginative, and escapist. Another difficulty

Banish the use of those four-letter words
Whose meanings are never obscure.
The Angles and Saxons, those bawdy old birds,
Were vulgar, obscene and impure.
But cherish the use of the weak-kneed phrase
That never quite says what you mean;
Far better to stick with your hypocrite ways
Than be vulgar or coarse or obscene.

    —Anon., *"Ode to Those Four-Letter*
      Words," 20thC

*Nature her custom holds, let shame say
what it will.*

    —*Shakespeare,* Hamlet

is that once having attained a certain popularity, they become so closely identified with the words they are meant to replace that they themselves come to be considered obscene. A euphemism's life is not an easy one. As Ernest Weekly pointed out in 1930 in his *Romance of Words*, the euphemism is by inevitable association doomed from its very birth.

Given the shifting supply of "good" words and the increasing demand for them, it's apparent that what is needed is a comprehensive venereal vocabulary, and we have it in *Bawdy Language*. Here is slang, rich and colorful; euphemisms, flowery, arcane, and remote; and quaint words rescued from Standard English, worthy of recycling. All are suggestive of the romanticism, cynicism, violence, and humor with which the actors, the parts, and the acts themselves have been viewed throughout history.

As noted earlier, it also includes words of the four-letter variety, without which we could not carry on our discourse. They are, after all, an integral and vital part of the lexicon. One of Murphy's Laws of Sex is that "Sex is a three-letter word, but it needs old fashioned four-letter words to convey its full meaning."

Bawdy Language does not eschew their use but instead calls for their judicious application so that readers and listeners might sample the great variety of expressions available without their senses being dulled by saturation.

*To gain the language,
'Tis needful the most immodest word
Be proclaimed and learn'd*
    —*Falstaff in Shakespeare's,*
        Henry IV Part II

Master *Bawdy Language* and you too will be able to talk dirty and command respect. Expand and sophisticate your venereal vocabulary. Obscenity, by itself, is the last refuge of the vulgarian and the crutch of the inarticulate **motherfucker.**

We begin with a survey of our sexuality. Another sex book? Spare us! Given the existing publications, journals, magazines and how-to-do-it manuals, we now have more knowledge than we know what to do with, spelling out in agonizing detail the technique and the joy of it all, and made so simple even a child can do it—with parental discretion, of course. However, there still remains one last step on the road to total sexual enlightenment: writing and talking about it properly. This is no simple task, for sex is easier done than said. To assist us in our quest, we turn to Book One, *The Erotic Tongue.*

The Big F

n the beginning there was **the act**. It was damn good fun but also somewhat scary. It struck fear and generated awe in those who experienced it. They surrounded it with mystery and circumscribed its use. When they later found a way to express themselves, they transferred the dread and awe to the word itself. The word closest to **the act** which reminds them most dramatically of their discomfort is the **Big F**, more commonly known as **fuck**.

I was walking along this fucking fine morning, fucking sun fucking shining away, little country fucking lane, and I meets up with this fucking girl, fucking lovely she was, so we gets into fucking conversation, and I takes her over a fucking gate into a fucking field, and we has sexual intercourse.
—An Australian "rigamarole" quoted by Wayland Young in Eros Denied, *1968*

My Word!

Whence came **fuck**? Nobody really knows. Some think it derives from the acronym for "For Unlawful Carnal Knowledge," maintaining that it was a form of legal shorthand for recording cases of rape and sodomy. Some trace it to the Puritan Massachusetts Bay Colony; others to medieval times. Further investigation, however, shows this hypothesis to be just so much **fucking** nonsense. There is no substantive evidence to support these claims, and it's further unlikely the word was ever an acronym given the many variations in its spelling.

Others argue that the word comes from the sound of the act itself: in and out, in and out, in and out—"ph-ck," "ph-ck," "ph-ck"—sounds only a trained ear could distinguish.

There is no consensus among serious students of the language. They used to believe that the word originated with the French *foutre*, or the Latin *futuere*, a theory now pretty much discounted.

If etymologists appear somewhat aroused by the topic, it's only because there are those who find **fuck**'s origins in the German *ficken*, to "strike, beat, knock, or bang," a theory that converges nicely with the fact that men today **hit on** a woman (make sexual advances). Over the years, synonyms have included **thump, smack, batter, stuff, punch, ram, jolt, cramp, poke,** and **wallop**—leaving little doubt as to how men conceived **the act**. *Ficken*'s roots are the Indo-European *peik*, meaning "enmity, evil,

maliciousness," the *p* becoming an *f* when it moved into the Germanic. It later made us "fickle," descriptive of one who shifts affections, initially in an evil, later a benign, fashion, as well as "fey," which is Old English *faege*, or "fated to die," which John Ciardi suggests may be at the base of the sixteenth-century slang to **die**, meaning to have an **orgasm**.

Ficken makes a strong case, but many now favor the Latin root *pug*, "to prick," giving us the Roman *pugil*, "boxer" or "puncture," and the link between sex and violence. The leading candidate, however, appears to be *firk*. The word was used widely and frequently from the eleventh through the seventeenth centuries, and was defined as "a sharp blow, or a thrust." It also meant "to stir up, cheat, move about briskly, to be frisky or jiggish."

There's also the Middle Dutch *fokken* and the Swedish dialect's *focka*, both of which signified thrusting and pushing as well as **copulation**, further pairing **sex** with force. While a small minority find its derivation in the Greek word *phuteo* for "sowing, planting, or begetting."

Any way you look at it, **fuck** appears to be a many-sided thing—the beginning of life, inconstancy, and random violence.

Written Off

Fuck was first recorded in the late fifteenth-century poem "Flen flyys," where it appears with a Latin inflection in alphabetically coded form. The sentence reads in translation: "They (the Carmelite friars of Cambridge, England) are not in heaven because they **fuck** the wives of Ely (a town near Cambridge)." The word later made the rounds of several sixteenth-century Scottish poems, and then, with the exception of the writings of the great seventeenth-century lech John Wilmot, Earl of Rochester (usually referred to as "Rochester"), it went underground. As late as the 1940s, writers frantically searched for cheap substitutes.[1] Norman Mailer relied on **fug** in *The Naked and the Dead* (1948). Not everyone was comfortable with the choice. On meeting Mailer for the first time, Tallulah Bankhead said, "I know who you are. You're the man who doesn't know how to spell **fuck**."

It wasn't until 1951 that the spelling of **fuck** was finally mastered, thanks to the ruling by the U.S. Supreme Court on *Lady Chatterley's Lover*. This gave the word new life. James Jones included it some 258 times in his original manuscript of *From Here to Eternity*, published that same year, though his editor, showing some restraint, edited it down to a mere 50. Overnight the word became the darling of contemporary novelists, leaving us all wondering what it was that people did prior to D.H. Lawrence. The literary world had learned how to **fuck** with a vengeance.[2]

If you had a million years to do it in, you couldn't rub out even half of the "fuck you" signs in the world.

—Catcher in the Rye, *J.D.Salinger*

Love at First Cite

Fuck's inclusion in dictionaries was also tortured and uneven. It first appeared in 1598 in Florio's English-Italian Dictionary, *A Worlde of Wordes*, but it wasn't until 1671 in a dictionary edited by one Steven Skinner that the word received an entry of its own in correct alphabetical order. What then followed was a series of erratic placements. Nathaniel Bailey (c. 1721) identified it as "a term used of a goat." John Ash (1775) called it "a low, vulgar word...to have to do with a woman." Francis Grose's *Classical Dictionary of the Vulgar Tongue*, published in 1785, featured a "f__k duck," the man who had care of the poultry aboard a ship of war. The word surfaced briefly in John Farmer and W.E. Henley's multi-volume *Slang and its Analogues*, a nineteenth-century survey of the common tongue, but disappeared from the single-volume abridgement.

You can search through most popular dictionaries of the nineteenth and twentieth centuries and nary a **fuck** will you find. It is absent from H.L. Mencken's masterful work on the American language. For years you couldn't find it in Webster's *New International Dictionary* or in the *Oxford English Dictionary*—the OED—the most comprehensive work on the language, one that prides itself on being "conceived in a scientific spirit." Makes one wonder, doesn't it, how they could care so deeply about words and at the same time not really give a **fuck**.

Not until the 1960s and '70s did the dictionary-makers finally acquiesce. **The Big F**'s formal coming out included *The Penguin Dictionary* (1965), *The American Heritage Dictionary* (1969), and at last the esteemed OED, in its 1972 supplement.[3]

By then, "nice" people had forgotten how to **fuck**, and the word had become our principal four-letter outcast. Mere mention of it caused flesh to creep and cheeks to flush. Few spoke of it openly.[4] Only the kids were telling it like it **fuckin'** is. And for them it was **beautifuckingful**, **far fuckin' out**, and **outta fuckin' sight**.

A Word of Caution

Unwelcome both at home and at work, many of the kids took the **Big F** to the streets. White kids simply expanded on **fuck**, distinguishing between the **fucker**, who initiated the act and the **fuckee**, the recipient.[5] They created the **fuckaholic** or **fuck freak**, one said to be **fuckstruck**, i.e., addicted to **sexual intercourse**. Not to be taken lightly was the supreme **fuckster**, one particularly adept at the act, constantly on the lookout for **fuckable** females, those deemed sexually ripe. There was also his female counterpart, the **fuckstress**. Both fancied themselves **fuckish**, always ready for it, and **fucksome**, sexually desirable. Obsessed with it also? Get thee to a **fuckery** (a **whorehouse**).

Black kids, on the other hand, created a whole new art form. They began with the **mean motherfucker**, a legendary figure who attained prominence in the sixties, as in **up against the wall, motherfucker!**

Before very long, its ranks swelled to include the **jive motherfucker**, the **dirty motherfucker**, and the exotic **muh-fuckah**. This is to say nothing of your basic, no-frills **mother** (also **mutha**).

Generally considered the worst forms of verbal abuse, these expressions can also be terms of respect, as when one street-corner man wishes to pay homage to another's toughness. They should, however, only be used with great care, or you too could end up calling for yo mamma. [5]

Fighting Words

It was on the battlefield where the **fuck** found itself most at home and was accorded the greatest respect. Young men who had been taught to eschew the **Big F** in word and deed because of its obscene nature were suddenly confronted with a greater obscenity—war. Knowing no other way to describe the **screwed-up** nature of things, they reached down into their souls and resurrected the forbidden **fuck**. Compelled to express the depth of their physical and mental misery, they truly felt **fucked and far from home**.

The experience repeated itself in World War II with appropriate comments about the military.[6] The original military **fuck-up** occurred in the British army around 1939 as an **MFU**, evolving into the great all-purpose **SNAFU (Situation Normal, All Fucked Up)** as well as a variety of mutant offshoots.[7]

The only phrase to survive the war and make its way into polite society was the **SNAFU**, though in a slightly "fouled-up" form. A survey of the political and social scene, however, shows things **SUSFU (Situation Unchanged, Still Fucked Up)**. A comment to which one can only add—**fuckin' A!** ("absolutely correct!" or "extremely good").

A Many-splendored Thing

Most people are familiar only with **fuck**'s violent side; few appreciate its complex character. **Fuck** is nature's all-purpose word, able to express every mood and capture the tenor of every occasion.[8] The only thing it isn't is simple, as with this **fuckin'** business.

Given the proper inflection, the word can express an entire range of sentiments:

Confusion:	**What the fuck?**
Despair and dismay:	**Fucked again**, or **truly fucked**.
Liberation:	**What the fuck!**

Tell Mr. Ross that I'm too fucking busy and vice versa.

—*Dorothy Parker, in response to a call from her editor*

Helplessness:	**Fucked by the fickle finger of fate.**
Concern:	**Doesn't anyone give a fuck?**
Surprise, dismissal, or rejection, with the help of various objects:	Oneself—**Fuck me!** Inanimate object—**Fuck it!** Helpless creature—**Fuck a duck!**
Futility:	**What the fuck?** or **Who gives a fuck anyway?**
Absence of meaningful action:	**Fucking around (about)**, or **Fucking off.**

Though it is anatomically **imfuckingpossible**, people constantly encourage others to go **fuck themselves**. They criticize books such as this as **unfuckingbelieveable, irrefuckingsponsible, outfuckingrageous** and **unfuckingrespectable**—though the author is just **fucking with their minds**. Knowing not what else to do, they offer to end the confusion by simply **getting the fuck out of here.**

> Joe (Larry Miller): How about a goodnight **fuck**?
> Emily (Elizabeth McGovern): Goodnight, **fuck**!
> —*The Favor*, 1992

Take My Word for IT

When we summarily dismissed **fuck** from our working vocabulary, we added more than 1,500 expressions to take its place. Eric Partridge, the noted lexicographer, remarked as to how the large number of phrases "bear witness to the fertility of the English language and to the enthusiastic English participation in the universal fascination of the creative act." Other critics saw the dismissal as a form of cowardice and hypocrisy.

Many of the substitute terms are vivid and expressive, oft-times ingenious. But none has proved more popular and inoffensive than **doing it**. For years everyone was **doing it, doing it, doing it**, and everyone knew exactly what **it** meant. Occasionally there was a screw-up, and somebody mistakenly took out the garbage, but for the most part, **it** came off as intended.

In 1934 the censors declared **doing it** "too suggestive" and banned **it, doing**, and **doing it** from the airwaves. This low blow deprived Rudy Vallee of the right to sing his greatest stage and radio hits, including "Let's Do It," "Do It Again," and "You Do Something to Me." Today, America is again **doing it**, with gusto. Of all the expressions we have for **the act**, the inarticulate favor **doing it** over all the others. Joan Rivers assured women everywhere that there's really nothing to **it**, "Just close your eyes, lie back, and pretend you're having an operation."

It couldn't be easier.

> *This is the way we say it in our time.*
> *When carnal and unmarried love is meant:*
> *I mean we do not make the double back,*
> *Or die: We sleep together. We conjugate.*
> —Winfield Townley Scott,
> "Sonnet XV," c. 1940

Though a lady repel your advance, she'll be kind
Just as long as you intimate what's on your mind.
You may tell her you're hungry, you need to be
*   swung,*
You may mention the ashes that need to be hauled,
Put the lid on her sauce pan, but don't be too bold;
For the moment you're forthright, get ready to
*   duck—*
For the girl isn't born yet who'll stand for "Let's
*   fuck!"*
*   —"Ode to Those Four-Letter Words"*

Do It Yourself

Doctors **do it** with patience
Lawyers **do it** briefly
Accountants **do it** figuratively
Publishers **do it** periodically

_____ **do it** _____

_____ **do it** _____

_____ **do it** _____

Dante **did it** divinely
Marx **did it** in a revolting fashion
Michelangelo **did it** on the ceiling
Moses **did it** on the rush
Sinatra **did it** his way

_____ **did it** _____

_____ **did it** _____

Making Do

In polite society they have their own ways of **doing it**, albeit in a drab and somewhat colorless fashion.

None is more popular than **making love**. Couples have been "making love" in the sense of paying court or wooing one another since 1580. They've been **making love** as we **do it** since around 1950, a meaning that wasn't even formally recognized in our dictionaries until 1976.

Another recent favorite is **having sex**, which has been used since the late nineteen-twenties or thirties. **Sex** comes from the Latin *secare*, "to cut or divide," and we first used the word to designate the two major categories of humanity we have come to know and love as male and female. According to Greek mythology, we began life as a perfect four-armed, four-legged he/she unit. Unfortunately, we were so taken with ourselves as works of art that our manner offended the mighty Zeus. He cut us down to size, severing us into two separate entities.

We later used the word **sex** not only for dividing the sexes, but to refer to qualities of being male or female. Over time we assigned specific attributes to each category. These distinctions were dutifully recorded in the esteemed OED, making it all very official. The male was described as "the better" and "the sterner" sex; the female as "the fairer," "the gentler," "the softer," "the weaker," and "the devout" sex. Women were also "the second" sex. For a period of time between the sixteenth and seventeenth centuries, when people spoke of "the sex," they had women in mind.

We obviously had a problem, and we called on the word itself to bridge the gap between the sexes. In the twentieth century we began to use **sex** to describe the means of forging a new togetherness, a way of helping us get our act together. Today, when we use the word **sex**, it generally refers to that unifying process.

Being with a woman often said it all, underscoring the closeness or coziness in the act. And there is no one closer than our **relations** (19thC). Men and women are also said to **be familiar with** (15thC) or be **on familiar terms with** one another. Before the fifteenth century some even considered them **overfamiliar**.

But such **familiarity** breeds **intimacy** nowadays. That began around 1884, with **people being intimate with each other**. Today, there is talk of people being **intimate** or **on intimate terms**. The nice part about it is you can also have intimates without necessarily **fucking** them.

I've only slept with the men I've been married to. How many women can make that claim?
—Elizabeth Taylor

You Should Know Better

You can't get any more **intimate** than by **spending the night with someone** or **sleeping with them**. We're been **sleeping with each other** that way since the ninth century, and celebrated it as such in poetry from Chaucer to Whitman. **Sleeping with somebody**, however, is not without its critics. Allan Sherman in *Rape of the A*P*E** noted, "Since time began nobody has been able to **copulate** while asleep. Even if it were possible it would be impolite."

It was especially easy to be **intimate** in the Old Testament. In those days all the more important people seemed to **know each other**. Of course **Knowing** a person was synonymous with **fucking** them, and the word was applied to both sexes. Men **knew** women, and women **knew** men. Later, we only had **knowledge of a woman** (c. 1425), where to **know** her was to love her. Knowing a man, however, came to count for very little, and self-knowledge, not at all.

A little knowledge continued to be a very dangerous thing. We eventually gained **carnal knowledge** (c. 1686), from the Latin *carnus*, "meat," which made it possible for us to know each other in the flesh, advanced students ostensibly being able to distinguish between eye of the round and chuck.

In God We Trust

They didn't know everything, however. The all-time Biblical favorite remained **to go in unto**, a phrase that appears liberally throughout the Old Testament. There are dozens of reference to it, as when, for example, Onan **went unto his brother's wife**. The expression is a real bell-ringer. It makes **the act** sound as romantic as pulling your car into your neighbor's garage.

You might not have guessed it from the Old Testament, but for the Jews, **fucking** has always been a matter of **doing the agreeable** (19thC)—no guilt, no pain, no anxiety. Good **sex** was considered a *mitzvah*, an exemplary deed. The most pious reserved Friday night for **doing it** with their wives, choosing the most holy day, the Sabbath, to perform this most sacred and blessed act.

Though they took seriously the injunction to multiply and be fruitful, Jews never sought to disguise or suppress the pleasure or its benefits. According to one Talmudic scholar, "It dissolves melancholy, calms bad temper and gladdens the soul... it cleanses the body...heightens heavy-headedness, and brightens the eyes...but in moderation." Enjoy! Enjoy! Take two and call me in the morning.

We're Cross with You

The Christian attitude toward **sex**, on the other hand, left everything to be desired.[9] It originated with the Church leaders and authorities, who did much to shape and influence future attitudes on the topic.

Each came at it differently. St. Augustine believed it a problem that began in Eden when we first unleashed our **concupiscence** (from the Latin for "to desire eagerly"), a strong and unnatural appetite previously subject to the dictates of the will, and he was most troubled by the lack of control that accompanied **the act**. Pope Gregory I was angered more by **the act** itself and that which impelled it than by the *voluptus carne*, the "pleasure of the flesh" which accompanied it and obscured its true purpose—**procreation**. For St. Thomas Aquinas, **sex** primarily offended his sense of orderliness, being contrary to the dictates of reason.

Before you could say "hellsfire, brimstone, and damnation," people began feeling guilt. Soon they found themselves **doing the naughty** (19thC), feeling naughtiness in the pleasure prior to, during, and subsequent to **the act**.[10] The medieval Church worked hard to eliminate guilt by simply cutting down on the number of occasions on which one might feel pleasure. It recommended abstinence on Thursdays in memory of the capture of Jesus; on Fridays in memory of his death; on Saturdays in honor of the Virgin Mary; on Sundays in memory of the Resurrection; and on Mondays in commemoration of the departed souls. **The act** was also forbidden forty days before Pentecost and Christmas, and was never to be performed on special feast days or during Lent. Thus was born the appointment book.

Those who made it dressed for the occasion. They donned the medieval **chemise cagoule**, a plain shift that totally covered the female save for a suitably placed hole through which the **penis** could perform its work, effectively generating new sinners for the Church to save.

Christianity has done a great deal for love by making a sin of it.

—Anatole France

Cleaning Up Your Act

It was easy for the Church to convince people that **sex** was a dirty business. Reinforced by the proximity of the sexual parts to, and their close association with, the process of elimination of waste, it was only a matter of time before sex came to be identified with the elimination process—a way of transferring from one individual to another such waste matter as may have accumulated in one's body.

Church authorities loved the image. It was perfect. Man eliminated into woman, and her **vagina** was the repository for his filth. This even sanctioned the role the **prostitute** played, likening her to a common sewer who helping carry away man's garbage. Chaucer's Parson wrote of **whores** "that must be likened to a common **gong** (a **toilet**) where men purged their **ordure**."

The theme was picked up in the language. Especially popular during the 1930s was the practice of **getting one's ashes hauled**.[11] A not unnatural thing, for when fires are raging, ashes are the natural residue. Someone has to remove them. After all, neatness counts, even in sex. It's another bond between sexual release and personal hygiene.

You'll find variations of this in contemporary blues songs, with references to how **my garbage can is overflowing** and requests to please **empty my trash**. We speak of **sex** as **easing oneself** (20thC), and **doing one's business** (20thC). Some even refer to **it** as **number three** (20thC), an apparent also-ran behind numbers one and two, **pissing** and **shitting** respectively.

Hundreds of years after Chaucer's Parson, a boy in Sylvia Plath's *The Bell Jar* described his first sexual experience with a **whore** being "as boring as going to the toilet." Phillip Wylie in *Opus 21* recounts how books of advice for young men attaining the age of desire sought to dissuade them from seeking the company of **prostitutes**. They employed not the toilet but the bathtub to make their point, asking indignantly, "Would you walk into a cheap hotel, find that the stranger before you had left the tub filled with dirty bath water, and immerse yourself in it?"

Sex is great, but it's really difficult to keep it clean.

Latin Lovers

As dirty as **it** is, men of the cloth love to talk about **doing it**. They are especially good at catching others in **the act**—but always in Latin. They never catch you **fucking**, only **copulating**, **fornicating**, **having conjugal relations**, or engaged in **coitus**. When not so occupied, you can find them sitting in judgment as to whether a marriage has indeed been **consummated**.

Copulation or **coupling** comes from the Latin *copulatus*, "being

Inter faeces et urinem nascimur.
We are born between fees and urine.
—St. Augustine

Love has pitched her mansion in the place of excrement.
—W.B. Yeats

linked or tied together"—a form of **sexual union**. *Conjugal* means "to join with," from *jugam*, "the yoke" (as many have experienced it). **Fornicate** (before 1300) originates with the *fornices*, the dark archways under the Roman coliseums where **ladies of loose morals** used to ply their trade. When many of the brothels of Rome later went underground, they became identified as *fornices*, making the goings-on into **fornication** and its practitioners into **fornicators**.

When in **coitus** or practicing **coition** couples simply "went together" (from the Latin *co* and *ire*). **Consummation** is sometimes the highest form (*summa*) of togetherness (*con*), thus saying it all as far as the Church was concerned.

You're An Animal!

The entire exercise, however, was not without value. Thanks to Christianity we uncovered our bestial nature. We were further assisted by the animals themselves. Sheep **tupped** (c. 1549), horses **covered** (c. 1535), birds **trod** (before 1250), foxes were **at clicket** (17th–18thC), dogs were **in line**, and deer and cats were **rutting**. It all sounded so good that before you knew it, we had appropriated these same expressions for ourselves. There we were, **bulling** (18thC), **hogging** (19thC), and **tomming** (19thC).

While the boars **served** (c.1577) sows; the bulls **served** cows, and the studs **served** mares, men and women were **in the service of Venus** (14thC). The quality of the service being as excellent as it was, it was only a matter of time before we sought to capture the moment in prose. Among the best examples of literary **service** is the scene in *Othello*, where Iago warns Brabantio that Othello and Desdemona are **getting it on** together.

> …Even now, now, very now,
> an old black ram is tupping
> your white ewe…
> You'll have your daughter covered
> With a Barbary horse
> Your daughter and the Moor are now
> Making the beast with two backs.

Standing Tall in the Saddle

Surely it was no surprise, then, to find ourselves **horsing around** (19thC), **playing at stallions and mares** (c. 1850). Some, however, put as much effort into preparation as in the ride itself. Many a man had to first **tether his nag** (17thC), **water his nag, take Nebuchadnezer out to grass**, and **play at stable my naggie** (19thC).

Ride as **fuck** was first recorded before 1250 and was Standard

Quoth she, "What is this so still and warm?"
"'Tis Ball, my nag, he will do you no harm."
"But what is this hangs under his chin?"
"'Tis his bag he puts his provender in."
Quoth he, "What is this?"
Quoth she, "'Tis a well where Ball, your nag, can drink his fill."
"But what if my nag should chance to fall in?"
"Catch hold of the grass that grows on the slip brim."
"But what if the grass should chance to fail?"
"Shove him in by the head, pull him out by the tail."

—Thomas D'Urfey, "The Trooper," in Songs of Wit and Mirth or Pills to Purge Melancholy, 1719

English for **the act** until around 1780. Man first **rode**, and later woman **got** or **had a ride** (19thC). For many it was a ride to remember. In *Antony and Cleopatra*, The Egyptian queen, thinking of her love far away at war, dreamily remarks, "O happy horse to bear the weight of Antony."

In a more contemporary vein, it was the topic of conversation between James Bond (Roger Moore) and Jenny Flex (Alison Doody) in the 1985 film, *A View to A Kill*: Bond: " I take it you spend quite a bit of time in the saddle." Flex: "Yes, I love an early ride." Bond: I'm an early rider myself."

There is nothing complex about **riding**. The man generally **mounts** (c. 1592) or **does a mount** and **rides the mare** (c. 1850), and the woman, well... But, as Dillard points out, in the black lexicon, **ride** refers with equal frequency to either sex in the active role. It's also been known to take many a strange turn. As noted by John Dryden in *Juvenal*, " How many boys that pedagogue can **ride**."

It's all good clean fun, but being with your neighbor's wife left you open to the charge of **riding in another man's saddle**, the **saddle** long having stood for the female **pudendum**.

My father was no jockey, but he sure taught me how to ride;
He said first in the middle, then you swing from side to side.
—Quoted in Le Roi Jones,
Blues People, c. 1963

Autoeroticism

The days of the horse and the **lascivious carriage** are over.[12] In its place we now have a **classy chassis** (c. 1940 for a well-proportioned female) and an entire sub-vocabulary to help maintain it, including the **valve job** (20thC, from the **vulva**), a **body job**, and a **lubrication**. What better place to **get your oil changed** than at your local **service station**? The basic parts include the **piston (rod)**, the **connecting rod** (both 20thC), and the **coupling pin** (19th–20thC).

It's all part of the American male's **sex drive** (1960s) —his all consuming love affair with things automotive.[13] He expresses his devotion to his vehicle by having it properly serviced—maintenance and repair work being done on it regularly. He **services** (1960s) his woman by **fucking** her when the mood hits. Everyone knows he caresses and pamper his car like a favorite mistress—or is it the other way around? e.e. cummings couldn't have agreed more

When my baby go to bed,
It shines like a morning star.
When I crawl in the middle,
It rides me like a Cadillac car.
—George Bill, "Scary Day Blues,"
early 20thC

...(having thoroughly oiled the universal
joint tested my gas felt of
her radiator made sure her springs were O.

K.) i went right to it flooded-the-carburetor cranked her

up, slipped the
clutch...

—from "she being Brand," 1926

He shakes my ashes
Greases my griddle
Churns my butter
Strokes my fiddle
My man is such a handy man
He flaps my flapjacks
Cleans up the table
Feeds the horses
In my stable
My man is such a handy man
Sometimes he's up
Long before dawn
Busy trimming the edges off of my lawn
My man is such a handy man
　　—Young Indian Jones and the
　　　Mystery of the Blues, *1992*

Making History

Its detractors could take nothing away from **it**s proud history. From time immemorial, **it** was **what mother did before me** and **what Eve did with Adam**. The commonfolk have been at **it** for centuries: **quiffing** (18th–20thC), **tiffing** (late 18th–early 19thC), **niggling** (c. 1465–1820), **snizzling** (c. 1923), **foining** (late 16th–17thC), **nubbing** (18th–early 19thC), and **nugging** (late 11th–mid 17thC).

When not so engaged you'd find them **jiggling** (c. 1845), **bouncing** (late 19thC), **shaking** (verb, 16thC; noun, c. 1860), and **humping** (c. 1760–1850). Taking great pains to be anatomically correct, they've been **belly-bumping, tummy-tickling, rump-splitting** (all 19thC), **joining faces**, and **rubbing bacons**.

Back in 1398, they loved to **swive**. Four hundred years later, they were **shagging**, originally an innocent expression for just "shaking about."[14]

The oldest expression in English for the **tickle-tail function** (17th–20thC) is to **sard** (c. 950) as in the old Nottingham saying, "Go teach your granddam to **sard**!"—a rank insult of the times and possibly the first recorded example of the "dozens," a remark somewhat equivalent to our own, "Your mother swims out to meet troopships!"

Doing Unto Others

Originally, **it** was just a **job** (16thC)—good work if you could get it. Over time, it came to be viewed as an act of charity, doing for those unable to do for themselves, as **to do a woman's job for her** (c. 1850). When woman's work was synonymous with the kitchen, one could **get her a handle for the broom** (18thC), **give her canister a rattle** (Robert Burns), **do some ladies' tailoring** (C. 1815), or **mend her kettle** (18thC).

Doing a woman's job is not without problems. It requires skill, dexterity, and determination. Many a fellow has started a **job** he later couldn't finish.

For many it's been a real **grind** (late 16thC), from the movement involved, giving us his **grinding tool**, her **grindstone**, and the **grinding horse** (all 19thC). One actively disposed to **the act** was said to be **on the grind** (19th–20thC). You'll find numerous references to **grinding** in books and songs from bawdy Restoration ballads to twentieth-century blues. Four centuries ago it was said,

　　Digbie's lady takes it ill,
　　that her lord grind not at her mill.
　　　　—Ladies' Parliament, 1647

By the 1930's, things improved, and Bessie Smith was singing,

> The woman has a grinder,
> The best one [she] could find.
> The man grinds her coffee,
> 'Cause he has a brand new grind.

Grinding proved so enjoyable it soon had a partner. Around 1669 **bumping** entered the language as a synonym for **copulation**. As noted by Mencken, in the days of burlesque, when a girl **bumped** she simulated the act by thrusting her hips forward. When she'd **grind** she'd "revolve her backside." Together they created the **bump and grind** (20thC).[15]

Write On!

Onward and upward, **it** soon evolved from a real **grind** into the highest form of communication. Once **it** entailed **conversation** (from the Latin *conversare*, "to keep company with") and **correspondence** (both 19thC). Before the era of the ballpoint pen, when a boss **did it** with his secretary or the clerical help, he **dipped his pen in the office ink** (20thC). On occasion, he didn't have the resources to finish his message. His **ink was run, his pen was done** (c. 1650). Alas, there was **no lead in his pencil**. Looking for assistance, junior executives today **take a dip in the secretarial pool**, hoping for some **shorthand service** (both 1990s).

Giving Them the Business

Words are cheap in a world based on money and politics, making it inevitable that we would have both **sexual commerce** and **business** in the nineteenth century. "Intercourse" originally referred to the normal flow of communications and commercial transactions between localities. But in 1798 we also discovered **sexual intercourse**. It proved so popular that **intercourse** developed a **traffic** of its own.

Since then most **traffic** has not been sexual, though an interesting intersection of the two meanings occurred during the nineteen-sixties when, for promotional purposes, Ralph Ginzburg had his magazine *Eros* postmarked from Intercourse, Pennsylvania— thereby putting the **Big F**'s stamp on the U.S. mails.

The Body Politic

Politically, most know Congress as a serious assembly or gathering of persons, but it's also been described as **amorous** and **sexual**

The Democrats are doing it to their secretaries, and the Republicans are doing it to the country.
—Joan Mondale

(16th–19thC). Few argued with the definition, as did James Boswell, who wrote in his journal, "I picked up a fresh, agreeable young girl called Alice Gibbs and we had a very agreeable **congress**."

Others also have found **congress** agreeable and amorous. The more famous congressional **liaisons** have included Elizabeth Ray with Representative Wayne Hays, and Fanny Foxe with Wilbur Mills. It appears that the highest position to which every office-holder aspires is that same **congress**. It is synonymous with the treatment given the American people by that body, as well as their extracurricular activities.

Do you know where your senator is tonight?

Pretty Please

When *The New York Times* and other august publications report such goings-on, they often describe them as **sexual favors** or plain **favors**. **Favors** traditionally are **granted** or **bestowed, lavished upon**, or **yielded**. William Safire, the columnist and wordsmith, defines such **favors** as the hats, bonbons, noise-makers and other souvenirs one brings back from an orgy.

Favors can be granted by both sexes. For a time, it was men who **did** or **worked their kind, did the act** or **deed** (c. 1230), or **did a kindness** (18th–20thC), but for the most part, it's been women who have extended every courtesy, helping make **courtesans** out of many of them. Often they've given everything save the final one. Moll Flanders proudly reported, "Though he took these freedoms with me, it did not go to that which they call the last favor." Makes you wonder, doesn't it, that **sex** might indeed be a favor of sorts.

Favors are generally helpful, but **connections** also help. Boswell reported trying to track down a certain "Signor Gonorrhea," finally narrowing his search to one of his many **paramours**. Confronting her with his condition, he then argued with her, pointing out, "Madam, I have had no **connections** with any woman but you these two months." As Boswell's experience reminds us, it's sometimes as important to miss **connections** as to make them.

Nice of You to Drop In

If all this seems too serious, perhaps you should simply treat it as fun. In *Gargantua and Pantagruel*, Rabelais had Grangouisier and Gargamell **doing the two-backed beast** together "joyfully **rubbing their bacon** against one another."

Shakespeare's characters **made the beast with two backs** and **groped for trout in the particular river**, an aspect of the sport that somehow eluded Sir Isaac Walton and most High School English teachers. More offbeat recreation had man **burying** or **dip-**

Fanny: There are words which sound better and are often used before company, instead of "swiving" and "fucking," which is too gross and downright bawdery, fit only to be used among dissolute persons. To avoid scandal, men modestly say, "I kissed her, made much of her, received a favor from her," or the like.

—The School of Venus, or The Ladies Delight Reduced into Rules of Practice, 1744

Well, it is sort of a favor. Isn't it? I mean when a girl lets you kiss her and, you know, go on from there—feel her up and you know, the rest of it—go all the way, and the rest of it. I mean, isn't it a favor? What's in it for her? I mean if she's not getting paid or anything?

—Jules Feiffer, Carnal Knowledge, 1971

These two did often do the two-backed beast together...in so far that at last she became great with child.

—François Rabelais, translated by Sir Thomas Urquhart, 1653

ping his wick (c. 1850). A contemporary parallel is **dunking the love muscle** (20thC), a great phrase that makes **the act** sound as if it were something akin to bobbing for apples.

Games People Play

Sexual athletes, front and center! It's time for **the first game ever played**, **the sport of Venus** (19thC).

It's the sport of the masses, **the national indoor sport** (20thC), **the old ballgame** (20thC), a game of inches where every young man **pitches woo** (1920s) and dreams of making a **hit** (mid 20thC).

It features something for everyone. For the young moderns there's **jogging**, **pole-vaulting** (both 18th–19thC), **broad-jumping**, **a bit of bouncy-bouncy**, and a little **one-on-one** (all 20thC), while historical buffs can play at **pushpin** (17th–18thC), **take a turn on the aphrodisiacal tennis court**, or opt for **a spot of Cupid's archery** (both 19thC).

You don't need a cast of thousands, either, only **a little o' the one with t'other** (18th–20thC). And it's so simple anyone can **do it**, merely a little **in-and-in** (17th–early 19thC) or some **in-and-out** (17thC).

Tennis Anyone?

Tennis? Not when you can play at

> **Two-handed Put** (18th–early 19thC)
> **Pully-Hauly** (late 18thC)
> **Pickle-Me-Tickle-Me** (mid 17th–18thC)
> **Cuddle-My-Cuddle** (D'Urfey)

or have

> **A Rootle**
> **A Poopnoddy**
> **A Squeeze and a Squirt** (all 19thC).

Le sporte is a French colloquialism for **fucking**—a game in which there is always a winner, **where you can lose the match and still pocket the stakes** (18thC). By mid twentieth century it definitely was not a matter of winning or losing—or even how you played the game—but simply a matter of **scoring**. Australians favored **a bit of socc'er**, the goal being to score between the posts. While American men strove to **hit a home run**, though most struggled to get to first base.

Take a Card, Any Card

If you're not up for sports, perhaps you'd settle for a quiet game of cards—maybe a somewhat unusual game called **Irish Whist**

AUBREY
BEARDSLEY

There hath a question been of late
Among the youthful sort;
What pastime is the pleasantest
And what the sweetest sport?
And it hath been adjudged
As well by great and small
That of all the pastimes none is like to
Uptails all.

—Thomas D'Urfey, "Uptails All,"
in Songs of Wit and Mirth, *1719*

(19thC). The woman **plays the jack against the ace**, and the **jack takes the ace**.

Jack has long been synonymous with the **he-thing**, and the **ace** (particularly **the ace of spades**) for more than three centuries has been identified with the female counterpart, from the shape and color of the **pubic hair**. When **jack takes the ace** the game is over—nothing else remains to be played.

All That Jazz

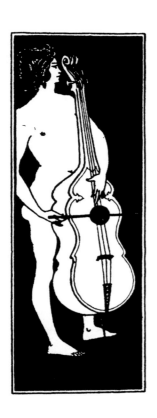

Cards aren't your bag, either? We could always **make beautiful music together**, starting with a little **fiddling about** (17thC, "caressing familiarly"), going on to some **strumming** (c. 1780) and some **tromboning** (late 1880s). The classic blend of sex and music is **jazz**, a popular expression from the thirties and forties for **doing it**—like the music, emotional, rhythmic, and improvisational. David Dalby, an authority on the African element in American English, finds the word's roots in *jas* and *jasy*, the core of which is "to speed up, excite, exaggerate, or act in an unrestrained way." The first jazz in this country was performed by black musicians in **bawdy houses**, firmly establishing the link between the music and **sex**. Streetwalkers later approached prospective customers with the line, "Hey, big boy, what about some **jazz** tonight?"

Jam and **jam session** have also been used in the same way. A lovelorn column in a British newspaper featured the following advice: "Quicker than a penguin sliding down an icicle, that's how quickly a **necking** session can turn into a **jam session**. And you're the one in a jam."

R&R

"Just so much jazz," you say. Perhaps you'd rather rock and roll, with thanks again to the black community. Dillard's study of the Blues led him to conclude that **rocking** correlated with the "less strenuous" activity identified with the female during **sex** and **rolling**, with the more violent actions of the male, especially the heightened activity just before or during **orgasm**. At least one such performer belied the traditional notion of just "rolling with it."

> I ain't tired of rollin'
> But I got so long.
> Mama I'm tired a rollin'
> But my time ain't long.
> When I roll my long time, mama, back East I'm goin',
> I say, I work so long so they call me rollin' stone.
> I been rollin' all night long;
> You can call it stayin', but I call it gone.
>
> —Lightnin' Hopkins Strums the Blues

Invitation to the Dance

Oscar Wilde called dance "a vertical expression of a horizontal urge." And a Gene Kelly you don't have to be to do the **mattress jig** (18th–19thC), the **reel o'Stumpie** (Scot., 18th–20thC), the **blanket hornpipe** (c. 1810), or the **four-legged frolic** (c. 1850).

The more experienced do the routine **box-step** (20thC) or the **matrimonial polka** (c. 1850). They're danced best to some **sheet music** (19th–20thC) or to the **tune of the shaking of the sheets together**—an old English country melody. Novices should take things a step at a time, They should never be rushed. It helps to think of dancing cheek to cheek as a form of floor play.

We have dance steps and sexual positions. Wayland Young in *Eros Denied* comments that both dancing and **fucking** are not a series of positions but, rather, a flow of movement. He considered the fact that we refer to sexual positions in this context the result of a blocked imagination.[16]

Sukey that danced with the cushion,
An hour from the room had been gone;
And Barnaby knew by her blushing
That some other dance had been done.
　　　—Thomas D'Urfey, "The Winchester
　　　　Wedding,"
　　　　in Songs of Wit and Mirth, *1719*

Tips of the Tongue

1. As the word most frequently exorcised from the airwaves, **bleeping**'s long been a favorite. Some found comfort in **fuck**'s abbreviated form, settling for **the F word**, an **effing** or an **f-ing**. Lord Byron gave a **fuhlke** (c.1820 of Don Juan) about it. Others **frigged**. As noted earlier, **frig** was originally a **rub-off**, but by the nineteenth century had graduated to the **Big F**. However, most people today prefer using it in a violent rather than a procreative sense, as in **frig it!** the boss **frigged** us! and you **friggin'** so and so. Those seeking comic relief and not taking any of it seriously, fall back on the Yiddish and simply **futz** around.

2. The silver screen took even longer. It wasn't until 1971, in *The Owl and the Pussycat* that Barbara Streisand became the first female superstar to say **fuck** in a major motion picture. Off the set, however, its use was commonplace. During the filming of *The Prince and the Showgirl* (1957), Laurence Olivier chided Marilyn Monroe for constantly arriving late, asking her, "Why can't you get here on time for **fuck**'s sake?" To which she replied, "Oh do they have that word in England too?"

3. **Fuck** attained full respectability in 1995 when Jesse Sheidlower, a lexicographer from Cambridge and editor at Random House published *The F-Word*. It is probably "the first dictionary devoted to a single word...containing several hundred variants and thousands of citations" (Williams, Alex. "One Frigging Great Lexicographer," *New York*. 30 Oct.95, v.28, n.43, p29). The author concludes that **fuck** is losing its

THE SCARLET PASTORALE

strength from mass exposure in both our oral and written tradition.

4. **Fuck** was even formally banned from the House of Commons
of Her Britannic Majesty's Parliament. As recorded in the
Manchester Guardian, the Speaker of the House, one George
Thomas, made clear where he stood on the matter.

> As long as I am Speaker I shall consider that an unpar-
> liamentary expression. None of us would use it in our
> own homes, and I hope that this House can maintain a
> better example to the country.

5. *Yo mama* and other such terms of abuse sprang from an exercise once popular in the black community called the "dozens"
(mother-rhyming), a game played on street corners by black
youth as a form of recreation or, as Rap Brown described it, a
popular form of recreation much "like white folks play Scrab-
ble." It was a verbal duel, the purpose of which was to
destroy your opponent with words. The dozens originated in
an African tradition where there is a great reliance on oral
expression, one in which people express references to one
another's mothers, often imputing incestuous relations as part
of the verbal give and take.

> I fucked your mama
> Till she went blind.
> Her breath smells bad,
> But she sure can grind.
>
> I fucked your mama
> For a solid hour.
> Baby came out
> Screaming Black Power.
>
> Elephant and the Baboon
> Leaning to screw
> Baby came out looking
> Like Spiro Agnew

> —H. Rap Brown, "Street Talk," in *Rappin'*
> *and Stylin' Out*, Thomas Kochman, Ed.,
> 1972

6. Brophy and Partridge who studied *The Slang of the British soldier* during wartime, remarked about its usage, that **fuck** was
"so common in its adjectival form that after a short time the
ear refused to acknowledge it and took in only the noun to
which it was attached."

7. It also spawned a host of lesser imitations, the best of which
include **COMMFU** (a **Complete Monumental Military
Fuck-up**), **FUBAR** (**Fucked Up Beyond Recognition**),
FUBB (**Fucked Up Beyond Belief**), **FUMTU** (**Fucked Up**

More Than Usual), **GFU (General Fuck-Up)**, and **IMFU (Immense Military Fuck-Up)**. Going international, we had the **Joint Anglo-American Fuck-ups (JAAFU)** and the **Joint Anglo-Chinese Fuck-Ups (JACFU)**. Things weren't completely hopeless, given the **SAMFU (Self-Adjusting Military Fuck-Up)**, but most tended to get completely out of hand, causing soldiers to scream **TARFU! (Things Are Really Fucked Up)** or **TAFUBAR! (Things Are Fucked Up Beyond All Recognition)**.

8. By 1874, **fuck** had also come to signify a person, usually a woman in sexual terms. The first recorded reference to it as a noun can be found in the OED, citing *Letters from a friend in Paris*: "I always held that dear mamma was the best **fuck** in the family, and in every way a most desirable and splendid creature." (OED, n., b., 1).

   In the twentieth century, **fuck** has been used in various other ways: as an impersonal noun in Henry Miller's once banned novel *Tropic of Cancer* (1948): "Nobody gives a **fuck** about her except to use her" (OED, n., 2); or as an intensifier in William Burroughs' *Naked Lunch* (1959); "How the **fuck** should I know?" (OED, n., 3).

9. Unlike Christianity, asceticism and self-denial have been alien to Judaism. As David Feldman noted in his study of Jewish sexual practices, the much discussed Judaeo-Christian sexual ethic "...is at the very least an untenable assumption."

10. Naughty once meant truly **naughty**. In the nineteenth century we had a **naughty house** filled with **naughty** girls all of whom were adept at **doing the naughty**. According to Farmer and Henley, "Working girls in large cities sometimes say they work for their living, but **do the naughty** for their clothes." The intensity of naughty has changed, but its core remains intact. **Doing the naughty**, a phrase from a bygone era, but one still very much with us. The song is over but the malady lingers on.

11. In Robert Gover's *One Hundred Dollar Misunderstanding*, Kitten, the **hooker,** plans her revenge on the college boy with one of her colleagues: "This time boff us cats gonna **haul his ashes**, an we is gonna haul 'em so far off he ain' never gonna find 'em agin."

12. There were other ways of hitching a ride. "Have you heard the story of the old Irish woman who was asked if she'd ever been bedridden? "Hundreds of times," she answered, "and once in a sled" (Stephen Longstreet, *The Pedlocks*, 1951).

13. Recent surveys show that 78 percent of men responding admitted to "loving" their cars; 63 percent actually talked to them. When asked what they would do if they had an extra

CLASSIC VINTAGE ROADSTER
40s all original, stored for ages now available for spin around the block. Need patient mechanic, good with his tools for quality ride. WF, HWP.
—*Seattle Weekly, 2002*

$500, the number one response from men was "buy something for my car." The top response from women was "buy something for my spouse/significant other."

14. **Shag** surfaced most recently on these shores in the title of Mike Meyer's Austin Powers sequel, *The Spy Who Shagged Me*. Until then Americans knew the word as a dance or something outfielders did when practicing catching fly balls. Now they could show their sophistication and be titillated by using one of the British synonyms for **fuck** as a double entendre.

    British wordsmith Michael Quinion suggests that Americans restrain themselves. In nineteenth-century Britain, **shag** was considered very vulgar and examples in print were rare except in pornographic writings. Things, however, are different today. Though it's categorized as low slang, **shag's** hardly in the same class as **fuck** in terms of shock value. Lots of young people use the term freely, while older ones consider it off limits, "at least in polite company." It's somewhat tasteless perhaps, but provides no cause for censorship of the movie title there.

15. Flash back to Elvis Presley, the "king of **bump and grind**." His performance of "Hound Dog" in 1956 on the Milton Berle show proved so provocative that it approached a national scandal. Under the threat of being bumped, Elvis's actions practically ground to a halt. There were no such gyrations when he went on the Steve Allen show, where Elvis moved nary a muscle, sedately singing to a transfixed basset hound, clearing the way for a future appearance with Ed Sullivan.

16. There's little blockage in today's dance craze known as "freak dancing." "Think girls bending over and rubbing their backsides against their partner in time to the beat. Think boys putting their hands on their dates' hips to pull them in closer still – then further away, then closer still. Now picture girls burying their faces into a second partner's midsection or gyrating over him as he lies on the floor." (*Washington Post*, May 18, 2002). Commented a high school principal, "If they didn't have their clothes on, you would swear they were **having sex**."

Sticks and Stones

f **sex** be an act, we all have parts to play with. As Florinda (Brenda Vaccaro) reminded Don Diego Vega (George Hamilton) in *Zorro, The Gay Blade* (1981): "...As the Alcalde's wife, I play many roles, but the people see only the part I play in public. Only a few select friends know my private parts." Most of us know them as the **carnal parts** (early 18thC), the **natural parts** (mid 19thC), the **naturals** (17thC), the **parts below** (17thC), the **underparts** (mid 19thC), the **privy parts** (c. 1565), the **private parts** (c. 1885), the **privates** (20thC), and the ever-favorite **genitals** or **genitalia**, from the Latin *gignere*, "to beget." In literate circles they're our **pudenda** (c. 1634), from the Latin *pudere*, "to shame"—giving us "that of which we are ashamed," which tells a lot about our feelings toward them.

Few speak well of these parts, many not at all. Even the great H.L. Mencken was struck dumb in their presence. He omitted any mention of them by name is his classification of the body parts—reasoning that there was no place for such items in a book meant to be read before the domestic hearth.

Well, the days of the domestic hearth are over, replaced by the age of sexual enlightenment. The times call for candor. Having found out everything about **the act**, it's now time we learned our parts.

Stand Up and Be Counted

Welcome to the club! Ours is exclusive. Women are simply not admitted. **Members** (c. 1290) in good standing include the **sexual member**, **the carnal member**, the **virile member** (18thC), the **male member**, the **privy member** (c. 1298), the **dearest member** (Robert Burns), and even the **unruly member**. It's not that we don't enjoy women, but our constituents come first. "Here's to the small circle of my female friends. May it never be entered except by an upright **member** (19thC toast)." Those unhappy with the decision can always protest as did Groucho: "I don't want to belong to any club that would have me as a member."

I'll tell you a little story,
  Just a story I have heard;
And you'll swear it's all a fable
  But it's gospel, every word.

When the Lord made father Adam,
  They said He laughed and sang;
And sewed him up the belly
  With a little piece of whang.

But when the Lord was finished
  He found He's measured wrong;
For when the whang was knotted
  'Twas several inches long.

Said He, "'Tis but eight inches
  So I guess I'll let it hang."
So He left on Adam's belly
  That little piece of whang.

But when the Lord made mother Eve
  I imagine He did snort,
When He found the whang He sewed her with
  Was several inches short.

"'Twill leave an awful gap," said He,
  "But I should give a damn,
She can fight it out with Adam
  For that little piece of whang."

So ever since that day
  When human life began,
There's been a constant struggle
  'Twixt the woman and the man.
    —Anon., "Whang," 20thC

Much luck to you members
Just try to never let me down
And keep to your place.
    —Thom Gunn, Das Liebesleben, *mid*
    20thC

That strives to stand that cannot go,
    That feeds the mouth that cannot bite.
It is a friar with a bald head
    A staff to beat a cuckold dead.
It is a gun that shoots point blank;
    It hits betwixt a maiden's flank.
A shift of cupid's cut,
'Twill serve to rove, to prick, to butt;
'Twas ne'er a maid but by her will
Will keep it in her quiver still.
    —Anon., "A Riddle," *18th–19thC*

A Stab in the Dark

We have more than 600 ways of referring to our **members**. Heading up the rolls is the right honorable **prick**, derived from the Old English *prica* for "dot or point." Its distinguished lineage goes back to 1592 and an OED citation: "The passing boye lifte up his **prick**." Three years later Shakespeare lifted it for *Romeo and Juliet*, causing Mercutio to pun, "The bawdy hand of the dial is now upon the prick of noon."

Prick was Standard English until 1700, after which it became a vulgarism, which is evidence of its popularity. Most recently, we have used it to describe a particularly offensive, irascible, or unscrupulous male. He's a rogue, a scoundrel, and a knave—one who under no circumstances can be trusted. **Prick** has also been an exclamation. The Spanish cry out, *"Carajo!"* The English-speaking world opts for "Gad!" "Gatso!" and "Gadzooks!" all corruptions of *carazo*, from the Italian *cazzo*, **prick**. Regardless of its common usage, the **prick** continues to be an outcast in polite society. As George Carlin noted, "You can prick your finger, but you cannot finger your **prick**."

Tails of Old

Of all our **members**, it's the **penis** that has won widest acceptance. It made its first recorded appearance in 1684 in a medical dictionary and over the years established itself as the most respected **member** in the field. It also has gained public exposure and access to places a **prick** could never go.

In truth, **penis** has an ignoble pedigree. Though it's a good Latin word, Ovid, the Roman poet and pornographer, had no use for it. Literally, **penis** means "tail" (Standard English for the part, mid 14th–mid 18thC)—and was a definite put-down. Freud, however, believed that women felt otherwise, elevating it to new heights when experiencing **penis envy**, an urge repressed at an early age to possess male power and exercise the male prerogative. A more succinct update in *Psychology Today* defines **penis envy** as "the desire to be red, wrinkled, and four inches long."

Simply Fascinating

Man has always been of two minds in dealing with his **prick**. It's been both an object of great pride and of great shame. In ancient times it was treated with reverence, worshipped as the source of fecundity and perceived to be the power behind motherhood, fertility, food and the seasonal cycles. In Egypt and Greece symbolic representations of it, huge **phalluses** (late 18th–20thC From the Greek for **prick**), were carried about in solemn religious processions. In Rome, images of **pricks** could be found everywhere. There were **pricks** at the doors of shops, **pricks** at the city gates, and **pricks** attached to the chariots of famous generals. Even drinking glasses and goblets were cast in their shape.

Believing that the **phallus** possessed magic powers and was especially effective in warding off the evil eye, the Romans also cast good-luck charms in the shape of male organs, which they wore about their necks. Supposedly, the evil eye became so taken with the sight of the **prick** that its attention was diverted from the intended victim. These charms were called *fascina* or "little bundles" from which we get the word "fascinating."

Things change over time, but no one knows why the **prick** remained a **penis** but ceased being fascinating.

For the Birds

A more modern contender for the top spot, and definitely trying harder, is the **cock** (16th–20thC). Many even consider it the most popular expression that we have for the **male organ**. Its origins, however, are in dispute. Consensus has it that the **cock** derives from the rooster, from its shape as well as its proud and active nature, originating with the Latin *coccus*, from *cocco-cocco*, the cock's cry. But John Ciardi, for one, disputed this derivation, basing his case on *kak*, Indo-European for the male **genitalia**. He argued that the **prick** influenced the word we have for the rooster, rather than the other way around.

Which really came first, the chicken or the...? No one knows for sure.

Winging It

Hardly your rara avis, the **cock** is part of a larger Greco-Roman tradition of putting wings on images of the **phallus**. The same instinct also gave us the **bird** in nineteenth-century England. In Italian the word *uccello* has the same meaning. You'll also find it on the highways of America where drivers **flip the bird**, raising their middle finger in tribute to each other's driving ability.

We have many fine-feathered friends in the States; they include the **canary** (20thC), found along the Eastern seaboard, and the Southern **pecker** (20thC), noted for its repeated rhythmic thrusts. Former President Lyndon Johnson had a special fondness for the latter; his credo being, "I never trust a man unless I got his **pecker** in my pocket." Having something important and personal on that man could only assure his compliance. Certainly, he could not stray very far under the circumstances.

In England, they say "keep your pecker up," to wish you "good health," from "peck," meaning "appetite," which is quite

Isn't it awfully nice to have a penis
Isn't it frightfully good to have it on
It's swell to have a stiffy
It's divine to own a dick
From the tiniest little tadger to the world's biggest prick
So, three cheers for your Willy or John Thomas
Hooray for your one-eyed trouser snake
Your piece of pork, your wife's best friend, your passing or your cock
You can wrap it up in ribbons, you can stuff it in a sock
But don't take it out in public or they'll stick you in the dock
...And you won't come back
      —*Sung by Eric Idle in* Monty Python's The Meaning of Life *(1983)*

understandable given how we peck at our food. The pecker has also long represented courage and resolution there. When someone asks you to "keep a stiff pecker," they're only encouraging you to keep your chin up and stick to the assigned task regardless of the difficulty. Keeping one's pecker up is very much a matter of pride in both countries, but for very different reasons

Watch the Birdie

Looks can be deceiving. Though the cock appears jaunty and confident, he's anything but cocksure. He may think of himself as a strictly all-male bird, but a close look at his history shows quite the contrary. Not only does this most masculine of birds have a feminine side to him, but, according to the lexicographer of black English J. Dillard, he once denoted exclusively the female organ in the black community of the Southern United States and the Caribbean. This usage originated in nineteenth-century England where women ofttimes used **cock** as a verb in a passive sense, as **to want cocking** or **to get cocked**. From there, it was a natural transition to refer to the female **pudendum** as a **cock**.

The male **cock's** stature has further been diminished by invidious comparisons with other birds, treating its appearance and character with even less respect.

> "Esther, have you ever seen a man?"...
> "No," I said. "Only statues."...
> I stared at Buddy while he unzipped his chino pants...He just stood there in front of me and I kept staring at him. The only thing I could think of was turkey neck and turkey gizzards, and I felt very depressed.
> —Sylvia Plath, *The Bell Jar,* 1963

Taking Flight

The **cock's** rise to the top has not been easy. Early in the nineteenth century a wave of anti-**cock** sentiment swept the land. It was part of a general purge of all language that was deemed offensive, transforming legs into "limbs" and bulls into "he-cows." **Cock** suddenly disappeared, not only from private conversations but from the family farm. Poultry farmers referred to their holdings as "boy birds" and "gentlemen fowl." In war, men pulled back the roosters of their guns. Thoroughly chicken about what others might think, the father of Louisa May Alcott, the author of *Little Women,* changed the family name from the more suggestive Alcox. And throughout all of this, folks had nothing to sustain them but a little rooster-eyed optimism.

Cock has staged a comeback, however. Though it's still not

a. Baileau Despréaux.

Before the barn-door crowing
The cock by hens attended
His eyes around him throwing
Stands for a while suspended.
Then one he singles from the crew,
And cheers the happy hen
With How do you do and How do you do
And How do you do again.
> —John Gay, song from The
> Beggar's Opera, *1728*

proper to bring him up in mixed company, the average male is cockier than ever. Impartial observers, however, still consider him "for the birds."

Little Things Mean a Lot

Cock and **prick** are especially vivid and evocative words. Most people, however, consider them obscene and socially unacceptable. Talking about them often occasions a violent reaction.

In response to our personal discomfort, and out of deference to the sensitivity of others, we often substitute a less emotionally laden term. **Penis** is a case in point. Latin lends class and respectability, and as a dead language, it threatens very few.

But the **penis** just wouldn't do. In its own lackluster fashion it failed to capture the true glory of a man's **organ**. As safe as the **penis** was, it was also incredibly dull, dull, dull.

Women compounded matters, rendering it somewhat nondescript as **it**, his **whatchamacallit**, and his **thing**. **Things** couldn't have been any worse, all **things** being equal.

Man tilled his fertile imagination, finding new ways to do his **prick** justice, extolling its virtues and singing its praises. He promoted it heavily as his **manhood** (20thC), though admittedly choosing a rather strange place in which to carry it. He reminded females that it was the **delight of women** (20thC), somewhat of an exaggeration, though it has been a source of amusement for them as a **toy** or **plaything** (both 20thC). On a more exotic plane, he encouraged woman to admire his **animated ivory** (18thC, John Cleland) and gaze longingly upon his **pego** (from the Greek for "fountain," early 18thC).

And what better way to keep a woman's body in tune than with a **whistle**, a **flute**, or an **organ**? The **flute** (18thC) traditionally has stood for a **prick**, all the way back to ancient Rome, and has created as much **marriage musick** (18thC, for children bawling) as has the **family organ** (18thC). What better entertainment is there than to see the man **in full orchestra** (late 19th–20thC, for **penis** and **testicles**)?

Man was determined to find the right metaphor, that none but himself should sell his **organ** short.

Funny You Don't Look Jewish

And it was man himself, along with his ambivalence toward his own **organ**, that contributed most to its decline and fall. Consider his **schmuck** and his **putz**, two of our more popular terms for the **prick**. Encouraged by Leo Rosten (*The Joy of Yiddish*), people believe them to be two rather nice words derived from the Yiddish

Judge: Did he introduce his organ?
She: It was more like a flute, *Your Honor.*
　　　　　　　—Anon., 19thC.

Better to be a king for an evening than a schmuck for a lifetime.
　　　　—The King of Comedy, 1983

"No, the mayor is not a coward, and the mayor is also not a schmuck."

   —Mayor Koch of New York City,
      *responding to a request that he pose
      with a tiger.*

via the German; their value further enhanced by their meaning as "ornaments, jewelry, or finery," the **putz** conveying the sense of being in full dress.

"What jewels!" you say. Not so. Lurking beneath the surface are the **shmuck**'s real roots, the Slavic *smok*, "snake."

So too is their usage riddled with ambivalence. Though they once had a positive connotation, they're used today primarily in the opposite sense. Man employs **schmuck** and **putz** not to praise his fellow man, but to humiliate and insult him, linking prototypes of the **penis** to male personalities in a particularly negative way and coming up with two separate types.

Your typical **schmuck** is a benign **prick**, gentle, inoffensive, and full of fun. In a playful moment, he will slip out of your BVDs and warmly rub against your thigh. He is the bed-wetter and the premature ejaculator. He gropes, muddles, and flip-flops about—and does an awful lot of plain dumb things. Though he's insecure and indecisive, most **schmucks** are lovable. Some people say, "I never met a **schmuck** I didn't like."[1] Others find them a real pain.

The **putz** is his antithesis. He's a nasty and immoral fellow who cares little for others. Ever combat-ready, he is constantly striking out against the world. A real **motherfucker**, there isn't a jockstrap that can contain him. **Putz** is the mindless Neanderthal, the embodiment of violence and immorality. When you call someone a **putz**, you're telling him that he's a real **prick**. The only thing worse is a **groisser potz**, a "**big prick**." The difference between a **schmuck** and a **putz**? It's as fundamental as the difference between Gerald Ford and Richard Nixon.

Sizing Things Up

Schmuck and **putz** suit many, but if it's size you fancy, you can't beat the Yiddish **schlang** (also **schlange** and **schlong**) from the German *schlange* for "snake." In *Portnoy's Complaint* (1967), the title character reminisced about his father's: "His **schlang** brings to mind the firehoses along the corridors at school. **Schlang**: the word somehow captures exactly the brutishness, the meatiness that I admire so, the sheer mindless, weighty and unselfconscious dangle of that living piece of hose through which he passes water as thick and strong as rope..."

Unfortunately, as definitive as it is, the **shlong** can also on occasion be ambiguous. Its second meaning as a "troublesome wife," can lead to such awkward constructions as "His **shlong** was uncooperative in bed." Caution is always recommended in use of these words. A **prick** in France is *bitte*, which in German means "please." Things can get somewhat confusing in the European Union, when you cross the border, forgetting where you are and what you are trying to say. So please be careful out there. Not everyone is familiar with the nuances of *The Erotic Tongue*.

Meat and Potatoes

There was no confusion when it came to food. It was both natural and inevitable that eating be a featured activity of *The Erotic Tongue*, with food itself playing the most important parts.

Man's bill of fare deals primarily with fine **meat**, either **beef** or **pork** (20thC), also used as a verb, as **to pork her**), as is your wont. There's also the **snorker**, Australian slang for a sausage, and the **tube steak**, a favorite of the cops in "Hill Street Blues," a popular TV show of the '80s.

But his **sweetmeat** (19thC) is often in such demand that there are times when you may have to settle for something less, perhaps a **weenie** (16thC) or a **sausage** (19thC), currently referred to in England as a "banger"—no doubt an innocent coincidence. Worse yet, you might have to make do with an old **hambone** (the topic of many an old blues song), some **marrowbone** (19thC), or even just some plain **gristle** (c. 1850). Not to be concerned, however; by the 1970s, it was fashionable to **jump a woman's bones**.

The main dish? **Meat and two vegetables**—the full spread. You can select from *une asperge* (Fr., "asparagus stalk"), or the unique **potato finger**. But we'd consider it especially crude if you suggested to the young lady that she **take a carrot**! Equally offensive is the French *Et ta soeur, aime-t-elle les radis?* ("And your sister, **does she like radishes?**" i.e., does she have a go at it?).

Fresh Fruit

There's no better way to bring dinner to a close than with something special. Perhaps some fruit? Cheeky lads making advances to town girls (c. 1905–1920) used to encourage them to "have a **banana!**" The phrase originated with an old British music-hall ditty, "I had a **banana** with Lady Diana," reportedly updated with the 1981 royal nuptials as "I had some fruit with the royal brute."

Bo Derek, America's sex symbol for the '80s, issued a similar invitation in her version of *Tarzan*. There we find her in the water face to face with the ape man. In one of the more memorable scenes in the history of contemporary cinema, she looks languidly into his eyes and coyly remarks, "I'm a virgin. You must be one too," while slowly—oh, so slowly—peeling a banana. Though this was a screen first, men have been **getting their bananas peeled** (c. 1930–36) long before Bo.

The Muslims also had the right idea, believing the forbidden fruit in the Garden of Eden to be not an apple, but a banana. But

Where's the beef?
   —*Wendy's Commercial, 1984*

From the tattered banana tree after waiting for months...
Unexpectedly, from the highest shoot, a huge Thing detached itself, leaving the sheath Curving, purpling, thrusting out an emergent Flower, that lifted...
   —*Charles G. Bell, "Banana," early 20thC*

what's a banana against Shakespeare's **poperine pear:**

> O Romeo, that she were, O, that she were
> An open arse [etcetera in some editions],
> Thou a poperine pear!
>
> —Shakespeare, *Romeo and Juliet*

That's "pop 'er in"—and possibly the single worst pun on **prick** in the history of Western literature.

May we also suggest the **sugar stick** or the **(ladies') lollipop** (both 19thC)? For those looking for something less explicit, we have some **pudding**, or **pudden**, from the **pudenda. Would you for an apple turnover?** (mid 20thC, teen-age wisecrack).

The Greeks and Romans favored **phallus**-shaped cakes, and the Egyptians, bread and pastries in the shape of both male and female **sex organs.** You could order them individually or joined **in union.** Hardly a thing of the past, since you can still find such exotic fare in specialized bakeries in our more cosmopolitan cities.

A fitting ending to a meal, which men described as the **dear morsel** and a **yum-yum** (both 19thC).

Making a Name For Oneself

Food is elemental, but people are number one. The ancients often gave the **phallus** image human features—face, hands, feet, all of which served to further emphasize its importance. It was also as a person, linguistically, that the **penis** most fully and truly came into is own. A noted nineteenth-century shopkeeper used to greet his more dandified customers with, "And how is our **small person** today?" This is hardly unusual, for in *The Erotic Tongue*, our parts play very real people indeed.

Why did man personify his **penis**, imputing to his **genitals** a life of their own? Lexicographer Alan Richter in *The Language of Sexuality* (1987) thought it helped the owner "to avoid responsibility for their actions." Officer Davis (Phil Hartman) in *National Lampoon's Loaded Weapon 1* (1993) surmised it was because "He didn't want a stranger making most of his decisions."

Whatever his motivation, man has assembled a gallery of greats on his behalf, employing dignitaries from the Bible, Mythology, the Classics, and the Imagination. There's somebody for everybody.

The master of ceremonies makes the initial introductions beginning with the Ancient world with **Julius Caesar** (c. 1840), the **Cyclops, Polyphemus** (19thC).

Those favoring the world of letters can opt for **Dr. Johnson** (18th–19thC). According to Eric Partridge, "There was no one that Dr. Johnson was not prepared to stand up to." Yet there's always someone to take up the challenge. In the film *Putney Swope*

He: Honey, would you like to see Oliver Twist?
She: Why not, I've seen it do everything else.
—Anon., *Victorian humor*

(1969), Putney's girlfriend tells him, "I'm going to **bend your Johnson!**" A somewhat disquieting and uncomfortable notion calling for some flexibility on the Doctor's part.

Biblical buffs might settle on **Old Adam, Abraham, Nebuchadnezzar** (c. 1860–1915), Conqueror of the Holy City, or **Nimrod** (19thC), the mighty hunter.

Followers of fiction have their **Sir Martin Wagstaff, Master John Goodfellow** (Urquhart), and **Captain Standish**, stout, "who made his dame cry out" (Joseph Ebsworth). On a more formal basis there's the **Rector of the Females** (Rochester), the **Captain of My Body** and **His Majesty in Purple Cap** (19thC).

Among the commonfolk, you could always reach for **Timothy Tool** (c. 1845), slip in **Daintie Davie** (19thC), or **Little Davy** (Scot. 19thC), and, as an act of charity, show **Old Blind Bob** the way—all quicker than you can say **Jack Robinson** (both 19thC).

I see your Schwartz is as big as mine...
Let's see how well you handle it.
—Dark Star (Rick Moranis), Spaceballs,
1987

You Can Call Me...

On a first-name basis, **Peter**, **Dick**, and **John** stand out. **Peter** began as *St. Peter*, who held the keys to heaven, but after he had used them regularly for a few hundred years, and clearly was no longer a saint, he was reduced to just plain **Peter**, a long-time favorite name for the **prick**. But **Peter** is nowhere as popular as he once was, having hit his stride among America's teenagers in the 1940s and '50s. In the Ozarks, however, he's still the word for the **family organ**. Vance Randolph, the noted folklore specialist, tells the story of a novice minister who both embarrassed and flabbergasted his congregation by innocently inquiring as to how many **Peters** were out there. It was a real gaffe. In that part of the country, one never refers to **Peter** in mixed company. A son is never named **Peter**. And nothing, but nothing, ever **peters** out.

John, the commonest name in the English language, has often given his name to the commonest **organ**, as has **Johnnie**, a favorite of "cultured" nineteenth-century females. We are told that women have also been hot for a man's **Jones** (20thC, U.S.), **John's** family name. But our featured performer is **John Thomas** (c. 1840), an old pet name for a flunky or a servant, an important figure in world literature who was also the hero of *Lady Chatterley's Lover* and without whom there would not have been a story.

"John Thomas! John Thomas!..."
"Ay," said the man stretching his body almost painfully.
"He's got his root in my soul has that gentleman! An' sometimes I don't know what ter do wi' him. Ay, he's got a will of his own, an' it's hard to suit him. Yet, I wouldn't have him killed."
"No wonder men have always been afraid of him!" she said.
"He's rather terrible."

Jack (19thC), a nickname for **John**, has also stood for the **penis**

and its **erection**, as has **Jock** (before 1790), from which we got the jockstrap by which today's male supports his **hanging Johnny**. Nothing—well, almost nothing—could contain a **roaring jack**. A **jack-in-the-box** (19thC) was your pop-up surprise, the **box** being the likeliest place in which a man might place it.

Though **John** apparently has fallen out of favor, it's **Dick** (since 1860) who continues to hang in there. This is one **Dick**, however, that is not derived from Richard. He originates with *dirk*, a short dagger used by sneak thieves in Old England. And its name derives from "Derrick," the notorious hangman at Tyburn Prison whose improved gallows design was the prototype of the modern crane, and who was evidently a real **prick** at that.

In the Name Of

There were however, more gentle sorts. In 1993, Disney released a film about the liberation of a trapped whale entitled *Free Willy*. It also released a slew of giggles in England where **Willy's** popular in yet another role—one of the reasons why Prince William is referred to as "Wills" there. Coincidentally, that same year, a resident of a state which proudly proclaims: "Virginia is for Lovers," Lorena Bobbitt, cut off John Wayne Bobbitt's **penis** in a marital spat. Seeking to put a human face on the story, *Newsweek* reported how the *Washington Post* referred to the severed organ as "Wally," "Alstaire," "King Gustav," and "Mr. Belvidere." It also noted a headline in The *Ottawa Citizen*: "Sad Saga of a Wife's Attempt to Free Willy."

Cutting a long story short, it's but one more example of the organ's need to make a name for itself. After all, **some of our best friends are genitals** (20thC). As Leonardo da Vinci, who himself lived without **sex**, reminded us:

> ...this creature has often a life and intelligence
> separate from this man, and it would appear
> that the man is in the wrong in being ashamed
> to give it a name or to exhibit it, seeking, rather,
> constantly to cover and conceal what he ought to
> adorn and display with ceremony.

LYSISTRATA.

Best Foot Forward

The personification of the **prick** represented its high point. But even then, men felt only partially confident. Few came to its defense. Except for Walt Whitman, who raised his **thumb of love**, others refused to even lift their **little finger** (19thC) on its behalf.

Finally, someone put his foot down—what psychologists call "displacement downward." None were more adamant than the authors of the Old Testament. If you can believe St. Jerome and his Vulgate translation of the Bible, all references the authors of the Bible made to the foot are nothing more than veiled allusions to the **penis**.

It's all very possible: in the Ancient East, **foot** and **leg** were familiar euphemisms for a man's **thing**. When a man **spilled water at a woman's feet**, he **ejaculated**. When he **washed his feet**, he actually bathed his **penis** in a woman's **vagina**. The man who suffered with **diseased feet** had in reality come down with **venereal disease**.

Don't have a leg to stand on? Try the **best leg of three**. But forget about the **hind leg**, an old Ozark expression for the **ass**. We've also had the **privy limb** since the thirteenth century and the **joint**, a contemporary black term that goes back to the nineteenth-century fowl and our inability to say "leg" in polite society.

This usage promises to kick off a whole new thing linguistically. There's no end of possibility what with getting a leg up on somebody, shaking a leg, and putting your foot in it. That, of course, is only if the shoe fits...

Stick to It

More than food, more than a plaything, more than a celebration of personhood or a small part thereof, the **prick** is also a highly useful instrument, even in its most primitive form—the **stick**. Whatever your shtick, we've got it: we have **joy sticks** (20thC), **dip sticks** (19thC), **cream sticks** (c. 1920), and **trap sticks** (late 19thC). We have **sticks** for every purpose and for every occasion. For musicians, **fiddlesticks** (c. 1800) to go with the **fiddle**, or the female **pudendum**. For leaders, the **scepter of authority** (18thC); for authorities, the **night stick** (19thC); for party goers, the **Maypole** (c. 1758), which truly was a symbol of **phallic** worship around which celebrants would dance; and for the religious, the **holy pole** (19thC) and the **pilgrim's staff** (18thC). Those inclined toward magic might prefer the **wand of love** (19thC)—a phrase that conveys the true wonder of the apparatus.[2] Satisfaction guaranteed. Thy **rod** and thy **staff** they comfort me. They should more than meet your needs as well.

...At winter's frost, or heat in June
The fiddle here is out of tune
Fiddles alone are not to blame.
The sticks must often take the shame;
Too often feeble, short or limber chosen.
And often fail for lack of resin.
    —*"The Question,"* New Crazy Tales, *1783*

Tools of the Trade

Sticks were also man's first **tools**, a popular term for the **prick** from the middle of the sixteenth century until the eighteenth. The **tool** remains an ever useful and versatile **instrument** (19thC). It's the **baby-maker** (late 19thC), or the **means of generation** (1791). In another vein, it's the **P-maker** or the **waterworks** (both mid 19thC) or a **hose** (c.1928, also a verb, meaning to **fuck**, c.1935 or "cheat," c.1941)—all very functional and no-nonsense.

So wild and wooly and full of fleas
Whose tool hung down below his knees.
    —Rudyard Kipling,
      The Bastard King of England

She can do more with a swipe than
a monkey can do with a banana.
  —*Iceberg Slim,*
     Pimp: The Story of My Life, *1967*

Would you in Venus' wars succeed then never
  shilly-shally stand
But boldly march up sword in hand. And that's
  the way to win her.
    —*Durfee, "The Rattle," 1766*

The penis mightier than the sword.
  —*Mark Twain*

The Dream Machine

The **tool's** utility has increased even further with advances in technology. Since the industrial revolution it has expanded to include all sorts of machines: the **grinding tool**, **the pile-driver**, as well as everyone's favorite, the **fornicating engine**, popularly known as the little engine that could.

Love's engine, or **machine of love**, is often described by the work it does: **bum-tickler** (18th–19thC), **quim-wedge** (19thC), **rump-splitter** (c. 1560–1800), **beard-splitter** (c. 1849), **bush-whacker** (18thC), **plug-tail** (mid 18th–mid 19thC), **kidney wiper**, **liver turner**, **womb brush**, and **tickle-tail**. As **love's engine** (19thC), the **organ** proved a smash hit. Starting as a **gentle tittler**, **jigger**, and a **wriggling pole** (19thC), it made its greatest impact as a **poker**, **rammer**, and **gooser**.

Best known for the force with which it hit, it produced the **dong**[3] (mid 20thC, Aust. And N.Z., "to strike" or "punch"), the **swipe** (20thC, U.S. black, "to deal a rather severe blow"), and the **whang** (19th–20thC, "to strike a heavy and resounding blow")— for many a woman, the final stroke.

Cutting Loose

But tools of peace easily became tools of war. It began with the sword, the *gladius* of ancient Rome whose effectiveness went unchallenged. Centuries later, the **sword** was but one weapon in **Adam's arsenal.** You could find everything there you might possibly need to carry love's battles to a successful conclusion: the **lance of love, love's battering ram, love's sensitive truncheons,** the **shafts of delight** (18thC), and **love's dribbling dart.** There were also **pikes, sabers, spears,** and **clubs,** all described with **love, pleasure** and **delight,** and all in the name of **Venus** or **Cupid.** Once we **broke a lance** with someone (19th–20thC), meaning to enjoy a woman. Nothing was more explosive, however, than the **artillerie de Cupide** or **de Venus** (19thC), "the arts and accomplishments of **venery.**"

In *The Erotic Tongue* we turn sex and war on their heads. Benign parts become instruments of war. In politics, implements of battle often become organs of peace. What next? A missile of Venus launched from love's pad—a double-duty weapon, allowing us to exit with both a bang and a whimper.

Great Guns!

Times change, as do our weapons. Most recently they go off with a bang; hence the need for training in their use. For that men join the army, and one of the first things they learn there is the difference between a rifle and a gun. Sergeants insist that you master the distinction. Those unable to do so are required to stand guard with one hand on their **penis**, the other on their rifle, loudly repeating this quatrain:

This is my rifle
This is my gun;
This is for shooting
This is for fun.

Men also learn to keep their weapons in good working order through periodic checkups, a.k.a. the **dangle-parade** (WWII, New Zealand). This all-inclusive drill includes **short-arm inspection**, a medical inspection of the **penis** while at rest, and **long-arm inspection**, while at "attention" (both WWII).

If "happiness is a warm gun" (the Beatles), it also has its downside. Though many take the necessary precautions, most men carelessly discharge their **weapon**. Many times, it's the woman who **draws their fireworks**, causing her to receive **a shot up the straight** (19thC) or **a shot twixt wind and water** (16thC), often leaving M'lady, you guessed it, in a **banged-up** state.

There are other problems as well. An overactive trigger finger can cause a man to **go off at half-cock**—a sober reminder that though power may grow out of the end of a gun, good **sex** is more than a one-shot proposition.

That's About the Size of It

"Generally speaking," Fanny Hill reminded us, "it is in love as it is in war, where the longest weapon carries it." So encouraged, man has gone to great lengths in describing his **rod** (19th–20thC). One of the more durable expressions we've ever known is the **yard**. It was originally a **stick**, but for almost two hundred years, from 1590 to 1780, **yard** was the most common literary term for the **prick**.

Most found the **yard** quite acceptable. As Eric Partridge noted, it never suffered the unfavorable social reputation of **cock**, **prick**, or **tool** and was always deemed an appropriate way of **getting** or **taking a woman's measure** (late 18th–mid 19thC).

To the goal of her pleasure she drove very hard
But was tripp'd up ere half-way she ran,
And tho' everyone fancied her life was a yard,
Yet it proved to be less than a span.
—Gravestone of one Sally Salisbury, 18thC

By 1850 it had become obsolete. Yet the **yard** lives on in every man's fantasy, though the details of the fantasy clash. We have the old adage, "Short and thick does the trick" (18thC), as well as Robert Burns's "Nine inch will please a lady," while contemporary folk hyperbole immortalizes **the man with the nine-inch prick**

Is that a gun in your pocket, or are you just glad to see me?
—Mae West

Here, Pistol, I charge you with a cup of sack.
Do you discharge upon mine hostess.
—Shakespeare, Henry IV, Part 2

"Is it our yard?" quoth she,
"Is this your tailor's measure?
It is too short for me
It is not standard measure."
—Ballad, 18thC

and a twelve-inch tongue who can breathe through his ears. In our world, however, it's the **three-inch fool** (*The Taming of the Shrew*) who clearly is the rule.

You're a Hard Man!

The size of our **members**, despite all the talk, varies most with the conditions. Ordinarily, it's nothing but a good-natured **flap-doodle** (late 17thC), **dingle-dangle** (c. 1895), or **twiddle-diddler**.

However, when hard times hit, the **bald-headed hermit** emerges as **Old Slimy**, a **mutinous rogue** sure to strike fear into the hearts of maidens everywhere. As the **belly ruffian** and the **terror of virgins**, he is clearly her **foe**.

When **the old man's got his Sunday clothes on** (19thC), he's at his finest and biggest. But it may be for naught; he's often dressed up with no place to go.

Rising to the Occasion

Some have interpreted this puffing up as arrogance, others, as an illness of sorts—an **Irish toothache** (19thC), the **horncolic** (mid 18th–mid 19thC), a **swelling**, or even **a hidden tumor**. But it's really nothing serious, only your everyday **erection** (1594) or **priapism** (1598), after Priapus, the Greek and Roman god of potency and virility, son of Aphrodite and Bacchus, who was always depicted as **tumescent** (1859). The commonfolk knew it best as a **stand-on** (19thC), a **stiff-and-stout** (mid 17th–20thC), a **hard-on** or **hard-'un** (adjective c. 1860, noun c. 1890), and, in times of want, a **hard-up** (late 19thC).

Oftentimes, it's unintentional, a social gaffe of sorts: a **boner** (19thC), or simply a **horn** (mid 18thC) for which no one in particular gives a toot.

Lucky Stiffs

Some may knock it ("a hard-on doesn't count as personal growth"), but for most men, the **prick** is a source of real pride. In the seventeenth century, they had both a **proud inclination of the flesh** and **grew proud below the navel**.

Early risers made it a **pride-of-the-morning** or a **morning pride** (both late 19th–20thC). Among the Maoris, a chieftain felt especially proud when he woke up with an **erection** prior to a battle. It was considered an extremely good omen.

It's all for the best he didn't know he was **piss-proud** (late 18th–20thC), that it was nothing more than a matter of urine retention. After all, pride goeth before a fall.

Now with your hand provoke my foe to rise.
—*Ovid*

Now pierced is her virgin-zone
Soon she feels the foe within it.
—*Rochester,* The Lucky Minute, *1670*

A standing prick has no conscience.
—*English proverb, 18thC*

When the prick stands up, the brain goes to sleep.
—*Yiddish proverb*

What Goes Up, Must...

Time to say good-bye? Say it with flowers. May we suggest the **flowery shrub**, the **sensitive plant** (c. 1779), **love's nectar-laden stalk**, the **man root**.

Few things stand as proud as the **arbor vitae** (c. 1732) in full flower. As Richard Brinsley Sheridan described it in *The Geranium*,

> How straight upon its stalk it stands...
> The tree of life, this tree that tempted Eve,
> the crimson apple hangs so fair.
> Alas! What woman could forebear? The tree by
> which we live.

But the fall is never far behind, and all fade after the heat. Rochester noted, "Now languid lies in this unhappy hour. Shrunk up and sapless like a withered flower."

A posy can turn a farewell into an until-we-meet-again. But with this wretched horticultural specimen added to our roster, our membership drive sadly concludes.

Wild Oaths

There are, however, some lesser items left to discuss. In the nineteenth century they knew them as **witnesses to one's virility**, and with good reason. **Testicles** (c. 1425) derives from the Latin *testis*, "witness," and *testiculus*, "the little witness"—related directly to "testify" and "testament," because at one time it was customary for men to pledge faith or swear testimony by holding or touching one another's **genitals**. The event is recorded several times—where else but in the Old Testament.

You'll find reference to such testimony in I Chronicles 29:24, where "all the heads and the mighty men and also the sons of King David have given a hand under Solomon the King," as a sign of their submission to his authority and a pledge of their allegiance. In Genesis 24:9 the servant was also off target when he placed his hand under Abraham's **thigh** when taking an oath.

You might consider the entire subject "detestable." In which case, according to John Ciardi, you'd be swearing against it, i.e., hating the subject from the bottom of your **balls**.

Hang It All!

Over the years, the little fellows have borne witness anonymously, in the shadow of their more famous counterpart, known only as **thingmajigs** (c.1880), **dojiggers**, **tarriwags** (17thC), **talliwags** (late 18thC), **whirligigs** (late 17th–early 18thC), and **twiddle-diddles** (c. 1786).

Q: What is the difference between dark and hard?
A: It stays dark all night.
—Anon., 1950s

The blowen was nutts upon
the kiddey because he was well-hung.
The girl is pleased with the youth
because his genitals are large.
—Anon., The Lexicon Balantronicum,
1811

At their best, they've hung in their well as **bobblers, swingers, pounders** (Dryden), and **danglers**. The man who was **well hung** (19th–20thC) was **hung like a bull**, a **stallion** (18th–20thC), or even a **rabbit** (20thC).[4] Those with lesser assets had little reason to crow, bring **hung like a chicken** (19thC). Far removed from the roost, today's urban male of undistinguished parts is **hung like a tic-tac** (tiny, popular mouth mints, 1990s)—leaving one anything but breathless.

A Real Gem!

Clearly, people set great value by them, but you'll never find them in Tiffany's—the **family jewels** (20thC), that is. John Cleland described them as his **inestimable bulse of ladies' jewels**, but they've also been everything from inexpensive **baubles** (19thC, **bobbles?**) and **trinkets** to previous **rocks** and **stones**. **Stones** is one of our more venerable words for the items, dating back to the twelfth century, but around the middle of the nineteenth century they came to be considered vulgar and deemed appropriate only in reference to the **testicles** of a horse.

Noah Webster left no stone unturned when he published his expurgated version of the Bible in 1833, transforming all references to **stones** into **peculiar members** ("peculiar," as belonging to one person only). In Deuteronomy 23:1, they became classified as top **secrets**, accompanied by the warning that "he that is wounded or mutilated in his **secrets** shall not enter into the congregation of the Lord."

More recently, **stones** are back in our good graces, while it's our **rocks** that we've been **getting off** (20thC, U.S.).

Rounding out our collection are **pebbles, marbles, agates**, and **goolies** (late 19thC, from "gully," a game of marbles). Naturally, we have **cherries, berries, nutmegs** (17thC), **marrons** (French for "chestnuts"), **love apples** (19thC), **avocados** (an old Aztec word for **testicles**), and little **acorns** from which grows the mighty oak. *Glans* is Latin for "acorn," which coincides nicely with the **glands, sex glands**, and **interstitial glands**, all favorite euphemisms from the 1920s and '30s.

The most interesting designation of all is the **nuts** (18th–20thC), often described as "tight" and "hard," though they are really soft and vulnerable. This leaves us all in a quandary when it comes to **getting one's nuts cracked**, a painful but pleasurable practice from the 1920s. Mencken reminds us that during the early twenties, **nuts** "had connotations that made [the word] seem somewhat raw," leading nice people to replace them with **nerts**, thereby **breaking everyone's nuts** in the process.

The Way the Balls Bounce

We're most nuts about our **balls** (10thC), the term by which we know them best. **Balls** have demonstrated exceptional versatility and service to the language. If you're looking for courage, look no further. It takes **balls** to acquit yourself like a man, often **balls the size of watermelons**. Even Hemingway's heroes required real **cojones** (Spanish for **balls**) in order to show grace under pressure. Ever so necessary, they're unfortunately not always sufficient. As Fast Eddie Felson (Paul Newman) reminded Vince (Tom Cruise) in *The Color of Money* (1986): "You've got to have two things to win. You've got to have brains and you've got to have **balls**. You've got too much of one and not enough of the other."

Newspapers seldom have **balls** in such matters. As part of a policy adopted in 1993–94, The *San Francisco Chronicle* suppresses even the hints it formerly gave readers to "offensive" words (e.g. **sh-t** or **a—hole**), choosing now to either omit them altogether or use in their stead "cute" equivalents, such as "Spaldings" (a trade name for sports equipment) for **balls**.

The oldest English word for the **testicles** that we have on record is the **beallucas** (before 10thC). We later had the **ballokes** (c. 1382) or **ballocks** and the verb **to ballock** (19th–20thC), from which we got our "Ballocky Bill the Sailor"—a **ballsy** old salt if there ever was one. Time and his yearning for acceptability would mellow him into the children's favorite, Barnacle Bill, with hardly a hint of his salacious character.

Truly **ballsy** but also somewhat **bollixed** or **balled-up** were the Skopts, a religious sect at the time of Catherine II and Alexander I, which initiated new members into the cult by searing their **balls** with a hot iron. For some unexplained reason, the sect died out— but their rites lived on, entering the language as our "baptism of fire."

Balls have also served us well as an important interjection, part of our long-standing tradition of using the better half of the body to register emotion. They express surprise and exasperation ("Nuts!") as well as incredulity and disappointment ("Nonsense!").

"Baloney!" you say? As Partridge reminds us, that word comes not from the sausage but from the Gypsy *pelone*—for **balls**.

Functionally speaking, it would be difficult to imagine the sports world without balls. Absolutely critical to most of our games, they are governed by definite rules as to their use. It's proper for men to play ball with balls provided by management, but it's forbidden that they play with their own **balls**. And when a ball bounces up and hits the catcher in the **balls**, it is said to "ring his bell," though the sound is that of a dull thud followed by a shrill cry.

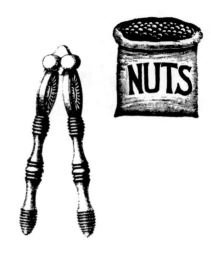

Hedy Lamarr: "I'll meet you in front of the pawn shop."

Bob Hope: "Okay, Dottie, and then you can kiss me under the balls."

> *—Sketch on* The Pepsodent Radio Show. *(Hope's line in the script was a simple "Okay.")*

Everyone has detractors, and there are those disrespectful of the **balls'** ties to the male ego. We call such women **ball-busters**, or **ball-breakers** (20thC)—terms which proved so popular, they are now synonymous with any extremely demanding person or activity. Such varying items as a job, a relationship, a tight parking space—all now qualify as **ball-breakers**.

Balls, however, finally achieved their deserved recognition as part of the vocabulary to the counterculture of the sixties when they became a full-fledged verb. You could now proudly proclaim, "I love **to ball** my old lady!" While the 1981 World Series was being played, the Rendezvous Cinema, at 54th Street off Seventh Avenue in Manhattan, a block and a half away from series headquarters, premiered a flick called *Ball Game*…rated X.

How really important are they? **Balls** are the ultimate motivator. Former Nixon aide and born-again Christian Charles Colson kept a reminder posted on a wall, "If you've got them by the **balls**, theirs hearts and minds will follow."

The Whole Bag of Tricks

Balls usually come handsomely packaged in an appropriate container, often a **bag**. For this reason, the word "bag" itself hasn't had an easy time of it. It was banned from use in Kansas during the 1920s because it reminded people of the **scrotum** (c. 1597), and was replaced by "sack" and "poke" in Appalachia for the same reason.

The sixteenth century favored the **culls**, either an abbreviated version of **testicles** or a variation of *culeus*, Latin for "bag." In Old English, the bag came disguised as a **cod** (c. 1398), encouraging countless scabrous puns. Shakespeare had us **changing the cod's head for the salmon's tail**. And Mark Twain grew it to monumental proportions as the subject of a long-suppressed poem, "The Mammoth Cod."

Man once carried his **fancy work** and all his precious **gear and tackle** in a sex glove called a **brayette** by the French (from the Latin *braca*, which is linked to the Aryan *bhrag*, a "covering for the loin and thighs") and a **codpiece** by the English.

Originally intended to protect him during combat, it became a popular objet d'art during the fifteenth to the seventeenth centuries. The glove was embroidered and colorfully decorated, often including fancy work, a pocket in which he also placed his handkerchief, loose change, and a piece or two of fruit, thereby rounding out his assets.[5] It was an outstanding addition to his wardrobe, inspiring admiration, speculation, and discussion as to what the bulge divulged. Borachio in *Much Ado About Nothing* mentions an imagined Hercules "where his **codpiece** is as massive as his club."

Today, a "well-filled crotch area" is called a **basket**, and the art of wearing tight pants to good advantage, **basket weaving**. Protocol suggests that good craftsmanship always be acknowledged directly to the **basket bearer**: "That's a nice **basket** you have there," or alternatively, **My, the Easter bunny's been good to you, hasn't he?** (**gay** lingo, 1990s). Others privately speak of a **bucket of balls** (mid 20thC), leaving everyone wondering when, if ever, man will learn to contain himself properly.

A Last Verbal Banquet

The orchid comes to us from *orchis*, the Greek word for **testicle**, based on the similarity in shape between the root of the plant and a man's **balls**. No one probably would have noticed if John Ruskin, the nineteenth-century writer and art critic, had not personally championed a cause to change the name, so angry was he that such a vile word should be used to describe so delicate and beautiful a flower.

His efforts, however, did not succeed. But it was a good try. Thus we had "**Orchids** to you, John!" an early twentieth-century curse, a later variation of which was, "**Testicles** to you."

Tips of the Tongue

1. Those who think smaller is more beautiful would use **shmekel**, the diminutive of **shmok**. Even this is not without risk, however, being easily confused with the verb, *shmecken*, "to taste."

2. For the man who has everything, there's **Aaron's rod**, the generator of not one but two miracles as recorded in the Old Testament. In Numbers 17:8, Aaron places it before the ark, and Jehovah causes it to bloom and bear ripe almonds. In Exodus 7:9–12, when he casts it to the ground, God transforms it into a serpent. The feat is also performed by Pharaoh's sorcerers, but, as a spectacular bit of showmanship, Aaron's rod-serpent swallows up all the others. It was the prefect symbol for the **penis**—the fount of all creative activity and the unassailable power that envelopes and engulfs all about it.

3. According to Anita Hill, Clarence Thomas' favorite video flick was *Long Dong Silver*. Who are we to argue with a Supreme Court Justice?

4. It's not just men. As Jonathan (Jack Nicholson) said to Sandy (Art Garfunkel) in the film *Carnal Knowledge*: "You think a girl

really goes for you and you find out she's out for your money or your **balls** or your money and your **balls**. The women today are better **hung** than men."

5. Stocking stuffing is not just a holiday tradition, nor something only men do. There's also **packing**, when a **lesbian**, flaunting her **butchiness**, wears an addition such as rolled up socks or a **dildo** in the crotch of her pants.

The Gender Gap

 o one particularly likes going into the **hole** (16thC), but this isn't your ordinary run-of-the-mill cavity. It's **your better 'ole** (16th–19thC), and ever since Eden the center of man's attention. His preoccupation with it has led him to embellish it: as the **sweet-scented hole** (C. 1690, Rabelais), the **touch-hole** (17th–20thC), the **aperture of bliss** (16th–20thC), and **your hole of holes** (16thC). He has also named it the **gap** (19th–20thC), **crack** (16th–20thC), **slot** (20thC), **cranny** (20thC), and **nook**, from which we get our favorite, **nooky** (or **nookie**, early 20thC), though some argue that **nooky** derives instead from to **nug** (17th–19thC) or to **nock** (late 16th–18thC), two of our more venerable expressions for **the Big F**.

Over time, your basic hole assumed new dimensions as the **crevice** (19th–20thC), the **bottomless pit** (18th–early 19thC), the **Great Divide** (c. 1925), and the **Grand Canyon** (20thC). It got religion with the **holy of holies** and the **temple of low men** (as opposed to the temple of **hymen**), puns calculated to bring us all to our knees.

Starting from Scratch

Nobody really knows where the **hole** came from, though Captain Grose, the roguish eighteenth-century lexicographer, had his own ideas about it. His version opens with an angel who had been employed in forming women, forgetting to cut off their **parts of generation**. Enter Lucifer who took it upon himself to set matters right.

Taking a somewhat direct approach to the problem, he placed himself in a sawpit with a scythe fixed to a stick in his hand and directed the women to straddle the pit. He then gave each the **mark of the beast** (c. 1715). The pit being too deep for the length of his instrument, tall women received only a moderate scratch, but little women, because their legs were so short and more within his reach, received a somewhat larger cut. The long and short of it?

*The portions of a woman that appeal to man's
　depravity
Are constructed with considerable care,
And what at first appears to be a simple little
　cavity
Is in fact a most elaborate affair.*

*Physicians of distinction have examined these
　phenomena
In numerous experimental dames;
They have tabulated carefully the feminine
　abdomina,
And given them some fascinating names.*

*There's the vulva, the vagina, and the jolly
　perineum,
And the hymen, in the case of many brides,
And lots of other little things you'd like, if you
　could see 'em,
The clitoris, and other things besides.*

*So isn't it a pity, when we common people chatter
Of these mysteries to which I have referred,
That we use for such a delicate and complicated
　matter
Such a very short and ordinary word.*
　　—Anon., cited by Peter Freyer,
　　　"It" in Mrs. Grundy, 1963

O gracious hymen!
Cure this dire mishap
Sew up this mighty
Rent or fill this gap.
　　—Robertson of Struan, Poems, *1746*

They both went home with an **everlasting wound** (17thC), known in some quarters as the **divine scar** (18thC).

The Devil, henceforth, was to be known as "Old Nick" or "Old Scratch;" and the **cunt**, as **slit** (17th–20thC), **nick**, and **gash** (both 16th–20thC).

As men saw it, women were left forever with an aching void. Soon men began employing these terms not only for the organ but for the sex act itself, and, unable to distinguish one from the other, for women collectively. This may have been the meanest cut of all.

Gimme a C!

M'lady's privates consist of a number of parts. Those which are featured most prominently are the **vulva**[1] (c. 1548, Latin for "wrapper"), and the **vagina**[2] (c. 1682, Latin for "sheath"). However, the whole world knows them better collectively as the **cunt**.

Cunt is a grand old word, not underground, not slang. You'll find variations of it in Old and Middle English, Middle Low and Low German, Old Norse, and Dutch. For years, it was believed that **cunt** derived from *cunnus*, the Latin word for the female **genitals**, but no one could explain how the *t* got into **cunt**. It was left for Eric Partridge to discover the word as related to the Old English *cwithe*, "womb," finding the root of the matter in *cwe*, (or *cu*), which signifies "quintessential physical femininity"—a root that appears in a host of words from "cradle" and "cow" to "queen" and "cunning."

Cunt has been taboo in writing and in speech since the fifteenth century. Between 1700 and 1959 it was considered obscene, and it was a legal offense to print it in full. John Fletcher, in *The Spanish Curate* (17thC), reminded us that to write *sunt* (Latin for "they are") with the *c* is "abominable"—creating a **fie-for-shame** (c. 1820) or a **hey-nonny-no** (c. 1690–1750). Shakespeare spelled it out clandestinely, and sneaked it by the bluenoses in *Twelfth Night* when Malvolio exults, "By my love, this is my lady's hand!, these be her very **C**'s, her **U**'s, '**n**' her **T**'s, and thus makes she her great **P**'s."

No ordinary four-letter word, **cunt**'s always been rather special. It's a "sexual energizing word," one which, according to Partridge, conveys "the sexual pleasure produced by a woman in a man and indeed all that woman-as-sex signifies to a man both physically and spiritually."

Daryl Van Horne (Jack Nicholson) in *The Witches of Eastwick* (1987) waxed philosophic on it as well, "A woman is a hole! Isn't that what they say? All the futility of the world pouring into her."

James Joyce had a different take, describing the Dead Sea in *Ulysses* as "the grey sunken **cunt** of the world." It was left to D.H.

It's a cavern of joy you are thinking of now
A warm, tender field just awaiting the plow.
It's a quivering pigeon caressing your hand
Or that sweet little pussy that makes a man stand
Or perhaps it's a flower, a grotto, a well,
The hope of the world, or a velvety hell.
But friend, heed this warning, beware the affront
Of aping a Saxon: don't call it a cunt.
　　—*"Ode to Those Four-Letter Words"*

Lawrence to capture its essence perfectly through Mellors, the game-keeper, in conversation with Constance Chatterley—a touch of poetic justice too that the **cunt** was "liberated" by the decision in the *Lady Chatterley* case, making it possible for us to see the word in print once more when the book was finally cleared for publication and distribution in 1959.

> "Th'art good cunt, though, aren't ter? Best bit o' cunt left on earth. When ter likes! When tha'rt willin'!"
>
> "What is cunt?" she said.
>
> "An' doesn't ter know? Cunt! It's thee down theer; an' what I get when I'm i'side thee; it's a' as it is, all on't."
>
> "All on't," she teased. "Cunt! It's like fuck then."
>
> "Nay, nay! Fuck's only what you do. Animals fuck. But cunt's a lot more than that. It's thee, dost see: an' tha'rt a lot besides an animal, aren't ter?—even ter fuck? Cunt! Eh, that's the beauty o' thee, lass!"
>
> —D.H. Lawrence,
> *Lady Chatterley's Lover*, 1928

The Generation Gap

Lexicographers, however, generally avoided any reference to it in their dictionaries, leaving a long-standing gap in the language. Francis Grose's *Dictionary of the Vulgar Tongue* met it halfway and awarded it four stars, ********, in his second edition in 1788, noting that the word came from the Greek *kovvos* ("bead" or "trinket") and the Latin *cunnus*. Then, adding insult to injury, he referred to it as "a nasty name for a nasty thing." Now really! For years, she was denied access to the OED. Only Partridge argued the injustice of her exclusion: "OED gave **prick**, why this further insult to women?" It wasn't until 1976 that it was finally given an entry of its own.

But even in its formal absence it has occupied a very special place in the English language. Not just "a bawdy **monosyllable** such as boys write upon walls" (Farmer and Henley) but the **venerable monosyllable** (pre-1788–pre-1915).

As Grose reminds us, there may be thousands of monosyllables in the English language, but there is only one that is the **definite article** (18thC).

Amo, amas,
I loved a lass
And she was tall and slender;
Amas, amat,
I laid her flat
And tickled her feminine gender.
> —Henry N. Cary, The Slang of Venery,
> *1916*

You Don't Say

However positive and reinforcing it could be, **cunt** has been a pejorative for women all the way back to the Roman times and the *cunnus*. According to Partridge, the word was used frequently by soldiers during World War I in such expressions as "You silly (or great) **cunt**." More recently, Dustin Hoffman called it to our atten-

The worse name anyone can be called is cunt. The best thing a cunt can be is small and unobtrusive: the anxiety about the bigness of the penis is only equaled by anxiety about the smallness of the cunt. No woman wants a twat like a horse-collar.
—Germaine Greer, 1971

tion while promoting his movie "Tootsie," in which he plays a man playing a woman. Displaying his newly raised consciousness on matters sexual, he noted, "If a man is obsessed with getting things right, he's called difficult. If I were a woman, I'd be called a **cunt**."

It's not unusual to insult people by identifying them with their body parts. Calling someone a **prick** is a commonplace insult, but we reserve use of the expression for males of a particular character, and not for men in general. **Cunt**, on the other hand, is not only a term filled with contempt and disdain, but it is applied indiscriminately, regardless of the person's character, insulting not only the person toward whom the remark is aimed, but all women everywhere.

Words Fail

Man has not only spoken ill of the **cunt** but has also described it in glowingly romantic terms. According to Karen Horney, the noted psychiatrist, this makes very good sense. Both approaches reflect man's deep-seated dread of the female **genitalia**; each in a different way helps allay this fear. By making little of the **cunt**, he convinces himself that there is nothing to fear from so mean an object. Through its idealization he insures the unlikelihood of harm from so divine a being.

And we have no shortage of superlatives to describe it. We have everything from **the dearest bodily part** (Shakespeare) to **the best part** (Earl of Dorset), **the best in Christendom** (Rochester), and **la belle chose** (Chaucer). For some, it's been just plain out of this world—as **in heaven** (18thC).

Yet that nagging fear is always there beneath the surface. It's also been **sheer hell** (18thC) and a **devilish thing** (18thC); so much so that many would dispense with the entire matter by putting the **Devil into hell** (18thC).

Some reserved judgment, as did John Donne with the **best-worst part**. Others extolled it as a **masterpiece** and featured it prominently as the **star** (16thC), depicted ofttimes as **pretty-pretty** (17thC) and indescribably **quaint**, as in Chaucer's "Miller's Tale": "Full prively he caught her by the **queinte**."[3]

At its lowest, this **cloven stamp of female distinction** (18thC) has been reduced to a **suck-and-swallow**, a **man** (or **fool**) **trap**, a **butter boat**, an **oystercracker**, and **sperm-sucker** (19thC). At the same time, it's been elevated to a position of power as the **controlling part** (19thC) and the **regulator** (late 18thC–19thC).

It's almost as though they forgot its more mundane functions as the **water box** (19thC), or **streamstown** (c. 1820–90), the **generating** or **brat-getting place** (19thC), the **nursery**, and the **bath of birth** (early 20thC).

The Lap of Luxury

Some such as Shakespeare simply settled for its general location, as in the conversation in *Hamlet*, act 3, scene 2:[4] "Lady," Hamlet politely asks Ophelia, "shall I lie in your **lap?**" "No my lord," Ophelia protests. Hamlet clarifies matters: "I mean, my head upon your **lap?**" She responds: "Ay, my lord." "Do you think I mean country matters?" (a dreadful pun as in "**cunt**-ree") queries the naughty Prince. "I think nothing, my lord," Ophelia uncomfortably avers. Hamlet retorts, "That's a fair thought to lie between maid's legs." Feigning innocence, Ophelia asks, "What is my lord?" Hamlet: "Nothing."

A Tough Slot to Fill

Most know the **cunt** best, however, by one of its more conventional aliases. Traditional favorites include the **quim** and **tail**. **Quim** (17thC) originates with the Celtic *cwyn* for "cleft" or "valley" and has that same *cwe* root noted earlier, while **tail** derives from the French *taille* for "nick" or "notch," the *vagina* having first turned **tail** during the fourteenth century in Chaucer's "Wife of Bath's Tale." Both have had their ups and downs, but none are more popular than **twat**, **muff** (both 17th–20thC), and **snatch** (20thC).[5]

Oh, the muff!
The jolly, jolly muff
Give me of muff great store
Red, black or brown, divinely rough
I honor and adore.
　　—Captain Morris, in Bee's Dictionary

　Twat's origins are unknown, and it has long been a source of mystery and puzzlement. No one was more confused than the poet Robert Browning, who stumbled across the word in an old Royalist rhyme, failed to understand its satiric intent, and came away with the impression that the **twat** was an article of clothing belonging to a nun. He liked the word so much that he proceeded to incorporate it, with that meaning, into his own, "Pippa Passes" (1841).

　Editors of the nineteenth-century edition of the Royalist rhymes changed the phrase from an "old nun's **twat**" to "I know not what." As far as we know, Browning's poem continued to make a habit of it. The **twat** also has the dubious distinction of gaining separate entry into the OED even before the **cunt** itself, in the totally male company of the **prick** and the **cock**, who gained access at the same time.

No money
No coney
　　—Massinger and Decker,
　　　The Virgin Martir, A Tragedie, *1622*

　Muff is more aptly likened to clothing ("Lost, lost and can't be found a lady's thing with hair all 'round"—Farmer and Henley), and a popular part of a seventeenth-century bridal toast: "To the well-wearing of your **muff**, mort!"—meaning "To the consummation of your marriage, girl!" Today, **muffs** are out of fashion, but as part of the ever-popular sport of **muff-diving** (**cunnilingus**, 20thC), they're still very much an in thing.

　Snatch was an illicit or mercenary **copulation** (17thC) before it got its present meaning. It eventually teamed up with **scratch** (which had become "money" c. 1930); and together produced the immortal couplet: "No scratch, no **snatch**!" Long before Visa and MasterCard, it was "No cash, no **gash**."

More Wise Cracks

We have more than 1,000 terms for the **vulva**. In the inner city, there's talk of getting some **trim** (from the 16th–18thC verb meaning "to deflower"). Earlier, they asked for the ever-popular **poon** or **poontang**. **Poontang** probably made it into the language through Creole from the French *putain* for "prostitute." That, in turn, originated with the Latin *puteus*, the well at which all came to drink their fill. Southern blacks could care less about its roots, always identifying the **poontang** directly with **pussy**.

> "Eye that poontang there," he said.
> "I could eat it with a knife and fork.
> Where I come from we call that
> kind of stuff 'table pussy.'"
>
> —William Saroyan, *Jim Dandy*, 1947

Pussycat, Pussycat, Where Have You Been?

It's for that same **pussy** that men truly go wild. This is one helluva pet—warm, cuddly, soft, and nice—a real pussycat who can turn into a regular tiger.

Given her profligate nature and her personal appearance, it was only a matter of time before our feline friend became identified with a woman's **private parts**. She first surfaced as a **pusse** in 1662 and is recorded for posterity in a toast of the period: "Aeneas, here's a health to thee, to **pusse** and good company." In the eighteenth-century they spoke of her **trotting out her pussy** (17th–20thC) and **giving her pussy a taste of cream**, or just **feeding the pussy**. **Pussy** was temporarily eclipsed in the nineteenth-century by **cat**, **chat**, and **mouser**. Later, we even had a **mousetrap**, but she always remained a little **pussy** (19thC) to those who knew her best. Come the twentieth century she began to make a strong comeback. By 1948, she was everywhere, and a very popular commodity at that. Alan Lomax cited her in "Mr. Jelly Roll":

> Papa's in jail!
> Mama's on bail!
> The baby's on the corner
> Shouting pussy for sale!

Her star was now fully on the ascent. The Fugs, an alternative rock band from the 60s, started their show by dedicating the music

Oh, the ring-a-dang-doo, now what is that?
It's soft and round like a pussycat.
It's covered with fur and split in two,
And that's what they call the ring-a-dang-doo.
        —Anon., 20thC

"to all the snapping **pussy** on the Lower East Side." They were soon joined by John Sebastian and the Lovin' Spoonful:

> Hot town, summer in the city
> Back of my neck feelin' dirty and gritty
> Cool cat looking for a kitty
> Goin' to look in every corner of the city
> —"Summer in the City," 1966

By the seventies, **pussy** had attained national prominence. T-shirts proudly proclaimed, "Happiness is a warm **pussy**," and dozens of books and hundreds of assorted icons were produced in its honor. In 1981, after twenty years under lock and key, the only complete Beatles recording never put on sale was finally released. Its title? "Leave My Kitten Alone."

Pussy rules the world.
—Madonna, 1990

Leave It to Beaver

The hard-working **beaver** also deserves a tip of the hat, as one who's labored in the shadow of the **pussy**. Its unofficial historian, Kilgore Trout, hero of Kurt Vonnegut's *Breakfast of Champions*, defined a **beaver** as "the photo of a woman not wearing under-pants and with her legs far apart so that the growth of her *vagina* could be seen." He went on to explain that:

> The expression was first used by news photographers who often got to see up women's skirts at accidents, sporting events, and from underneath fire escapes and so on. They needed a code word to yell to other newsmen and friendly policemen and firemen and so on, to let them know what could be seen in case they wanted to see it. The word was this: "Beaver!"

Its origins are elusive. One theory is based on guilt by association, **beaver** having once been slang for a **hat** and a **beard**, both of which also did time as **cunt**.[6]

Others looked to women's underwear. When women's panties first appeared in the sixteenth century, their primary purpose was to protect the wearer from the cold. The first undergarments were made of warm material—flannel, cotton, velvet, and, you guessed it, beaver skin. Given only rare glimpses of reality, you can under-stand how the confusion arose in man's mind.

Be kind to animals, kiss a beaver.
—Army saying, 20thC

Hear her say, "Ward you were really hard on the beaver last night."
— Viagra ad, nytimes.com, 2003

What's Up Doc?

The pussy and the beaver have both done yeoman service in *The Erotic Tongue*, but what animal to better represent both reproduc-tion and the **vagina** than the rabbit? The French even speak of a sex maniac as **une chaud-lapin**, a "hot rabbit."

Have you heard the one about the rabbit who
washed her thing and couldn't do a hare with it?
          —*Anon., Maledicta*

We know it best in its obsolete form,—**con(e)y**, **cunny**, or **cunnie** (17thC), all of which are coincidentally, diminutives of **cunt**. **Coney** rhymes with **bunny** (18thC), a word that originated in Scotland for the tail of the hare. It was later shortened to **bun**, which also attained considerable popularity as the female **genitalia**. Rather than having to rub a rabbit's foot, sailors in the eighteenth century, prior to embarking on long voyages, would **touch bun for luck**, a ritual that proved even more popular than knocking on wood.

You Can Call Me...

It was only a matter of time before the **cunt** emerged as its own person. But we have fewer personal names for it than for **prick**. Most have only limited usage and none have attained the prominence, popularity, or instant recognition of a **John Thomas**, a **Dick**, or a **Peter**.

There's little rhyme or reason to the names for the **cunt** except for the cockney rhyming slang that gave us **Berkeley Hunt** (She's a real **Berkely**!), **Joe Hunt** ("Don't be such a **Joey**!"), and **Charlie Hunt** ("That bloke's a **Charlie**!")—all of which rhyme with guess what.

However, men spoke fondly of **Miss Laycock** and **Miss Horner**, perhaps of nursery-rhyme fame (both 19thC), and women of their **Little Sister** (19thC), their **Granny** (20thC), and their **Aunt Maria** (before 1903). Intimate relations aside, she's always been a good **chum** (19thC).

Such knees, such thighs
And such a bum
And such a, such a modicum.
          —*Cotton, "Scoffer Scofft," 1675*

They also knew her as **Madge** (c. 1780) and **Mons Meg** (from the cannon with the huge aperture at Edinburgh Castle) as well as **Mary Jane** (c. 1840) and **Lady Jane** (c. 1850) who, together with **John Thomas**, provided most of the action in *Lady Chatterley's Lover*. But this is also one lady with a good bit of **tomboy** in her. John Taylor, in "The Water Poet" (1643), wrote of her "playing **tomboy** with her **tomboy**."

For the most part, people prefer that she remain anonymous. An old British ballad reminds us, "Such delicate thighs and that shall remain nameless between" (17thC). There's also **her thing**, **what-do-you-call-it**, **what's her name**, **what's-its-name**, and **you-know-what** (all 18thC). In 1772, a fellow named Bridges sadly mused, "I wish I'd never touched **her what-d'ye-callum**."

Well, what d'ye know about that!

Long Time, No C

As with the **prick**, the **cunt**, when not a whole person, has been made a small part of one. But whereas we displaced the **prick** downward, things were looking up for the **cunt**. In the eighteenth century you might have heard an angry fishwife scream, "I'll knock six of your eight eyes out." An ophthalmologist's dream. The other six, as detailed by a lexicographer of the time, included two **bubbies** (also called **big brown eyes** in twentieth-century U.S. Southern slang), the **navel**, the **pope's eyes** (the **asshole** and the **pisshole)**, and the **cunt**.

In a somewhat upside-down view of the world we saw the **cunt** as the **long eye** (c. 1850), the **nether eye**, the **upright wink**, and the **dumb squint** (all 19thC). It was further distinguished as **the eye that weeps most when best pleased** (G.A. Stevens). The **long eye** was characteristically shortsighted and often caught by surprise. Seeing his **thing** for the first time often proved to be a real **eye opener** (19th–20thC).

The whore laughs with one eye and weeps with the other.
—Pietro Arentino, 16thC

Look Ma, No Cavities!

No need to stand there with your mouth wide open. Wipe off that **upright grin** (19thC)! Not believing in a **mouth that cannot bite** (18th–19thC), men suffer from the classic male phobia of *vagina dentata*, fearing that when the **penis** is inserted into the **vagina**, it will be bitten off.

Psychiatrists tell us that men who dream of teeth in the **vagina** are expressing a fear of women and emasculation. Those so afflicted might consult their analyst for treatment or undergo an approved program of dental care. Any friendly lexicographer, however, could tell them that they are confusing her **bite** (late 17th–early 19thC) with the Anglo-Saxon *byh*, the fork of the legs.

On one account you can relax. Your secrets are safe with it. As the **nether mouth** (late 16thC), it's **the mouth that says no word about it** (18th–mid 19thC). But don't expect it to express appreciation. It's also **mouth thankless** (mid 16th–early 17thC)—take, take, take, and never a sign of gratitude.

What's Cookin'?

There was a time when, after a hard day's work, the man of the house would come home to find his wife with skirt raised before the fireplace—**warming the old man's supper** (18thC). That, however, soon gave way to the **oven** (18th–19thC). **Oven** was very much in vogue as the **cunt** during the eighteenth and nineteenth centuries. Some think it originated with the Old English proverb, "No man will another in the **oven** seek, except that him selfe have been there before."

Atop the oven, the standard family fare was **la soupe et le boeuf** (19thC, "beef stew"), the **conjugal ordinary** (19thC). Some men preferred **being in a woman's beef** (18th–mid 19thC); later, **in her mutton** (19thC). It was **mutton** (c. 1670) that truly proved

*But if my oven be over-hot
I date not thrust it in, dear,
For burning of my wriggling pole
My skill's not wirth a pin, sir.*
—Thomas D'Urfey, The Jolly Tradesman, 1720

Nothin' says lovin' like something from the oven.
—Pillbury Flour commercial, 1960s

to be his **meat** (late 16thC), especially when served **laced** (c. 1575–1860), **split**, or **hot** (both 17th–19thC).

A Different Angle

One man's meat, however, is another's **poisson**. For **C-food** (20thC) fanciers there's always **a bit o'fish** (18th–20thC). Fish has long been identified with the **she-thing**: "Two things smell like a fish, and one is a fish," a derogatory term for a woman taken from the supposed odor of the **vagina**. Joe Turner's, early rock and roll song, *Shake, Rattle, and Roll*, featured the line," I'm like a one-eyed cat peepin' in a seafood store," where the one-eyed cat is the **penis** and the seafood store, the **vagina**. The Beatles' "Penny Lane" featured **fish and finger pie**. **Fish** also made it into contemporary **gay** slang for a **heterosexual** woman, **fish and chips** (1990s) being the wife and kids of a male lover.[7]

Some, however, prefer **oysters** (19thC), named for their shape and garniture as well as their reputation as an aphrodisiac, to say nothing of **bearded clams** (20thC), very close in appearance to the real thing and a very popular item at that.

Green with Envy

If it's veggies you fancy, you'll love her **greens**. It used to be that people **got, gave,** or **had 'em** (19thC). Both men and women were **on for their greens**, and men were **forever after 'em. Fresh and curly greens** were a special delicacy. Men used to swear by them. "S' help my **greens**!" they used to say.

Either way, if it's **head** you're after, you won't be disappointed if what's in **the grocery basket** (19thC) turns out to be **cabbage**.

Cabbage in nineteenth-century England was the **cunt**, creating a vegetable fancier known as the **cabbage man**, also lending an added touch to the French term of endearment, "mon petit chou, "my little cabbage."

Somehow, **cabbage**, with the same meaning, found its way across the Atlantic and into the black dialect of the 1920s and '30s, before finally making its way into the white community. When children asked the inevitable question, "Mommy, where did I come from?" the standard reply was, "I found you under a cabbage leaf." In England, little girls came from under the **parsley bed** (17thC) and little boys from under the **nettle** or the **gooseberry bush. Parsley** came to represent the pubic hair and the **parsley bed** the **she-thing**. Men waited their turn to **take a turn in the parsley bed**.

But why stop there? If **cabbage** and **parsley**, why not also a **cauliflower**? Grose recounts an incident in a court of law where a woman used that vegetable to make reference to her **private**

I was never so scar'd since I
pop'd out of the parsley bed.

   —*Ward,* London Spy, *1719*

I got a sweet woman;
She lives right back of the jail.
She's got a sign on her window
"Good cabbage for sale."

   —*Jelly Roll Morton, "Lowdown Blues"*

parts. Taken somewhat aback and amused by so far-reaching a metaphor, the judge countered by suggesting, "You might as well have called it an artichoke."

"Not so, my lord," replied she, "for an artichoke has a bottom...a **cunt** and a cauliflower have none."

Branching Out

What's a meal without fruit? And what better place to look than the **orchard**, a traditional symbol of fertility and virility? There you'll find **the fruitex vulvaria** (19thC), **the fruitful vine which bears flowers every four weeks and fruit every nine months** (19thC). Help yourself. Take an **orange** (17thC) or **shake the plum tree.** The **plum tree**, according to Shakespeare, has long been man's favorite. We are all said to have fallen out of the **plum tree** at birth. Something "plum" is considered the ultimate—hence its connection with the **cunt**. And for a **plum**, no man will hesitate going out on a limb, especially with two strong ones to support him. Its not like he's without a proper tool. Every man comes equipped with his own personal **plum-tree shaker.**

I was never stained but once falling out of my mother's plum tree.

—Marriage of Wit and Wisdom, *1547*

Forbidden Fruit

Don't give a fig? Aristophanes, in his play *The Peace*, encourages us otherwise:

> Now live splendidly together
> Free from adversity
> Pick your figs
> May his be large and hard
> May hers be sweet.

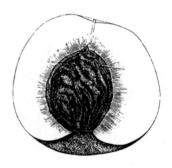

Since Adam and Eve both reputedly covered their nakedness with a fig leaf, the fig has come to be identified with the **vagina**, the **penis**, and even **the act** itself. The appearance of the split fig added further to the case because it so closely resembles the lips (the **labia**) of the **vulva**. In Italy, the *fica* is a common gesture of contempt: thrusting the thumb between the middle and index fingers. Originally, it was used as a good-luck gesture to ward off evil spirits. Today, it's yet another way of saying, "**Fuck** you!"

How Sweet It Is

Concluding your meal with your just desserts, you might try something from the **sugar basin** (mid 19thC) or from among the **hymeneal sweets** (19thC): a **bit o'jam**, a **cookie (**both 19thC) or perhaps some **jelly roll** (20thC). **Jelly roll** is a popular Southern Black term. You'll find references to it in many blues songs of the twenties and thirties, as well as in the literature of the period.

We also have some plain **jelly** (19thC) serving a dual role as both **cunt** and an attractive female. Both **jelly** and **jelly roll** have also done extensive service in black jazz lexicon as nicknames for men who loved both women and their parts. They both began as Standard English, took on a sexual connotation, and then later merged with elements of African verbal translation. David Dalby, a student of African elements in American English, traced it back to the Mandingo *jeli*, a minstrel who gained much popularity with the women by his delightful use of words and music. What a dream combo we'd have with Jelly Williams on bass, Jelly Thompson on guitar, and Jelly Roll Morton on piano. M-m-m-m-m!

W.C. Handy gave **jelly roll** his own personal endorsement: "I'm most wile about mah **jelly roll**!" Thomas Wolfe also attached special value to it: "'What's—what's he going to give you a dollar for?' he muttered, barely audible. 'Jelly roll,' said Ella Coperning." (*Look Homeward Angel*, 1929).

Pot Luck

All that talk about food. But where's a lady to put anything? It's not like she doesn't have any options. Around the house, there's many a **canister**, **pan**, **bucket**, **chalice**, or **box**. The **box** has been around since the seventeenth century and is still in use today. Doggerel of the 1950s reminded us,

> "She's got no cherry, but that's no sin
> She's got the box the cherry came in."

Thinking outside the box, things also went to pot, creating the **melting pot** (19thC), the **mustard pot** (19th–20thC) and the **honey pot** (18th–19thC).

Opting for simplicity, she might favor a nicely shaped **pipkin** (17th–19thC), a small earthenware pot, and for that special occasion, **the miraculous pitcher that holds water mouth downward** (mid 18th–19thC).

However, M'lady's been known to draw the line against certain arrangements. According to Grose, eighteenth-century maidens were heard to complain, "I will not make a **lobster kettle** of my **cunt**!" (c. 1795–1800), a reply frequently made by the **nymphs** of Portsmouth when requested by a solder (a "red-coat") to grant him a favor.

Mind Your Business

Inevitably, one comes around to that which puts the food on the table. Ever since Adam made the first entry at **Eve's customhouse**, men have reduced her and **it** to a marketable commodity, speaking of her business as the **leading article** and her **stock-in-trade**.

My daughter's a girl of reputation, though she has been seen in your company, but she's resolved never more to venture her pitcher to the well.
—William Wycherly, Love in a Wood, 1672

There is more than a hint of this in eighteenth-century England. When a young lass bent over somewhat injudiciously, a true gentleman would avert his glance and gently warn her, "Take care Miss, lest you show your **money**." Nell Kimball, the Great American Madam, was one who realized its earning potential. Reminded that most women were either unaware of it, or chose not to treat their **money** as such, she quoted her Aunt Letty, "Every girl is sitting on her fortune, if only she knew it."

Saving it for marriage used to enhance a woman's value. It was once said that a woman without a dowry at least possessed a **Cambridge Fortune**. Cambridge was interchangeable with the city or town of your choice. Her wealth consisted of a **windmill** and a **watermill**—the **ass** and the **cunt**, respectively. An **Irish inheritance**[8] was a **Tipperary Fortune** which included not only the above, but **tits** as well, making her the precursor of today's well-endowed woman.

...When gently I lay'd her,
She opt a purse as black as coal
To hold my coin.
—From an Old Broadside ballad, 1720

Gimme a Ring Sometime

Counted among a woman's most precious possessions and the counterpart to a man's **family jewels** was **cupid's ring** (mid 18th–19thC), also called **(Hans) Carvel's ring** (c. 1700), after the medieval doctor who slipped it on one night in his sleep. According to Grose, the good doctor dreamt of receiving a ring from the Devil which, as long as he wore it, would insure his wife's fidelity. "Hans took the ring...and thrust it beyond his joint. 'Tis done,' he cry'd... 'What's done, you drunken bear,' cried his wife. 'You've thrust your finger God knows where!'"

Woman cannot make living with left leg
Woman cannot make living with right leg
But between them she do all right.
—Pseudo-Oriental wisdom, c. 1950s

Lover's Lane

A fine dowry is one way to a man's heart; another is through his stomach. But there is yet a shorter and more direct route. Admittedly, not one of the smoother routes to travel, it happens to be one of the more **agreeable ruts of life** (19thC). In fact, the **vagina** is the one body part of *The Erotic Tongue* that's actually had a street named for it. Peter Freyer, the British authority on prudery, researched a Gropecuntlane, a street name appearing in London, York, North Hampton, Wells, and Essex in England in the thirteenth and fourteenth centuries. Further study revealed it to be "a common name for a dark and disreputable passage."

As forbidding as it sounds, there's little to fear in taking a walking tour of the area, providing you apply the proper terminology and exercise the necessary discretion in following directions.

Hit the **road** (17th–20thC), take a turn on **love lane** (19th–20thC). Though on first sight it might appear a **blind alley**, it is the **Main Avenue** (both 19th–20thC). If you don't believe it, check out the **traffic** (19thC for "sexual activity"). After a brief stretch on **Leather Lane**, proceed with caution, for the **road to paradise** quickly converges into the **road to a christening** (19thC)—a sudden turn that could be disastrous. Keep on **the straight and narrow**. At the fork check out all signs. Do not make a mistaken turn onto the **old dirt road** (19th–20thC), known also as **Hershey-Bar Road** (20thC).

Going All the Way

At last there's cause for celebration. We've finally come to the **end of the sentimental journey** (18thC), which also happens to be **home**. The connection goes back to the very last word in Laurence Sterne's 1786 book, *A Sentimental Journey Through France and Italy*, which ends with "So I stretched out my hand and caught hold of the *fille de chambre's* _____."

It may not look like much, but whether you call it the **thatched house under the hill** (c. 1770–1850) or the **mansion of love** (19thC), it's there you'll find **the rest and be thankful** (19thC–20thC), and a retreat from the hurly-burly of the outside world.

Could there be a better place to settle in? Henry Miller thought so: "Perhaps a **cunt**, smelly though it may be, is one of the prime symbols for the connection between all things. To enter life by way of the **vagina** is as good a way as any. If you enter deep enough, remain long enough, you will find what you seek."

Your Place or Mine?

With luck, the keeper of the **premises** will have **rooms to let** and be willing to take in a **lodger** (19thC for a **penis**). The quality and the location of the rooms vary. Most prefer the **front parlour** or the **front room** with the **front window** (both 19thC). But you may have to make do with the **front attic** (19thC) or the **cellar** (Richard Brome). For all, there's the convenient entryway at the **front door** (18thC, John Cleland) or the **portal of love**.

It's the door they're all looking to **get in**. Some sought to force matters by **picking the lock** (18thC) as well as boasting of it: "Here's the lock of all locks and unlocking the same" (G.A. Stevens, *Songs Comic and Satyrical*, 1788). Many a man applied his **key** (18thC **penis**) directly, a very special **key** that young girls especially feared, frequently described as **the key that lets a man in and a maid out** (18thC).

Is This Trip Necessary?

There are men, however, who quest for adventure. It is they who prefer to idealize and romanticize the **vagina** as a faraway and

Please, Mother, Open the door!
　　—Cocky boys calling out to the girls,
　　　early 20thC

When a door has once been broken, it is hard to keep it shut.
　　—Anon., 19thC

…License my roving hands and let them go
Before, behind, between, above, below,
Oh, my America, My Newfoundland.
　　—John Donne,
　　　"To His Mistress Going to Bed"

exotic land to be reached only after a long and difficult voyage. The strangeness of the geography makes it seem distant and remote, perhaps even foreign. Only when she **spreads her pretty map** (Alex Comfort, 20thC) do parts unknown reveal themselves. The explorer can now make out the **Antipodes** (19thC), the **Midlands** (C. 1820), the **Low Countries** (18th–mid 19thC), and the **land down under**. The easiest way to find it is to **go south**, somewhere **'twixt wind and water** (16thC).

The entire trip is a joyful excursion. There's pleasure not only in sailing toward foreign parts, but in the ecstasy experienced at the moment of arrival and the romance and mystery of exploration.

Once there, man can discover the romance, color, and charm of **nature's tufted treasure**. Take a dip in the clear, deep pool in the **forest glade** or the **shady spring** (Bridges). View the awesome **hymeneal waterfall** (George Baker), the spectacular **oracular portcullis** (James Reaney), the **living fountain** (Robert Herrick). Retire to the exotic **downy cave**, **love's pavillion**, and the **mystic grotto** (all 19thC). Pass through the **postern gate** to the **Elysian Fields** (Herrick). Frolic in **love's playground** (19thC). Take a turn in the **breathtaking Grove of Eglantine** (Thomas Carew) and the historic **Orchard of the Hesperides** (Christopher Marlowe).

And thanks to new direct flights and special stopover fares, he can also include in his trip a breathtaking excursion through the **Cyprian Strait** and the **cloven inlet**, round **Cape Horn** or the **Cape of Good Hope** (both 19thC), while anchoring in the majestic **Botany Bay** (19thC).

I wish I was a diamond ring
Upon my Lulu's hand
And everytime she scratched her ass
I'd see the promised land.
　　—Anon., Lulu, 20thC

How Does Your Garden Grow?

The **promised land** features many scenic wonders. Shakespeare's Venus encouraged Adonis to roam in both the **high delightful plain** and the **sweet bottom grass**.

"I love your hills and I love your dales," John Keats reminded us. Our scenic tour reveals a slight incline known as **Mons Veneris** ("Mount of Venus" in Latin), known also as **Pill(i)cock Hill** (16thC), **Mount Pleasant** (c. 1880), or **Shooter's Hill** (late 19thC). There you'll find the **green grove**, the **green meadow** (c. 1850), the **(front) garden** (16th–19thC), often described as **the gentleman's pleasure garden** (19thC).[9]

Amidst it all appears the **beauteous flower** (19thC), the **flower of chivalry**. If you should check the **bush**, in it you'll find a **bird's nest** (for both the **pudendum** and **pubic** hair). It could be that of the **magpie (18thC)**, the **cuckoo (18th–20thC)**, the **goldfinch** (before 1821), the **dove**, or the **phoenix** (c. 1640). A famous nest is this. It's the **nest in the bush** (18thC), one widely celebrated in prose, poetry, and drama.

With your arm kisses on my lips,
How could I stay your hand;
The veil was lifted and by faith,
You viewed the promised land.
　　—Anon., "The Rehearsal," 1895

Her legs opened wide
My eyes I let down steal
Until that I espyed
Dame Nature's Privy Seal
　　—Farmer, Old Songs, Merry Songs, 1897

I must another way,
To fetch a ladder, by the which of your love
Must climb a bird's nest soon when it is dark.

—Shakespeare, Nurse in *Romeo and Juliet*

Letting Your Hair Down

Here's to America, land of the push,
Where a bird in the hand is worth two in the bush.
But if in that bush a fair maiden should stand,
Then a push in the bush is worth two in the hand.

—Anon., 20thC

Tired of beating around the **bush** (mid 19thC)? Looking for closure? It's not always easy. John Ruskin found the **bush** to be an insurmountable obstacle. Because of it he was unable to consummate his marriage on his wedding night, so shocked was he to find his teenage bride, Effie, sporting a growth of hair above **love's triangle**. Why it was enough to raise the **nether eyebrow** (19thC). Another sportsman might have taken a **shot over the stubble** or, better yet, **taken a turn in it** (19thC). Others would have tickled her **scut** (16thC), long considered her **tufted honor** (17thC, Urquhart). But not John!

Obviously, our Victorian long-hair had never heard about **fluff** (19thC), the **fleece** (17thC), the **short-hairs** (20thC), the **belly** or **quim-whiskers** (19thC), the **silent beard** (18thC), the **twat rug** (19th–20thC), the **snatch thatch** (late 18thC), the **lady's welcome mat**, or the **cunt curtain**.

It is not fit the silent beard should
Know how much it is abus'd...for
if it did, it would...make open its
sluice to the drowning of the low countries
in an inundation of salt water.

—Sir Thomas Brown, Works, 1704

If That Don't Top Everything

They had entirely different problems two hundred years earlier when a smallpox epidemic resulted in considerable fallout in the most exotic places. Thoroughly embarrassed by their baldness, women fashioned artificial hairpieces known as **merkins** (**merkin** also being a long-standing name for the female **genitalia**, 17thC).

Merkin is still with us today in a different capacity. The name of the President of the United States in the film *Dr. Strangelove* was Merkin Muffley (**cunt cunt**). A curious turnabout, given that Presidents have traditionally been seen as **pricks** rather than **cunts**. Interesting too, that a **cunt** should be the only voice of restraint and moderation during a time when the world was perched at the brink of nuclear destruction. At any rate, the original epidemic passed and the fashion faded, leaving us with such phrases as the **quim wig** and the **ladies' low toupee** (both 19thC)—and the traditional organ still in charge of the oval office.

If dresses get much shorter
Said Mary with a sob,
I'll have two more cheeks to powder
And one more place to bob.

—Ditty from the 1920s

This Bud's for You

The Erotic Tongue would be less than complete if it failed to mention more than the **vagina** or the **vulva**. We haven't even touched upon the **clitoris** (c. 1615), a part which Aristotle considered "the foundation and the fountain of sexual love in the female." First discovered by Renaissance anatomists in 1559, Realdo Colombo called it a "pretty and useful a thing" (*De re anatomica*); two years later, however, Gabriello Fallopio, of tubular fame, disputed its priority.

Sinastari, a Roman inquisitor of the early sixteenth century, took things in an opposite direction, fantasizing about women with elongated **clitorises** raping men. He also claimed that only women with excessively large **clitorises** could engage in **sodomy** with one another. If a charge was brought against a woman, competent midwives should examine her to ascertain if her **clitoris** was enlarged. In the late nineteenth and early twentieth centuries it was a commonly held belief that an "enlarged" **clitoris** signified one prone to engage in various forms of female "degeneracy," black women's sexuality, and **nymphomania**—black women, **lesbians**, and **nymphomaniacs** all being grouped together as possessors of a "primitive" sexuality.[10] Though sexologists such as Havelock Ellis disputed the theory, most doctors of the time clung tenaciously to the belief.

Today, we're much more enlightened on the topic. Though it's widely recognized as woman's source of **self-pleasure**, we still have few words to describe it.

The reason, clearly, is that men have never tolerated rivals particularly well, and the **clitoris** (popularly known as the **clit**, 20thC) is no exception. At one point they didn't bother with it at all, dismissing it as the **penis muliebris** (19thC, medical terminology meaning "a female **penis**" from the Latin *mulier*, "woman"), thus reducing it to a vestigial organ, a weak homologue of sorts, something about as useful as a man's nipples.

Freud demeaned it further, considering the **clitoral orgasm** a stage of infantile sexuality, woman's developmental goal being to move from the **clitoral** ("infantile") to the **vaginal** ("mature").

More recently, it's Freud who's been deemed immature. As Natalie Anger pointed out in *Woman: An Intimate Geography*, the **clitoris** has some 8,000 nerve fibers—double that found in the **penis**. "**Penis envy**?" she inquires, "Who'd want a shotgun when they could have a semiautomatic?"

Others practiced character assassination upon the word itself. Searching for its derivation, etymologists linked the word to the Greek *kleiein*, "to shut or close," implying that something or somebody was being shut out. Wayland Young, in *Eros Denied*, asks us to take a closer look and see if the **clitoris** really does shut or bar access to the **vagina**, inquiring, "What forced such derivation but that it should be barred or shut." This when they could have chosen *kleitos* for "renowned, splendid, or excellent," or even settled for the somewhat neutral *kleitoris*, "the small hill."

Men's anatomical perspective was also cockeyed, likening it to the **ear-between-the-legs** and the **shame tongue** (direct translation from the German). Others settled on the nondescript **button**

No man should marry until he has studied anatomy and dissected at least one woman.
      —*Honoré de Balzac, La Physiologie du Marriage*

I said, "Give it to me baby, you don't understand
Where to put that thing
Where to put that thing
Just press my button, give my bell a ring!"
      —*"Press My Button (Ring My Bell),"*
      Blues Song, 1936

(19thC) or **little bud** (Edmund Wilson, *Memories of Hecate County*, 1951). The French call it **la praline**, a "sugared almond," from its similarity in shape. Baskin-Robbins later contributed inadvertently—hitting the spot with "pralines and cream."

As a person, it's held several positions: the **goalie** (20thC), always keeping his eye on the puck; the **little ploughman**, supervising the proper sowing of the seed; and the **peeping sentinel**, guarding love's treasure against intruders.

It's also been the solitary adventurer—the **little boy** (or **little man**) **in the boat** (c. 1908, Can.)—adrift upon the **open C** (mid 19th–20thC).

After the grandiloquent terms for the **vulva**, it's quite a letdown. The **clitoris** not only comes up second best but ends up sounding like an outtake from a TV commercial.

Tickle Your Fancy?

The **hymen** (c. 1615) comes off somewhat better. We know it best as the **cherry** (20thC), which describes both the thin membrane stretched across the **vagina** and identifies the bearer with **virginity**. [11] Those who still have it are also described by the fruit, a term that's used for men as well ("He's still **cherry**" or "still got his **cherry**," even though it's an anatomical impossibility). **Cherry** was originally a nineteenth-century term for a young girl, a time when it was still believed that all girls were intact. Other terms include the favored **maidenhead**, which preceded the **hymen** (13thC), the **virgin flower**, the **darling treasure**, the **jewel without price** (all 19thC), but also, unfortunately, **the perishable commodity** (Cleland).

Hymen himself was a Greek god of marriage who lent his name to that unique membrane. He also gave us "hymns," originally special songs sung on the wedding night to invoke his blessings on the marriage. Some also believe them to be shrieks of pleasure given off by the bride the moment she bade **hymen** adieu. Most, however, consider them cries of pain. **Defloration** tears the **hymen** and hurts like hell. There's really nothing to sing about.

Dis-Organized

Women's **organs** have never had an easy time of it. They were always considered something less than, or a variation of, the man's.

Dr. William Acton, a noted Victorian sex quack and self-styled authority, published an opus in 1857 entitled *The Functions and Disorders of the Reproductive Organs in Childhood, Young, Adult Age and Advanced Life Considered in Their Physiological, Social and Moral Relations.* All without a single mention of woman.

I have an intense desire to return to the womb; anybody's.

—Woody Allen

The **ovaries** are another case in point. We didn't even know them as such until 1662 when Johannes van Horne, a Dutch professor of anatomy, tired of the standard references to them as "the female **testicles**."

Angry over the manner with which women's **organs** have been dealt? Looking to vent your spleen? But only if you're a man. According to Hippocrates and the ancient Greeks, the spleen was the organ of the body responsible for melancholia, what we now know as depression. To treat a man for depression, the physician would make a small incision in the general area of the spleen, allowing the unhealthy vapors to escape. Woman's melancholia was another matter altogether. No small incision for her. Her problems were said to be located in the womb. The Greek word for womb is *hysteria*, and in order to cure a woman of her hysteria they insisted on removing the entire womb, an operation that we now know as a "hysterectomy."

And that, dear reader, finally brings down the **cunt curtain** (19thC).

Tips of the Tongue

1. And what of the **vulva**? Though the **vulva** is the proper word for woman's external **genitals** and the proper counterpart to the **penis**, few ever speak or write of it. Instead it's the **vagina**, the internal organ that connects the **uterus** with the outside of the body which we're always talking about. Many times what people call the **vagina** is really the **vulva**.

   Dr. Mildred Ash, a noted psychiatrist, in an article in *Maledicta, The International Journal of Verbal Aggression*, expressed shock at the absence of **vulva** from our vocabulary. She viewed this as more than an oversight but part of the general deprecation of the female **genitalia**, concluding that women avoid its use because they are ashamed of its "ugliness" and its close association with the obscene **cunt** and because it also reminds them of the lack of a **penis**. Men prefer using the **vagina** because by reducing it to a hole of sorts, "It enables them to master their fear of people who have no **penis** and do mysterious things like **menstruate** and have babies." Typical of this is the remark made by Andrew Dice Clay in *The Adventures of Ford Fairlane* (1990), "What's the definition of a **vagina**? The box a **penis** comes in."

2. The **vagina** can speak for itself. It has done so extensively since its Off Broadway debut in 1996 in *The Vagina Monologues*, by Eve Ensler. As noted by a *Times* drama critic, Ms. Ensler captures its essence beautifully as a metaphor for female loss, passion, and terror but also appreciates it for what it is—a source of pleasure, pain and an object of hatred

as well as desire. Her play also set a precedent as the first of a new genitourinary genre on the Great White Way, including *Urinetown*, *Puppetry of the Penis*, and *Menopause, the Musical*.

3. It's also generated much wordplay. Geoffrey Chaucer, you should pardon the expression, had a ball with **cunt**, punning on the word unmercifully off of *queynte*, meaning "curious," "strange," or "artful" and *queynt*, "quenched." Since Chaucer's time, the two meanings have diverged and become spelled differently, leaving things simply "quaint." But the bad puns continued. British poet Andrew Marvell (1621–1678) wrote in "To His Coy Mistress," that after her death:

    ...then worms shall try
    That long-preserved virginity,
    And your **quaint** honor turns to dust
    And into ashes all my lust

4. The Bard laps it up in a number of other productions as well. In *King Henry VI*, Part III (act 3, scene 2), the Duke of Gloucester refers to it. In act 4, scene 3 of *Othello*, where Emilia speaks to Desdemona. In *1 Henry IV*, 3.1.226–27, where Hotspur calls to his wife, "Come, Kate, thou art perfect in lying down. / Come quick, quick, that I may lay my head in thy **lap**." It also proves a great place to take a nap in *King Henry VI*, Part II (act 2, scene 2), when the Duke of Suffolk tells Queen Margaret how difficult it is to leave her, alluding to "a pleasant slumber in thy **lap**."

5. Less well known but also popular are **quiff** (from to **fuck**, 18th–20thC) and **ginch** (from early 20thC slang for a woman). Earlier it could fit you to a T as the **teazle**, the **tuzzy-muzzy** (c. 1700 and the **tirlry-whirley** (late 18thC–early 19thC). Robert Burns wrote movingly how "Ye wrought a hurley-burley in Jeanie Mitchell's **tirley-whirley**." While in Victorian England they employed the **motte**, a popular cant word and one favored by Frank Harris in *My Secret Life*. "I should have guessed her full sixteen, had it not been for the little hair there was on her **motte**, and the delicate pink small cut and tight **penis** hole." **Motte** comes from the French from an obsolete word for "round" or for a "moat." Later when it became synonymous with a prostitute, she became a **moth**, a mispronunciation perhaps or, as some thought, in tribute to her brief life and protective coloration.

6. There are also contemporary references to a **beaver-shooter**, one concerned with looking at a woman's genitals, and a **beaver shot**, a glimpse or a photograph of them, also known as **split beaver**.

7. Smell all too fishy? There is a basis for it. The Greek *delphos* means both "fish" and "womb." In Christian theology the fish

is a phallic symbol, and in many cultures, it is also considered an aphrodisiac. The **cunt's** also been known as the **fish pond** (20thC), where a man employs his **fishing rod** (20thC). Frustrated in his quest for **fresh fish**, he'll make a trip to the **fish market** (19thC, **whorehouse**), making sure to wear his **fish skin** (20thC, **condom**). Combined with the earlier references to **groping for trout in the peculiar river, the cod's piece, and changing the cod's head for the salmon's tail**, it should be quite an outing. All potential anglers should be aware, however, that the **rod of love** is worthless without a good line. When all else fails, fish your wish.

8. The Irish have always been on the butt end of sexual language. They and the Dutch were to the eighteenth and nineteenth centuries what the Polish were to the twentieth. In addition to the **Irish fortune**, there's also an

Irish Wedding:	**Emptying a shit-house**
Irish Confetti:	**Semen**
Irish Root:	**Penis**
Irish Toothache:	**Priapism** (i.e., to get one's Irish up)
Irish Dip:	**Sexual intercourse**
Irish Clubhouse:	**Brothel**

9. Being in a woman's garden elicits a wide range off responses. Some stand in awe, as in Aristophanes' *Lycistrata*: "Yet, I never saw a lawn so primly kept." Others take matters immediately into their own hands: "Love's meadow happy Dick with nature's **scythe** was mowing." (Dick and Kate , from *The Rattle*, 1766). Not even improper equipment held man back. Old English folk songs and ribald ballads forever encourage him to **cut her grass**, or **mow her field**, "even though his **scythe** be bent and broke."

10. In 1918, a dancer sued the publisher of a journal for libel for an article linking her name with the heading, "Cult of the Clitoris." The publisher's defense rested on the assertion that she could not possibly been libeled in that no one knew what a **clitoris** was.

    When the dancer herself was questioned whether she knew the term, she answered, "Yes, but not particularly." The author of the article swore he had tried to find a title "that would only be understood by those it should be understood by." He added how he had telephoned a village doctor to whom he mentioned the word and was told that it "was a superficial organ that, when unduly excited or overdeveloped, possessed the most dreadful influence on any woman, that she would do the most extraordinary things," adding how "an exaggerated clitoris might drive a woman to an elephant."

A Doctor testifying on the publisher's behalf said that he had shown the term to fifty or sixty friends, none of whom knew its meaning (presumably most of these were fellow Doctors). He added," Of course clitoris is a Greek word; it is a medical term...nobody but a medical man or people interested in that kind of thing, would understand the term." (Lucy Bland, 'Trial by Sexology? Maud Allen, *Salome*, and the "Cult of the Clitoris Case" in Lucy Bland and Laura Doan, eds., *Sexology in Culture: Labelling Bodies and Desires*.)

11. Virginity once meant more than the condition of one's cherry. According to Gordon Rattray Taylor's *Sex in History*, the Romans distinguished between *virgo*, "an unmarried woman," and *virgo intacta*, "a woman who had never known a man."

Ditto for the Greeks, to whom a **virgin** was a woman who had opted for personal autonomy instead of submitting herself to the narrow caged life of marriage. **Virginity** was considered less a physical state than a way of being. A woman getting married was seen as selling her independence, causing others to say she had "lost her **virginity**." The only way to restore it was **to sleep with** a god, leaving most men out. Men for the most part continue to be infatuated with the notion.

As Tamra Broder (Anjelica Huston) noted in the film *Enemies, A Love Story*, "Men love virgins. If every man had his way, every woman would lie down a prostitute and get up a virgin." Leave it to the **gay** community to come up with the solution—a **born-again virgin** (1990s), i.e. a **hetero** having his first **homosexual** experience.

Spare Parts

Mammary Lane

ur treatment of women remains incomplete. While rummaging about through love's attic you'll find the greatest assortment of odds and ends since the Olde Curiosity Shoppe: Nicely shaped **jugs** (early 20thC), hand-crafted **love handles** and **knockers** (both 20thC), a **pair of (Cupid's) kettledrums** (c. 1770–1850), some restful **chest and bedding** (c. 1785, nautical) and, for the autoerotic set, a pair of **headlights** (20thC). All neatly arranged on a **rack** (1990s).

Upon closer examination, you'll see that this mixed bag from the past consists of nothing more than **breasts**. If it seems like **breasts** have been around forever, you're not far off. They bounced their way into the language about the year 1000, coming from the Indo-European *bhreus*, "to well or sprout," starting life as an Old English *breast* and a Middle English *brest* before finally settling in to the form we know today.

But it's the **bosom**, a word that appeared about the same time that's proven more acceptable. According to its ancient Indo-European origins, the **bosom's** nothing more than the space between the arms. Nothing much, but you'd have to admit that it filled the space nicely. Around the middle of the nineteenth-century, **breasts** fell out of favor, and "nice" people stopped referring to them. When you were invited out for turkey dinner and you wanted to express your preference for white meat, you always asked for turkey **bosom**, never the **breast**.

Over time, the **breast** came to be perceived as increasingly impolite to the point of being considered savage, and the **bosom** as refined and gentile. **Bosoms** had a brief, wild fling as **bazooms** (mid 20thC), before ultimately reverting to their conservative character and traditional spelling.

As acceptance of **breasts** declined, other substitutes were tried,

The woman's breast nourishes the child and gladdens the father.
—The Koran

Drebin: "Lt. Frank Drebin of the Police Squad."
Monique: "Is this some kind of bust?"
Drebin: "Very impressive, but we need to ask you some questions."
—Naked Gun 2-1/2, The Smell of Fear
1991

A woman has bosoms, a bust, or a breast,
Those lily-white swellings that bulge 'neath her
*   vest*
They are towers of ivory, sheaves of new wheat,
In a moment of passion, ripe apples to eat.
You may speak of her nipples as small rings of fire
But by Rabelais' beard, she'll throw fifteen fits
If you speak of them roundly as good honest tits.
*   —"Ode to Those Four-Letter Words"*

And tho' I let bobbies oft
Finger my bubbies who think
When they kiss them that they shall possess me.
*   —"Wooburn Fair," in* Farmer, Old
*   Songs, Merry Songs, 1897*

including the **top**, the **torso**, and the **chest**. The **chest** was adopted by many, including a twentieth-century stripper who promoted herself and her wares as "Evelyn West and her treasure **chest**." But such efforts proved a total **bust**, a general term for the upper part of the body including the head, shoulders, and upper chest when speaking of a sculpture, but reduced to the **breasts** when referring to a woman.

Breasts, however, wouldn't take it lying down. They fought back valiantly, finally making a remarkable comeback in the 1920s. Today, they are quasi-respectable. They still occasion a twinge or two when mentioned publicly, but for the most part appear to be holding their own.

Tit for Tat

In and around the locker room there's little talk of **breasts**, but lots of conversation about **tits**. **Tits** is a charming word that suggests many things. George Carlin once proposed a new crackerlike snack treat from Nabisco: "You can't eat just one!" We prefer **tits** as the family dog, small, warm, cuddly, and benign—not unlike the little pooch sitting dutifully with his ear to the RCA phonograph.[1] "Here **tits**! Nice **tits**! G-o-o-o-o-od **tits**!"

Historically, breasts began as **teats** (c. 950), not becoming **tits** till around the seventeenth century, later spinning off the likes of **titties** (c. 1740) and **diddies** or **diddeys** (c. 1780). Once they referred solely to the **nipples** (c. 1530); today they describe both soft protuberances situated on the thorax of the female.

Tits have been considered vulgar since the nineteenth century; it is now considered gauche to tell a lady what lovely **tits** she has. But it's especially difficult to remember that in England, where when your mind is wandering, **your tit is in a trance**.

Lenny Bruce once found himself in such a state, fantasizing how he entered Eleanor Roosevelt's bedroom and found her changing her clothes. "Haven't I got beautiful **tits**?" she asks him. "You sure have," he replies. "Do you work out or anything?"

I'll Drink to That

Call them what you may, to the little sucker born every minute, it's all academic. When he's looking to quench his thirst, he heads straight for the **mountains**.

There you'll find him, cozying up to the **dairy arrangements** (c.1923), chug-a-lugging at the **baby's public house** (c. 1884), or taking lunch at **Café la Mama** (c. 1970). Functioning as such they're the **mammary glands** or **nature's fonts**, long used as the **milk bottle**, the **milk shop**, and the **milky way**. They're also the

toora-looras (c. 1909), as in the Irish lullaby "Toora-loora-loora." When the service is slow, baby's sure to let you know. The child's cry goes "bu-bu-bu," from which we get the ancient cant word, *bub* for "to drink" as well as **bubbies** (late 17th–20thC), **bubs** (19thC), **boovies, boobies,** and **boobs** (all 19th–20thC).

In the tradition of good service, older terms for breasts include the **dugs** (c. 1530), from the Danish *daegge,* and the Swedish *daegga,* "to suckle a child." Though **dugs** have long represented **teats** or **nipples**; the OED now considers their use as applied to woman "contemptuous."

The **paps** (c. 1200) also had their day, originating with the first sounds made by a baby, identified with its call for food and its main source of nourishment, the mother's **breasts. Pap** later became synonymous with food that was soft or liquid, providing us with the word for something of very little substance, "pap," as well as a name for the food itself, "Pablum." This is to say nothing of *poppycock.,* a detailed explanation of which may be found in *The Book of the Toilette.*

More Food for Thought

Young or old, we all need a balanced diet. What better way to get each day off to a rousing start than with a good breakfast? Our morning menu includes **muffins** (20thC), **pancakes** (19thC), **flap-jacks** (20thC), and **dumplings** (c. 1709), as well as the specialty of the house, **deux oeufs sur le plat** (20thC, "two fried eggs up").

Rounding out our meal, we've got fresh fruit. You can select from **oranges à l'étalage,** ("oranges on display"), **grapefruit** (20thC), **watermelons** (H. Allen Smith), **honeydew melons** (20thC), **clusters of grapes** (Song of Solomon), and a **lovely bunch of coconuts** (c. 1909). We have no raisins or prunes, but if you look real hard you'll probably spot an occasional **lemon** (20thC) or two.

It's all **eye-pleasing fruit** (Sir John Suckling, 17thC), **love's strawberries,** and **apples.** And how do you like them apples? **Apples tipped with coral berries** (Carew), **ungathered apples** (Wright, 20thC), **two fair apples, fragrant, sweetly savor'd apples** (Francesco de Barberini, 14thC), **apple-knockers** (c. 1940's), **twinn'd apples round and small** (Cornelius Gallus), and **fair apples in their prime.** As well as something from the **apple-dumpling shop** (late 18th–19thC).

Thanks for the Mammaries

The French used to say, "**Jactons d'entrée des Roberts!**" "Dig those **boobies!**" (*Roberts* has been a nursing-bottle trademark

Then those twins, thy strawberry teates, curled, purled cherrilets...
        —Joshua Sylvester, Miracle of the Peace, 1599

Please let me squeeze your lemons
    While I'm in your lonesome town
Now, let me squeeze your lemons, baby
    Until my love comes down.
        —Charlie Pickett, "Let Me Squeeze Your Lemons," early 20thC

since 1888). In Australia, they praised her **norks**, from Norco Cooperative, Ltd., a major processor of dairy products. American men prefer **whatta pair!** (mid 20thC) and **TNT!** (**two nifty tits!**, mid 20thC).

But these aren't just ordinary playthings to be casually fondled and then tossed aside. They're a **classy pair**, a **matched set** with a splendid history.

In the 1930s and '40s, they were virtually inseparable as **the twins**. In the nineteenth century, they were **les deux soeurs** (the two sisters, a.k.a. the twin sisters) as distinguished from **les deux frères siamois** (**the Siamese twins**—i.e., the **balls**) and more recently, **The Pointer Sisters**, after the pop singers of the time. They've also been named **Charlies** (c. 1840), after Charles II's many mistresses, noted for their opulent **charms**, and **Langtries** (c. 1880–1900, society slang) from Lily Langtry, the famous singer and actress, and one of the most beautiful women of her time. Her name became so synonymous with beauty that the most attractive women in the British colonies were addressed as "Mrs.Langtry." **Langtries** first denoted lovely eyes before making a natural progression to the **breasts**.

In a more contemporary vein, Mae West's pointed remarks are still with us, and so is her name as cockney rhyming slang for **breasts**. She gave her name to the war effort during WWII for life jackets "that bulged in the right place," twin-turreted tanks, and twin-lobed parachutes that malfunctioned. Other cockney slang for breasts includes **Lewis and Witties**, **town and cities**, **Jersey cities**, **Bristol cities** (most commonly referred to as **Bristols**), and **thousand pities**—all rhyming with **titties**.

Eventually, **breasts** attained seniority as the **elders** (17thC, Eng.; c. 1920, Aust.), bringing to mind the story of the woman who had two tattoos, smiling portraits of two former lovers, one on each breast. How she feared the moment of revelation on her wedding night. But when the disclosure was made, her husband took it in stride. "I'm so glad you're not upset, dear," she said. "No need to make a fuss," he commented philosophically. "They may be smiling now, but in a few years, what long faces they'll have."

Magritte

Poetry of the Spheres

The poets were especially fond of them, immortalizing them forever in marble and alabaster.

Geographically, they've been **East and West**, **globes** (c. 1860), **hemispheres**, and **points of interest** (both 19thC). Naturally, **pleasant eminences**, **chalky cliffs** (both Shakespeare); **mounds of lilies**, **twin orbs**, **orbs of snow** (all Cleland); and **nature's fonts**, as well **as two rounded hillocks** (Thomas Heywood, 17thC), **ivory hills** (Cleland); and **hills of paradise**.

Bustin' Out

Breast interest and competition peaked in the States during the forties and fifties, when sweater girls, pin-ups, and movie stars were all bursting at the seams, vying for the honors. It was the heyday of Marilyn Monroe, Sophia Loren, and Silvana Mangano. Howard Hughes used every bit of his engineering genius to design and build a **bra** for Jane Russell with an uplift rivaling that of his famed aircraft. And teenage boys spoke enthusiastically about her **gazongas**, **goonas**, **snorbs**, **hooters**, **wallopies**, and **bazooms**. Big **breasts** were sure winners. At every contest we also had our also-rans: recipients of the **booby** prize included the **droopers**, the **hangers**, and the **swingers** (all 20thC), also known as **saddlebags** (20thC) and **tobacco-pouches** (Fr. *blagues à tabac*).

Breasts were now an object of passionate concern. In America women rubbed in proteins and turned to surgical augmentation; silicone injections produced **silicones** or just plain **cones** (late 20thC), also known as **bolt-ons** or **built-ons**. In Europe, they spread on an exotic ointment, a special muck consisting of oysters, caviar, and mud from the bed of the sea. Other approaches were deceptively simple. Joan Rivers' solution was to merely coat the **breasts** with sugar and water, lie **naked** in the sun, and pray for killer bees.

See Jane Russell shake her tambourines and drive Cornell Wilde.
—*Tag line for preview of* Hot Blood, *1956*

...They and their ilk [hucksters who exploit love and sex] now turned every billboard and even kiddies' comics into peep shows. Furthermore, it is the upper half of women, the infants' half, that has gotten most of their attention, and I sometimes marvel how it is, with all these misdirections sprawled about, that the birthrate has risen so.
—*Philip Wylie,* Generation of Vipers, *1958*

Uplifting Thoughts

But behind every pair of **breasts** there was a man. It was men who set the standards for the **Breast** Betterment League and determined when a pair was ready to face the world. They described women who qualified as **well developed** (19thC), **(well) stacked** (mid 20thC), **(well) endowed** or **zaftig** (20thC, Yiddish for "juicy, luscious, overweight in the right places"). Later, they said a woman was **well built**. The phrase originated in the 1930s, a time when many a public bathrooms was going up, especially in parks and recreation areas, as part of the WPA. Given men's way with words (especially about women) and the pleasure they take in the bathroom and bathroom phrases, it was only natural that they'd link her architecture to that of the the **privies** of the time which were of truly solid construction. Hence the ultimate tribute, **built like a brick shithouse** (20thC). What finer compliment could a woman hope for?

Literate men, however, would have little to do with such phrases, opting instead for more gentile expressions such as **buxom**. **Buxom** derives from the Old English *bouen*, "to bow," and was once an innocent word used to describe a person of either sex who was humble, submissive, obedient, tractable, and easily bent— qualities any lord would be happy to find in his peasants.

By the sixteenth century the word had begun to be applied specifically to a powerfully built female field hand. It later made a quantum leap to her appearance, and today refers to any woman with a shapely **full-bosomed** figure.

Our Cups Runneth Over

Making it to the top: getting to be considered **buxom** or **built like a brick shithouse** was never easy. You first had to put your **glandular endowments** (19th–20thC) through a period of rigorous discipline when they were forced to take up temporary residence in a **training bra** (c. 1950s). We can only surmise that this was a time when they learned to sit and heel on command. Those that made it reached their final destination, the full **bra** (c. 1934) or **bras** (c. 1910), more formally known as a **brassiere** (c. 1912).

The **bra**, or something like it, has been in use for over 6,000 years but really didn't come into its own until the turn of the twentieth century. The first formal application for a patent on the garment was filed on February 12, 1914, by Mary Phelps Jacob, also known as Caresse Crosby, who fashioned a prototype using some ribbons, thread, and two handkerchiefs. She later went into full production, but lacking adequate publicity. her **brassiere** business sagged and Mary was forced to sell her company to Warner Brothers Corset Company for a mere $1500.

After World War I, the donning of the **bra** became synonymous with the chucking of the corset, long considered the restrainer of the female and the mainstay of her oppression. The **bra** allowed women to both liberate their bodies and assume a host of activities, both work and play, previously open only to men.

The word **brassiere** derives from the French *bras*, "arm," and the *bracière*, "arm protector," raising serious question as to its true contents. The French themselves appear equally squeamish in discussing such matters, referring to the garment as *un soutien gorge*, "a support of the throat."

Over the years, we've known the **brassiere** by many names. Originally, it was a **bust bodice** (c. 1829), a **BB** (c. 1920), or a **bust-girdle** (c. 1904). An early manufacturer proudly advertised three basic models: The **Dictator**, which suppressed the masses, the **Salvation Army**, which lifted them up, and the **Yellow Press**, which made mountains out of molehills. More recently, we've had a **booby trap**, a **breast bucket** (20thC garment-industry expression), a **flopper-stopper**, a **hammock for two**, and an **over-the shoulder boulder-holder** (all mid 20thC).

Encouraged by men, women have used them to also exaggerate their **bra-sets** (20thC) with the aid of **palpitators**, also known as **palpitating bosoms**, and **patent heavers** (all late 19thC), **gay deceivers** (early 20thC), and **falsies** (mid 20thC). We even briefly

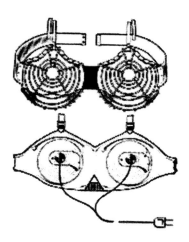

In the last couple of weeks I have seen the ads for the wonder bra. Is that really a problem in this country? Men paying enough attention to women's breasts?

　　　　　　—Hugh Grant

had the **Rawhide bra** from the TV series of the same name (1959–66) whose theme was "head 'em up, move 'em out;" though Australian men preferred the **sheepdog** who "rounded them up and pointed them in the right direction."

Much of the **bra**'s thrust towards acceptance occurred under the stewardship of Ida and William Rosenthal, who went into business as the Maidenform Company in the 1920s as a protest against the notorious flat-chested flapper girls of the Roaring Twenties. Ida was the actual inventor of **brassiere cups**, designing **bras** for every female figure from the budding teen to the mature matron.[2]

As popular as **bras** have been, they momentarily fell out of fashion in the sixties with the **ban-the-bra** movement, during which time they were either burnt or consigned to the trash can. Again, ironically, in the name of liberation.

Please Bare with Us

Banning the **bra** turned out to be a huge flop. But from the male perspective, that wasn't necessarily a bad thing. Sizing up a woman was always considered easier without it. Even better was when she was **sporting her blubbers** (late 18thC), **flashing** or **displaying her charms** (18th–20thC), or **airing her dairy** (18thC). Getting an eyeful, however, has often been a matter of being in the right place at the right time.

Historically, **breasts** have gained their greatest exposure as woman's status in general has grown; the lesser the oppression, the greater the view. The Renaissance blatantly adored, emphasized, and displayed naked **bosoms**, though their revelation was restricted to ladies of nobility and propriety who bared their **bosoms** but were sufficiently modest to mask their faces.

Décolletage or **cleavage** became high fashion in seventeenth-century France, where it was even given a special name, "the well of sanctification or dedication." We later knew it as the **mammaelar trench** (19thC) and the **great divide** (20thC). Later surgical advances turned it into the **silicon(e) valley** (1990s).

In Victorian England, women bared nothing—even in front of their husbands in the privacy of their own bedrooms. Today, anything goes. Since the second half of the sixties, we've favored the designation **topless**—a trend begun by waitresses, dancers and shoeshine girls which quickly spread to other sectors. Variations now include **semi-topless** (pasties), and the all-encompassing **topless-bottomless**.

The media continue to feature the **breasts** on **jiggle shows** as part of **T and A.** (both late '70s) for America's *R and R.* But we haven't had any new terms recently. Perhaps at long last, the American male's obsession with the **breast** has simply peaked—or better yet, gone flat.

Mammie: "What are you gonna wear?"
Scarlett: "That."
Mammie: "No you won't. You can't show your bosom before three o'clock."
—Gone with the Wind, *1939*

I'm going to whip his _____.
    —Jimmy Carter speaking of Ted Kennedy
    as reported in The New York Times,
    June 14, 1979

There was a young lady named Glass
Who had the most beautiful ass—
  Not round and pink
  As you might think
It was gray and had ears and ate grass.
    —Anon., 19thC

Real Bummers

And lastly, we have the parts we share in common.

It was the early days of the "Tonight Show," and Steve Allen was placing his customary "cold" phone call to some unsuspecting party on the outside. The woman on the other end answered with the name of her firm, Big A Cleaners. Allen paused and then smartly inquired, "How much will you charge to clean up my **big A**?" The audience roared delightedly.

Everyone knows the **big A**, but it wasn't always an abbreviated version of reality. It came into the world whole as a full-blown **arse** (c. 1000), and was Standard English until the second half of the seventeenth-century.

However, the word proved so popular that it came to be considered vulgar. Driven underground, it was reduced in print to an ar__ or an a__se, occasionally even a _____ or an a***.

Complicating matters further, people began to confuse the **arse** with the similar-sounding four-legged beast of burden. For years, **ass** had been an acceptable euphemism for the **arse**, but now, it was too close for comfort.

Dictionary makers were also quite diffident on the topic. Samuel Johnson originally included **arse** in his *Dictionary of the English Language* (1755) as did Francis Grose, in his *Classical Dictionary of the Vulgar Tongue* (1785). But when someone asked the good Doctor its meaning, he referred to it as **the part on which we sit.** His questioner responded, "Do you mean a chair, Doctor?" This helped spawn a host of functional designations: the **sit-me-down** (19thC), the **sit-upon** (19thC), the **rumble seat** (c. 1920s), the **seat of honor**, **shame**, and **vengeance** and the plain old **seat** (all 19thC), there being no better place for your favorite **flesh-cushions** (Cleland).

The literary world thought it best to also sit it out. The last writer to spell **arse** in full until 1930 was Jonathan Swift, in his *Battle of the Books* (1704), when the spider asked the fly, "Do you think I have nothing else to do in the devil's name, but to mend and repair after your **arse**?"

Out of this confusion emerged the **A-double scribble** (19thC) and the plain old **A** (c. 1855). For more than two hundred years, the word was treated in this **half-assed** manner. Finally in 1930, with very little fanfare, it was printed again in a book by Frederic Manning entitled *Her Privates We*. The privates, incidentally, referred not to female **genitalia** but to Her Majesty's soldiers. No one made a big thing of its return; in fact, hardly anyone cared. But the **ass** was at last made whole again.

Today, when push comes to shove and we wish to speak delicately of it, what do we fall back on, but our **arse**. We had come full circle. The word had become a euphemism for itself.

Turning Tail

Everything should have been perfectly clear. But American men still didn't know which end was up. They chased **tail** with ardor and passion, often settling for partial satisfaction with a **piece of ass** (20thC), a telling commentary both on their mental health and their knowledge of women's anatomy.

This confusion is characteristic of the multifaceted character of the words in *The Erotic Tongue*, often playing not one, but several parts. Consider not only the **tail**, but the **gig** (or **giggie**), the **keester**, and the **buns**, all of which have at various times stood for different sexual parts. Thoroughly confused by it all, men apparently decided that the only safe way was to treat them all with equal affection.

The **tail** (14thC) comes from the Indo-European, describing the appendage at the rear end of an animal. In England, it began life as a **prick**, evolved into an **ass** during the fourteenth century, later becoming a **cunt** and a taboo expression around 1750. In the States, **tail** took a different route, quickly making an **ass** of itself.

Gig started off as a **wanton** (17th–18thC), reaching midlife (19th–20thC) as a **rectum**, as in "Up your **giggie**!" And toward the middle of the twentieth century began to settle in as a **vagina**.

Other multi-sexual words include the **keester** (**cunt**, early 20thC, **ass**, mid 20thC), and **bun**. **Bun** had already done itself proud as the **cunt** early on (late 17thC), coming as it did from the **bunny**, but in the plural, designating an **ass**, it probably derived from the bakery shelf and its relationship to **tarts** and other assorted pastry.

In the singular, however, **bun** still refers to the **cunt**, even as a bakery item. This includes the hot-cross buns, on which some put the sign of the cross, to help soften their erotic character.

What's a **bun** anyway without dough? Without it we'd never be able to get off our **duff** (mid 20thC). That's because the *gh* in "dough" was once pronounced like an *f*, the word itself meaning "the soft and spongy part of anything."

Ever had a piece of ass?
Turn it over, there's
Pussy on the other side.
—*Graffiti, Brown University*

Stepping to the Rear

The **ass** is a dependable part that holds up its end of things. As the **seat** (19thC), it certainly knows its place.

It would be wrong, however, to think it just rests there. This is a hard-working part that quietly goes about its business at the orifice, functioning as the **shithole** (19thC), the **brown bucket** (20thC), the **dirt road** (early 20thC), and the **poop-chute** (20thC). However, there's little recognition paid its work, and no more insulting a remark than being called "a **fucking asshole**." Nothing personal, it's just one person's opinion, and as Dirty Harry Calla-

Ten percent of the people at UNC have hemorrhoids.
The other ninety percent are perfect assholes.
—*Graffiti, University of North Carolina*

han (Clint Eastwood) reminded us in *The Dead Pool* (1988), "Opinions are like **assholes**; everybody has one."

Getting Off One's Ass

With an arrow so broad,
He shott him into the backe-syde.
—Joseph Ritson, ed., "Robin Hood," 1795

The entire experience proved so puzzling, some could no longer locate what they were looking for. They looked to the **backside** (16thC), the **posterior** (c. 1614), the **rear end** (c. 1920s) or the **behind** (described in the OED as something "in the rear of anything moving" or "the rear part of a person or garment").

Not knowing where else to turn, they came up with the **lower back** (late 19thC). Things were now desperate. In 1912, British papers recorded news from South Africa of a certain Lord Methuen who had been wounded in the **fleshy part of the thigh**. Most thought this all **very ass backward** (or **bass ackward**, both 20thC), a somewhat strange expression used to describe something that's askew or out of sync. So too with the expression itself, **ass-forward** being a much more accurate description of the condition.

I really didn't do anything to my backside.
—Australian pop star Kylie Minogue reacting to tabloid reports that she had plastic surgery done to her posterior, 2002

Global Perspective

The **ass** was slowly becoming alien to us. From France we borrowed the **derriere**, made especially popular by women's magazines in the late nineteenth century. From Germany and Eastern Europe, via the Yiddish, there emerged the **tochis** (early 19thC, also **tochus, tochos, tochis, tokus**, etc.) from the Hebrew *takhat*, literally, "below." Softening the guttural "ch" made for the more affectionate **tush** or **tushy** (both 20thC). It also spun off the **toches lecker** (aka **TL**) or **ass kisser** as well as the remark, **Kush mir in toches (kiss my ass)**, a request people have been making since the sixteenth century. The appropriate response? **Tough toches!** meaning "too bad, or tough luck!"

I've had it up to my keister with these leaks in the press.
—Ronald Reagan, summer of 1983. His speech-writer substituted keister for tush.

It was also the Germans who saved our **rump** (mid 15thC) from *rumpf*, "the trunk of the body." But it's the Italians we can thank for the **labonza** (mid 20thC), a word for **ass** popularized by Jackie Gleason, having magically migrated from its original Italian meaning of "stomach."

It was the **keester** (also **keister, keyster, keister, kister**) (mid 19thC), however, that truly got us into Dutch, from *keest*, "kernel" or "core"—the best part of anything, and a further reminder of the respect it is due.

Rear View Mirror

Not everyone was sure. The **ass** blended so well into the background, people found it difficult distinguishing it from other familiar objects.[3] In 1862, reference was made to army officers so drunk, they **did not know their ass from a musket**. Most frequently, people don't know it **from a hole in the ground** or **from their elbow** (both 1930s).

Further complicating matters were its many varieties.[4] Heading the list was the **hard ass**. We first heard of him in 1876 when Native Americans described General Custer as "Long Hair and **Hard Back Sides**."

He's nothing, however, compared to the notorious **bad ass** (c.1956)—known far and wide as one tough customer. At his worst, he's a **lean mean bad ass** or the **baddest badass** (both 1970s).

At the other end of the spectrum there's the benign **paper ass** (c.1953) who's talking nonsense or hiding behind regulations; and the **candy ass** (1950s) who's soft and weak.[5] The proper response to these negative types is to never react in kind. It's much more effective to just turn the other cheek.

Getting a Boot Out of It

No one likes a wise ass. So says the conventional wisdom. Yet the answer to many of life's dilemmas lies hidden within the inner recesses of this humble part. It reminds us what is truly basic.

These fundamental teachings come from the Latin *fundus*, "bottom" and *fundare*, "to base firmly" making for the **fundament**, "a groundwork or underlying principle," and yet another synonym for the part on which we are so firmly based. What better way then for coaches and teachers to stress the "fundamentals" than by **kicking ass** (also **butt** or **tail**, all 1960s)?

When you **kick ass**, you assert yourself or beat up on another. It's the fullest expression of the competitive spirit.[6] Always a serious matter, during the seventies it also became fun. Not only people but things **kick ass**. Doing so transforms them into an extremely fine experience. A certain CD or movie can really **kick ass**. It can also be an adjective as in, "This is a **kick-ass** book."

Backsliding

Kicking ass is not without risk however. The **buttocks** (14thC), "the two fleshy protuberances forming the lower and back part of the trunk," especially take its lumps—from *butt*, "the bottom," "the thicker end of anything," a swelling caused by the Indo-European *bhau*, "a bruise."[7]

This can easily result in that nagging malady known as a **pain in the ass**, a simple nuisance which can easily become a major problem. Left unattended, you could end up with your **ass in a sling** (mid 20thC). Internal questions should be referred to your **proctologist**, a student of the **anus**, from the Greek *proktos*, for

*Rectitude: The formal dignified demeanor
assumed by a proctologist immediately before he
examines you.*

—*Washington Post,* "Alternative meanings
for words," 2002

that particular organ. A Brown University medical sociologist reports that **proctologists** are commonly referred to in the profession as **Rear Admirals**. Coincidentally, Dr. Reinhold Aman, editor of *Maledicta*, noted that when former President Jimmy Carter was treated for a hemorrhoidal condition in 1978, the attending physician was Dr. William Lukash, a real Rear Admiral in the U.S. Navy.

Ass in an Uproar

There are psychological difficulties as well. Many people **drag ass** or find their **ass is dragging** (1930s). They had the same problem back in 1780: "My **arse** hangs behind me heavy as lead." (Farmer and Henley). Many are probably suffering from the syndrome known as **anal cranial inversion** (1990s), "having one's **head up one's ass**" (1940s), what in its more advanced stages is known as **anal retention**—the tendency to keep it there.

The Bottom Line

Ridden with physical and psychological problems, the **ass**, like Rodney Dangerfield, "gets no respect." People everywhere call it stupid. There's something about it that just does not sit right. In the anatomical hierarchy it is considered the dregs, the pits, if not the absolute **bottom**.

There seems to be no end to the calumny. When it was time for Shakespeare to make the weaver in *Midsummer Night's Dream* into an ass, what did he call him but **Bottom**. No matter, **Bottom**'s tops in our book. As **balls** are the repository for courage, the **bottom** is the seat of endurance. In eighteenth- and nineteenth-century England, it was synonymous with grit and perseverance, good soldiers often being described as having "a great deal of **bottom**."

It may well be our lowest part, but **bottom** comes directly from the old English for "ground" or "soil." Its Indo-European roots meant "to place firmly and securely." When you rest on your **bottom**, you're on pretty solid ground.

That's more than we can say for the Soviet Foreign Minister who, at the Vienna Summit Conference several years ago, attempted to use the word in a toast to the wife of the U.S. Secretary of State—without a translator. "To a gracious lady," he said. "Up your **bottom**."

Esquire magazine hit rock bottom in 1943–44 when the Postmaster General threatened to curtail its circulation for printing such suggestive words as **backside**, **bottom**, and **bawdy house**. **Bottom** needs no defense. We've known it as the sitting part of man since 1794. Its distinguished progeny include **botty** (19thC),

b.t.m. (late 19thC), and the **booty**, as in the 1984 disco hit, "Shake Your Booty!"

A Bum Rap

Despite the **bottom**'s excellent lineage and its deserving a fair shake, most people still treat it as a no-good **bum**. The **bum**'s been with us since the late fourteenth century, but around 1790 it fell into disrespect, and since 1840 it has been made to feel especially unwelcome in England. When the Al Jolson film *Hallelujah, I'm a Bum* opened there in 1930, the Lord Chancellor, Britain's public censor, had it retitled, *Hallelujah, I'm a Tramp.*

The American tramp, however, had nothing to do with the English **bum**. The British **bum** has been an **ass** since the late fourteenth century, and its origins are thought to be onomatopoeic. It couldn't be a contraction of **bottom**, which wasn't used in that sense until later. The American **bum**, as hobo, goes back to the German *bummeln*, "to loaf or loiter" and the *Bummler*, "an idler or loafer," who didn't appear here until the first major wave of German immigration during the 1850s.

Only occasionally do the two converge, as when you "give someone the bum's rush," picking up a loiterer or trouble-maker by the seat of his pants and throwing him off the premises. There's also a "bummer," a real bad experience (c. 1960s), and a possible tie-in with the earlier *bummler*. John Ciardi passed on an intriguing bit of folk etymology suggested by *Musical Heritage Magazine* (May 2, 1977), attributing *bummer's* origin to the famed eighteenth-century organ-maker, Johann Jakob Bommer, "whose organs were so much admired they gave rise to the expression "It's a real Bommer."

Unfortunately, so's the explanation.

The Real Bad Ass

Bums are also people. Our gallery of infamous **bums** include the notorious *Roby Douglas*, a mythical nineteenth-century nautical figure noted for his "one eye and a stinking breath," as well as *Gluteus Maximus*, "the notorious blowhard Roman general." Another hostile figure was **Heinie**, the endearing diminutive of Heinrich that also doubled as amalgam of Heinrich and **hind end**, used in a derogatory fashion to designate a German soldier or a person of German descent during WWI. Not taken seriously, all these **bums** were treated simply as nuisances, written off as **a pain in the Frances** (19th–20thC).

The standard response to such discomfort is, "Ask my **Nancy!**" (c. 1810–1910). This, however, is not an especially effective

Like a mauve carnation, puckered up
And dim it breathes, meekly nestled
*   amid the foam*
Damp, too from caresses tracing the
*   smooth dome*
of creamy buttocks up to the innermost rim
*   —Ode to the Asshole, Paul*
*   Verlaine and Arthur Rimbaud*

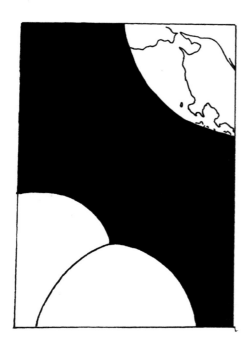

recommendation since **Nancy** is generally not capable of answering back, although on occasion, **Brother Round Mouth** (c.1810–70) has been known to speak.

Let's Face It

Appearances notwithstanding, there's no disputing the **ass's** fine disposition. Just look at that **Sunday face** (c. 1860), decked out with its **broad smile** and its **vertical grin** (18thC). Few will ever forget the classic mouth, those **two fine cheeks** (mid 18thC), **and ne'er a nose.**

Some have likened its roundness to a **moon** (mid 20thC). The French even refer to it as **la lune**. It's also been active as a verb as when an avid female fan of the New York Yankees in the summer of 1980 **mooned** for the players on the team bus—showing her "admiration" for them.

Still can't see it? Obviously a problem with your **blind eye** (18thC). Check it out through the **monocular eyeglass** (c. 1860–1910). Foresight may be flawed, but hindsight is always 20/20.

Sitting Pretty

Well **tickle my Toby!** (c. 1675) or **kiss my blind cheeks** (17th–20thC) if a closer look doesn't show our **tush** to be really friendly, and none more so than dear **Fanny**. In England she was originally a **cunt** via Fanny Hill, the high-flying heroine of John Cleland's raunchy eighteenth-century novel, *Memoirs of a Woman of Pleasure*.

In America, however, she's always been the **butt** of our jokes. Derived from the *fundament*, she's been shortened and punned successfully into **funniment**, **fun**, and **funny**, before finally becoming **Fanny**. There was, however, nothing funny about her problems in the States. As late as 1929, she found herself on B.F. Keith's list of expressions that vaudeville performers were not allowed to use on stage. Ever versatile, they landed instead on **the part that went over the fence last**, the **caboose**, and **where the sun never shines.**

Today she's out from under that cloud. Well respected, accepted by all, **Fanny** now travels in the best of circles, accompanied by the **tush** and the **derriere**.

Bottoming Out

Still displeased with the choices? You could always fall back on your **prat** (16thC), a fine word originating with the Old English *praet* for "prank," which, in addition to being an **ass** also doubled as a **vagina** during the nineteenth century. It was from the first meaning that many a vaudevillian and silent-film star developed his pratfalls, building entire comedy routines about them. There being no better way to guarantee a laugh than by falling on one's **ass**.

Show biz also provided the **bippy** (mid 20thC), made famous by Steve Allen from *bipinnate*, "having two parts equally distributed on the sides of a common axis." The **bippy** is a no-risk body part, one known for its reliability, as close as you can get to a sure thing. As Allen might have remarked:

"Bet your sweet bippy?"
"I'll see you and raise you two cheeks."

The End

Repent, the **end** is near. Time to **bust ass** (c.1937), **get the lead out**, **shake your ass** (c.1927), and **get your ass in gear** (1940s). As the sun sets on beautiful **Spice Island** (c. 1810–50) and the **moon** begins to rise, we weigh anchor from **Dilberry Creek**, also known as **Sinkhole Bay**, and set sail for the **Hinterland** and the **Western End**.

It's no easy feat to negotiate the **Windward Passage**, what with those treacherous gale-force winds. But ours is a sturdy vessel, wide in the **bow, poop**, and **stern** (late 16thC), with the requisite **porthole** and the extraordinary **fantail** for the overhanging portion of the **stern**, from which some think came our **Fanny**—all very nautical, but nice.

It's with a touch of sadness that we leave behind those magnificent promontories those, "plump, smooth and prominent, form'd luxuriant tracts of luxuriant snow that luxuriantly fill the eye..." (Cleland), **pleasant eminences** (Shakespeare) that have encouraged us all to scale new heights.

"In what part of her body stands Ireland?"
"Marry, Sir, in the buttocks. I found it out by the bogs" (latrine).

—*Shakespeare,* The Comedy of Errors

Tips of the Tongue

1. Can't see it? A few years ago a story made the rounds of a young woman in a bikini who was bathing in the surf when a particularly violent wave hit her and swept off the top of her bathing suit. To avoid embarrassment, she embraced her nakedness with both arms. As she was making her way to shore, a young boy stopped her and innocently inquired, "Lady, those sure are cute little puppies. You suppose I could have the one with the pink nose?"

    This is to say nothing of our other animal friends, making for the **cat's head, cats and ditties** (cockney rhyming slang) as well as the **two young roes** from the Song of Solomon.

2. Beginning in 1949 and running for 20 years, the company created one of the nation's most uplifting and successful ad campaigns. Offering prizes up to $10,000 for situations in which

women might wear their product, they asked women to fill in "I dreamed I _____ in my Maidenform bra." Entries included: I dreamed I took the bull by the horns... and I dreamed I rode in a gondola... "I dreamed I went to blazes..." was illustrated by a girl in **bra**, fireman's helmet and boots, swinging from a fire engine.

3.   Other confusing comparisons include not knowing it **from a stalk of bananas** (1930s), **a hot rock** (1930s), **third base** (c.1955), an **armpit** (c.1962), a **pork sausage** (c.1970), a **rifle barrel** (c.1972), the **back side of a checker board** (1970s), **ice cream** (1980s), a **pitchfork** (1985) or a **jug of apple cider** (1970s).

4.   There's even more out there in the wild kingdom. We have the well-known **horse's ass** (c.1865), a persistent or obnoxious fool who annoys people by getting **on their ass**. That's bad enough. But even worse is getting a pesky **bug up your ass**, making you feel outright irascible. **Up to your ass in alligators** (1960s)? You're simply overwhelmed by a multiplicity of demands. Not to worry. Most of these matters are **not worth a rat's ass**, being of little value. There's no better way to register your indignation, than by screaming, **"In a pig's ass!** not at all, never!"

5.   Master of the expletive, Richard Nixon labeled his Secretary of the Treasury a **candy ass** when he balked at using the tax system to punish citizens Nixon considered "enemies," thus reprimanding him or **chewing his ass out** (1950s) publicly. **Chewing other people's ass out** is often a favorite pastime of our Presidents. George W. Bush chewed out Adam Clymer, a **New York Times** reporter, describing him to Dick Cheney as a "major-league **asshole**." The Associated Press proved to be an even bigger one, however, reporting only how Bush "disparaged Clymer."

6.   Everyone **kicks ass**. At one U.S. Open, tennis star Pete Sampras said that by staying aggressive, he hoped to "**kick** (his opponent's) little **ass**." During the 1984 campaign, Bush the Elder told a longshoreman in Elizabeth, New Jersey, "We tried to **kick a little ass** last night." When questioned about it, he characterized it as an "old Texas football expression."

7.   The medical profession has always treated the **ass** as a part worthy of concern. Though they were less interested in it as a whole than in its component parts. In addition to the **buttocks**, they had the **anus** (since mid 17thC), "the posterior opening of the alimentary canal," and the **rectum** (since mid 16thC), "the large end of the bowel connecting to the **anus**." Muscularly, the **gluteus maximus**, the largest of the muscles in the **buttocks**, and the lesser ones known as **medius** and **minimus**.

Different Strokes

he mother of the household stands outside the bathroom door hyperventilating. A gentle knock. No response. Knocking escalates into a rapid rhythmic tempo, becomes a pounding, finally degenerates into a series of irregular thuds. A shrill scream and the all too familiar refrain, "What are you doing in there?" Inside, oblivious to it all and comfortably ensconced against the outside world, is you-know-who doing **you-know-what**.

> Little boy sits on the lavatory pan,
> Gently caressing his little old man.
> Flip, flop, into the tank,
> Christopher Robin is having a whank.
>
> —Anon, 20thC

Swinging Single

The parts can be a whole lot of fun when put together properly, but individually they're also a source of enjoyment.

Playing with oneself (18th–20thC) is a worthwhile activity for both sexes and one of the most rewarding of all the sexual practices. In terms of orgasmic efficacy, it seldom fails us. Alfred Kinsey reported that 95 percent of the time it is successful, with 75 percent of the participants attaining **climax** (20thC) in less than four minutes. Yet some consider it **wasting time** (20thC), as does Richard Spears (*Slang and Euphemism*), who arbitrarily lumped all 127 synonyms for the act under that heading.

Detractors apparently didn't realize its potential as the source of real **self-pleasure** (20thC) and the ultimate expression of **self-love** (20thC). Why, even the Germans consider it *Selbstbefriedigung,* "self-satisfaction."

As this branch of uncleanliness, viz., Sinning with a person's own Self, is the most general of any Sin of Impurity...instructions concerning it are the most wanted in the world to awaken the Guilty, and deter the Innocent and Unwary from falling into it, through Inadvertence or Ignorance.

> —The Crime of Onan or the heinous
> Vice of Self-Defilement with all its
> Dismal Consequences, *1724*

"With whom did you first do it?"
"I was alone at the time."
> —Woody Allen

Self-love? Why not? George Carlin tried it and so enjoyed the pleasure of his company that he sent himself flowers afterward.

The Yanks are Coming

Most men who **play with themselves** generally **jerk off** (19th–20thC). The basic all-American **jerk-off** consists of a motion that is quick and suddenly arrested, a stop, a sudden pull, throw, thrust, or twist: one, two, cha-cha-cha. You **bring it up by hand**, **bring it down by hand**, and **bring it off by hand** (all 19thC). For variation, you may **jerk jelly**, **jerk juice**, or **jerk iron** (all 19thC), as you are disposed.

In second place we have the **jack-off**, from **Jack**, an old person-ification of the male organ. The British, on the other hand, mostly **whank off** (19th–20thC), also **whank, wank, wank off, whang**, and **whang off**. No one really knows where the **whank, wank**, or **whang** come from, though a good guess might be a combination of "whack" and "bang."

Alexander Portnoy, Crown Prince of the **hand-job** (20thC), favored none of the above, preferring instead to **whack off** (20thC). Portnoy's **whack-offs** are of legendary proportions. He soloed at fifteen on the 151 bus from New York. They still talk about his famed three-finger **hand-job** with staccato half-inch strokes up from the base.[1]

Success didn't come easy for Portnoy. It took hours of hard work, determination, discipline, and practice, to say nothing of an understanding mother.

> Now this time don't flush, do you hear me, Alex?
> I have to see what's in the bowl.
>
> —Philip Roth, Mother Portnoy in *Portnoy's Complaint*, 1967

Doing it by the Book

Though **masturpation** has a brief fling in 1621, officially it's **masturbation** (c. 1766)—one of those elusive words that etymologists can't seem to get a grip on. Some think it originates with *manus*, Latin for "hand," and *stupare*, for "defile," hence "to defile by hand." A nice theory for moralists, but one which could give us *manustrapation*, and a chorus of st-t-tuttering acned teenagers. Others, including the authors of the venerable Oxford English Dictionary, found its roots in *mastitubari*, which they translate as "to disturb the male member," though some believe that it is not the *member*, but the seed (*mas*) that is disturbed. Either way, a simple act appears to have left the entire scholarly community in a highly agitated state.

Love thy neighbor as thyself.
What am I supposed to do—jerk him off, too?
—Rodney Dangerfield, 1982

I'll come and make love to you at five o'clock.
If I'm late, start without me.
—Tallulah Bankhead

The good thing about masturbation is you don't have to dress up for it.
—Truman Capote

The World's First Jerks

Masturbation has a long and distinguished history, and we're at no loss for words to describe it. Ancient Egyptian papyri reveal how Atum-Ra created the universe when he "**frigged with his fist and took the pleasure of emission.**" He is said to have cried out, "I was the one who **fucked with my fist and milked with my hand.**"

Self-manipulation (19th–20thC) was sanctified among the Egyptians and an important part of their rituals. True believers were encouraged to engage in the practice to provide food for the gods and to ensure a fertile land.

According to Gordon Rattray Taylor's *Sex in History*, rivers were an especially important part of the gods' work. The sacred Nile represented the **masturbatory ejaculation** of the god Usiris, who controlled the rise and fall of the river by "**alternate continuous manipulation and regurgitation of his gushing genitory.**" But the Nile was not unique. For devout Hindus, the Ganges flowed from the throbbing head of the divine **lingam**, as did the Sea of Soma. And among the Assyrians and the Babylonians there was a particular deity noted for having "**fertilized the fertile crescent with his superfructiferous seed by a torrential act of self-stimulation.**"

It was an exciting time when man literally had the whole world in his hands.

We have reason to believe that man first walked upright to free his hands for masturbation.
—Lily Tomlin

Crafty Southpaws

The Greeks and Romans also felt especially comfortable with the practice. Juvenal, Diogenes, Laertius, Ovid, Scioppius, Pliny, and Aristophanes all wrote freely and openly on the topic, with seemingly little stigma attached to it. But the right hand apparently didn't know what the left hand was doing, and **masturbation** soon came to be considered "sinister." That's Latin for "the left hand," the hand most closely associated with **masturbation** and other "unclean practices," such as wiping after **defecation**.

Any wonder that the word has come down to us through the years associated with evil doings, or that left-handed baseball pitchers are considered particularly flaky?

Waste Not

But for the best source of **masturbation** lore, you have to turn to the Old Testament. There you'll find the story of the granddaddy of them all, the man who allegedly started the practice, the person many consider **Mister Masturbator**: Onan. Ironically, though his name is closely identified with **self-manipulation**, the truth as revealed in Genesis 38:9 is that he never once raised a hand on his own behalf.

Onan and Er were both sons of Judah. One day, God got so upset with Er's behavior that he upped and slew him, leaving Er's widow alone and unattended. Hating to see a good woman barren and going to waste, and in keeping with the Levite tradition, Judah turned to Onan and said, "**Go in unto** thy brother's wife and marry her, and **raise up seed** to thy brother." **A bit of home gardening**, as they say in the trade.

For God's sake, Onan **went in unto** his brother's wife, which also translates as **he fallowed her field**, but knowing that the seed should not be his, **left her unseeded after plowing**, i.e., he spilled it on the ground. Medieval rabbinical scholars described the act as **threshing within and winnowing without**. Masters and Johnson call it **coitus interruptus**. Whichever, what he did proved so displeasing that the Lord slew him on the spot. And mistakenly, Onan's boo-boo came down to us through the centuries as **the solitary evil**.

Onanism (18th–20thC) was man's first somewhat unoriginal sin: both a fall from grace and a nasty spill.[2]

Bible Thumpers

Masturbation never sat well with the ancient Jews. **Self-abuse** (early 18thC) was the basis for the banishment of Ishmael, and God caused the great flood in part because of the actions of Noah's contemporaries who **spilled their semen on trees and rocks** and constantly **abused their fountains**.

The act once even brought down the house. While a crowd of thousands watched, Samson, captive of the Philistines, was forced to **make sport of himself**. Pained, blinded, and humiliated, his last words to Yahweh were, "May I be avenged to the Philistines for **the draining of my fountain**."

Samson had let it all hang out. Accordingly, he is described in ancient Hebrew as a *sahug*, **a phallus-beater**, a term also found in Job 12:4 and Jeremiah 20:7. This translates also as a "laughing stock." Our contemporary equivalent is a **jerk**—one whose brains have been addled through **masturbation**.

Good to the Last Drop

It was no laughing matter to the Jews. "Friends of the Foetus"—the contemporary anti-abortionists who mark life from the moment of conception—have nothing on their Hebraic precursors, who considered the **seed** the beginning of life.[3]

This led to a number of rabbinical prohibitions against behavior likely to lead to **masturbation**. Males were advised not to touch the **penis** while **urinating**. They were also warned against wearing tight pants, riding bareback, having lascivious daydreams, and looking at one's own **sexual member** or that of another. It was also recommended that a boy sleep on his side rather than face up.

With all these warnings and restrictions, is it any wonder that Jewish boys aren't any good with their hands? Or that in nineteenth-century England they referred to the practice as **cynic friction**, **keeping down the census**, and **simple infanticide?**

God'll Get You for That

Never to be outdone by Judaism, Roman Catholicism made such sexuality its special concern. In the seventh century, Theodore of Canterbury issued a penitential for offenders against morality in which he recorded a variety of forbidden practices, including **masturbation**. By the twelfth century, the Church's anti-sex campaign was in high gear.

Though **masturbation** trailed far behind the other **unnatural vices**, it outranked in seriousness **fornication**, an offense deemed more serious than murder.[4] The penitential codes contained twenty-five paragraphs on the topic of **self-abuse** by lay people and even more for cases when the sin was performed by the clergy. As far as **rape, adultery**, and **incest** were concerned, it was no contest. **Masturbation** was the winner, hands down.

If God had intended us not to masturbate, He would have made our arms shorter.
—*George Carlin*

Doing It Religiously

Almost as if in reprisal, people began striking back at the Church through language. Some struck a blow directly by **boxing the bishop**—believing at first "glans" that the top of the **penis** resembled a bishop's miter.

Others took a more exotic approach. **Boxing the Jesuit and getting cockroaches** is an anticlerical expression dating back to the eighteenth century. It originated with sailors and was defined by a lexicographer of the times as "a crime much practiced by the reverend fathers." It was yet another way of saying that man cannot live by a fistful of Hail Marys alone. To **box** is to enclose, as with one's hand. No one really knows, however, why the Jesuits were associated with such activity. Speculation is that it was their high standing in the Church and their propensity for manipulation.

As to cockroaches (perhaps nothing more than a wretched pun on **cock**), why not? If God can visit boils, locusts, famines and the like upon us, cockroaches are certainly not beyond Him. Cockroaches may well be an important first sign. Check with your friends. Do they show any of the primary symptoms? Has hair begun to grown on their palms? Have they started going bald? Are their eyes bloodshot; their brains going soft?

Getting cockroaches merely clinches the diagnosis. Reach out to your friends. Plead with them to stop before it's too late. Encourage them to drop Dear Abby a line. Have them see their clergyman, seek out professional help, or, if the condition persists, an exterminator of their choice.

A Penance for Your Thoughts

"When the flesh rebels against the spirit," asked a monk of his Prior, "What do you do?" "I take my breviary and read it through," he replied. "And I," said a sanctified frater, "jump into cold water." "For my part," observed a young fellow listening in, "I settle the matter at once without ceremony: I knock the brains out of the evil one."

—Sexual humor from Victorian England

Some were so angered by the Church's attitude that they turned violent. They even went so far as to **shoot the bishop** (19thC), a form of mayhem also known as a **wet dream** (19thC), which the Church deemed a serious offense. The penalty for **shooting the bishop** was singing seven penitential psalms, to be done immediately after rising from the debauched state, followed by another thirty in the morning. If the offense occurred while falling asleep in church, the guilty party was required to sing the entire psalter. No provision appears to have been made for those who were tone deaf.

Night Time Is the Right Time

It was only an **involuntary seminal emission** (19thC), but when the evening air is thick with activity, you're talking about a case of **nocturnal pollution** (17th–19thC) and perhaps the need for an environmental impact statement.

Shakespeare hinted at the personal consequence of **masturbation**, referring to it as **the means of weakness and debility** (*As You Like It*). Not much later, scientists and medical men such as William Andrus Alcott cited the proven effects of indulging in **self-pollution** (early 17th–19thC). Their litany of resultant ills included St. Vitus' dance, idiocy, apoplexy, blindness, consumption, and hypochondria.

Man who go to bed with problem in hand wake up in the morning with solution at his finger tips.

—Teenage babble, mid 20thC

Claude François Lallemand, a nineteenth-century professor of medicine, cited the practice as causing the genitals to deteriorate, the spermatozoa to decrease in number and vigor, and the muscles, particularly in the heart, to weaken. "All sensations decrease, sight is endangered, the mind is threatened, and the usual end result is idiocy and death."[5]

A contemporary of his, British scientist Sir William Acton, assured us that although widespread and out of hand, **pollution** could be controlled. His program: a cold-water enema at bedtime and cauterization of the uretha with silver nitrate. And if that didn't work, the patient should tie a cord around the **penis** before retiring. But only if he was truly at the end of his rope.

A Vice for the Lovelorn

The world took a major stride toward sexual enlightenment when authorities began to treat **masturbation** as an appropriate subject for medical study. We even had new terms for the practice, such as **autoeroticism** (also **autoerotism**, 19th–20thC, popularized by Havelock Ellis), **manual orgasm** and **ipsation** (both 19thC), making it more a technical than an anti-theological exercise.

But though the experts thought they had separated sexual behavior from theology, and introduced it as a subject for scientific study, it still remained a moral issue, **a vice, secret and solitary.**

For screwing's always fit to spout
And VD you can moan about
But whanking hasn't any clout
　　—*Charles Thompson, in John Whitworth,*
　　　　editor, The Faber Book of Blue Verse,
　　　　1990

Misspent Youth

Parents soon joined the Church and the authorities in trying to curb the practice. Mothers and fathers considered it their sworn duty to prevent their children from **throwing a tantrum** (17thC) and **going off with their marbles.** Father strapped his son's **privates** into a small metal cage prior to bedding him down for the night, so as to insure a hands-off policy. Just in case, Dad kept the key close by if nature should inopportunely call in the middle of the night. More elaborate cages came equipped with accessories— spikes which surrounded the perimeter or tiny bells which went off should an **erection** occur.

Harriet Beecher Stowe warned parents "that certain parts of the body are not to be touched except for purpose of cleanliness, and that the most dreadful suffering comes from disobeying these commands" (from her book on domestic science, designed "to help American women maintain economical, healthful, beautiful and Christian Homes"). Victorian nannies admonished their charges, "If you play with it, it will fall off." But the beat went on. Kids continued to practice **paw-paw tricks** and **pinch the cat.**

A hundred years later, American children were still playing at **pocket pool.** There was simply no suppressing it. In the 1940s, a favorite children's radio program was "The Buster Brown Radio Show." It featured Froggy, the gremlin who upon the request, "Plunk your magic twanger, Froggy," would transport us all to storyland. Little did parents know that **plunking one's twanger** was part of a tradition that has been carrying kids on erotic journeys since the seventeenth century.

It's called in our schools "beastliness," and this is about the best name for it...should it become a habit it quickly destroys both health and spirits; he (the boy) becomes feeble in body and mind, and often ends in a lunatic asylum.
　　—*Robert Baden-Powell, founder of the*
　　　　Boyscouts

Present Arms

Little boys grow up into big boys, and the military was right there to pick up where Mom and Dad left off. **Mounting a corporal and four** (late 18thC for the thumb and four fingers) has always been a **soldier's joy** (19thC), though army rules prohibited the recruit from playing with his **weapon**.

By the twentieth century, sergeants began disturbing the **blanket drill**, greeting the dawning of each day with "Hands off **cocks**, feet in socks!" Also, "Drop your **cocks** and grab your socks"), favorites both in this man's army and the R.A.F. There's nothing like military discipline to make men come clean.

Pound for Pound

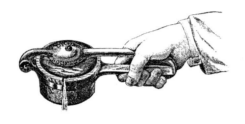

If talk of weaponry has you nervous, remember, **masturbation** is a rough business. It is, after all, the practice of **self-abuse** (early 18thC), and man's approach to the subject is anything but gentle. Some would even characterize it as downright heavy-handed. Over the years, man has **pulled it** (19th–20thC), **beat it** (20thC), **shook it up** (19thC), **flogged it** (20thC, Aust.), **pounded it** (20thC), **whacked it** (20thC), and **tossed it off** (late 18th–20thC).

Manual Arts

Man was always quick to acknowledge the source of his pleasure, handing plaudits to **five-finger Mary, four sisters on thumb street, Mrs. Hand and the five fingers, Mrs. Palm and her five daughters**, and **Lady five fingers**.

As he became more metaphorically adept, he began to **pull his wire** (19th–20thC), **pump his pickle** (20thC, Can.), or **jerk his gherkin** (mid 20thC). For simpler minds, a little rub did them fine. **Frigging** (from the Latin *friccare*, "to rub," 16thC) was a favorite—one of the oldest and most durable expressions for the act. English boys still used the term far into the eighteenth century, providing them with many a memorable moment. One student later reminisced of "fanciful delights…**frigging** in the school **necessary**."

Beastly Behavior

Many chose to consign such roughhousing to the barnyard. There, **bird in hand**, a man might **fight** or **jerk his turkey** (19thC) or **dash his doodle**. **Doodle** (mid 18thC) is a child's appellation for a **cock**, derived from the sound of its crowing, "cock-a-doodle-doo." A **doodle-sack** is the likely female repository for said **doodle**; and a **doodle-dasher**, a man given to habitual **self-manipulation**.

C.B.'ers today compound the mayhem by **choking the chicken**. Anyway you look at it, that's still using your **doodle**, ole buddy!

Once having put such fowl play behind him, a young man could also **come his mutton** (18thC), **mutton** being one of those great all-purpose words for both male and female sex organs. **Coming one's mutton** has long been a popular sport for lonely winter nights, though a form of recreation farmers acknowledge only sheepishly.

Today, there's a whole new, exciting world outside the farm. For outdoor recreation, try your hand at **fishing for trouser trout** or **flogging the dolphin** (20thC).

Why the poor dolphin? Why pick on it? Was it a matter of shape? Native intelligence? Leaping ability? Was it an accident or was it done on porpoise? No one knows.

But if you can **flog the dolphin**, there's no reason why you can't also **gallop the antelope** (20thC).

The origin of the latter remains especially obscure. We know from the mating habits of the antelope that when a stag is frustrated in his efforts to win a female, he **masturbates** by rubbing his antlers rhythmically against a tree, often as much as three or four times a day. Truly **horny**! Though this sheds new light on the **stag party** and **stag films** (both 20thC), it still leaves us very much in the dark on **galloping the antelope**.

Hold Everything!

When all else fails, you can always
> **Beat the pup**
> **Spank the monkey**
> **Pump the python**
> **Peel the eel**.

So dear reader, why not try your hand at it?
> **Slam the seal**
> **Blast the bear**

> _____ the _____

> _____ the _____

> _____ the _____

CAUTION: If your momma doesn't get you, PETA may.

Poetry in Motion

Others sought to lend a defter touch, hoping to capture the rhythmic nature of the act. They encouraged us to **beat the meat, slam the ham**, and **flog the dog** (all mid 20thC).

And if alliteration turns you on, you can always **paddle the pick, pound the pud**, and **pull the pudding**. If that doesn't suit you, **pull the pick** and **paddle the pudding**. No need to stop there! Why not also **paddle the pick**, **pull the pud**, and **pound the pudding**? It still beats lifting that barge and toting that bale.

Few can handle their meter better than Allen Ginsberg:

> Pope my parts
> Pop my pot
> Poke my pap
> Pit my plum.

> —from "Fie My Fum"

Having One's Hand Full

Tired of **playing solitaire** (20thC)? Nobody said you had to do it alone. Ordinarily a do-it-yourself proposition, the game can also be played by two, as in **chopsticks** (20thC, U.S.), after the piano exercise of the same name in which hands are crossed over. Three or more persons constitute a **circle jerk** (20thC, U.S.), the original theater in the round.

Those fearful of taking their lives into their hands can always find outside help. You can turn to **Second-Hand Rose** or your friendly **fricatrice**. She's descended from the **Ladies of Lesbos**, whom Catullus described as standing at the crossways and in alleys "to **jerk off** the high-souled sons of Rome."

In Merrie England, a female **masturbator** of men was called a **shagstress** or **a milk-woman** (both 18thC). The price list in a particular eighteenth-century **brothel** featured a bargain two-guinea job by "a young agreeable person, sociable, with a white skin and soft hand. Polly Nimblewrist from Oxford or Jenny Speedy-hand from Mayfair." Today? Get thee to a massage parlor and ask for a **local**. It needn't be costly. The nice part about it is that you can spend whatever you like.

Lady Be Good

And what of women? A whole chapter and hardly a mention. Both men and women **play with themselves** (18th–20thC). Though the language of **self-help** (20thC) is expressive, we have only a few isolated phrases describing women engaged in the activity. Heading the list is to **jill off** (as opposed to **jack off**). Unlike men who are into the more violent aspects of the activity—beating, banging, flogging, slamming, and whacking—women are just **diddling about** or **rubbin' the nubbin'**. This kinder, gentler approach finds her **petting her bunny**, **tickling kitty** (also her **clitty** or her **crack**) and **stroking the flower** (or the **lizard**, also a male term). Hard at work, she's **digging for clams**, **polishing her pearl**, or **waxing the bishop**. The closest a woman ever gets to violence is **whipping her wire** (or her **cream**) or **spanking the monkey**, the latter being a favorite of men as well.

Historically, few people have taken female **masturbation** seriously. There's little reference to the practice in Judaism, and Roman Catholic manuals of sexual ethics that treat male **masturbation** as "a grave moral disorder" simply dismiss female efforts as acts of mere **lewdness**.

It's been a well kept secret.

In 1846, Mary Gove Nichols, a lecturer on hygiene, shocked her audience by publicly revealing that women also did it. In 1877, Dr. John Harvey Kellogg of Battle Creek, Michigan, brother of the man who introduced modern breakfast foods to the world, snapped and crackled with indignation as he popped the question, "Do you know what your children are doing?" He then provided thirty-nine telltale signs to help parents determine if their young ones were into vice. For girls, those which were particularly telling included lack of breast development; pimples on the face or, especially, on the forehead; fingernail biting; eating clay, slate, pencils, plaster, chalk, and other indigestibles; and habitually moist, cold hands.

Critics warned of dire consequences: the grave, the madhouse, or, worse yet, the **brothel**. There were caveats galore, but few phrases to describe the sin itself.

Is it that for a woman, sex without a man was inconceivable and hence...well...uh...not conceivable? Or was it because men who for so long controlled the written word, deliberately excluded that which did not flatter their king-size egos?

If you'd believe man, this delicate creature's sensibilities exist on a higher plane. Her life's joy is in pleasing him. She is either his sweet madonna, or his very own **whore**. There's no way she could enjoy existence apart from him. As for seeking sexual pleasure? And without him? Absurd! Finding it by herself? **Balls!**

Finally, women have begun taking matters into their own hands.[6] But man has been slow to come around, finding it especially difficult to accept the idea of women's **self-pleasure**. He is now on the spot. Though groping for an answer, he still can't put his finger on it.

You can lick our chops, but you can't beat our meat.

—Sign in a butcher shop, Providence, Rhode Island, 1980

I Have To Hand It to You

Dependency on the **penis** has often limited woman's options, forcing her to make do with whatever was close at hand. The stiffest competition to the **penis** came from the **dildo**, both as a noun (17th–20thC) and as a verb (17th–18thC), meaning "to arouse a woman by digitation and fondling of her privates."

Its origns are somewhat unclear. Partridge thinks **dildo** originated with the Italian *diletto*, "delight." The OED finds its roots in "a particular kind of tree or shrub with cylindrical form."

Dildos were once made of ivory, glass, porcelain, and wood,

Twelve dildoes meant for the support
Of aged lechers of the Court...
Some were composed of shining horns,
More precious than the unicorn's.
Some were of wax, where ev'ry vein,
And smallest fibre were made plain,
Some were for tender virgins fit,
Some for the large falacious slit,
Of a rank lady, tho' so torn,
She hardly feels when child is born.

—"Dildoes," Samuel Butler, 17thC.

often beautifully decorated and dressed with handsome leather covers. Some even came with a leather squeeze bag which one could fill with tree sap. Today, they're made of soft latex with a rubber squeeze bulb. We've experienced them in many different ways. In the nineteenth century, they were everything from a **bientateur** (Fr., "do-gooder"), and a **godemiche** (from the Latin, "I enjoy myself"), to a **consolateur** (of which which there is little to be said).

Good Vibes

Help is on the way. Recent years have seen the introduction of technology to **masturbation** with **vibrators** (also called **cordless massagers**) and an array of **sexual aids**.[7] Women employing them are said to **catch a buzz** or **digitize**, though any of the expressions for female **masturbation** will also do. For that special call, simply **dial O on the pink telephone**.

Truly electrifying! But you ain't seen nothin' until you've tried **Accu-jac**, the trade name for a device that in time should, deservedly, become generic. It's surely nothing to shake a stick at, and it's **bi-sexual** to boot.

Accu-jac features an "external mode" for men that powers a clear, pliant sheath which slides up and down the **penis**, and an "internal mode" that powers a six-inch **dildo** whose speed and length of stroke can be controlled. It's all completely automatic, with a control panel that provides the option of varying the length of the stroke or depth of penetration as well as the speed of the air-flow and alternating massage. The unit can be used by one person or up to four simultaneously, depending on the model and the options, and you may select the male sleeves from six different shapes and nine different sizes and from two different **dildos** for the internal mode.

The marriage of technology and the time-proven art promises to call us all to new heights of **self-pleasure**. The final stroke. We have seen the future, but it is clearly out of our hands.

Why did God create man?
She knew a vibrator couldn't carry out the garbage.

—*Anti-male sentiment, 1990s*

Tips of the Tongue

1.   The high point of Alexander Portnoy's adventures occurred when he took a pound of fresh liver from the refrigerator and **jerked off** into it. Afterwords, he washed it thoroughly and put it back. Even so he felt guilty. "My God," he thought, "I **fucked** my family's dinner."

     Portnoy's Complaint was America's first best seller on **masturbation**. Shortly after it was published, Jacqueline Susann, author of *Valley of the Dolls*, a sleazy pot-boiler of the times, appeared on the *Tonight* show to plug her latest work.

Host Johnny Carson asked her what she thought of *Portnoy's Complaint*. "It's a great book, " Miss Susann said. "But I wouldn't want to shake hands with the author."

2. When asked why she had named her canary "Onan," Dorothy Parker answered, "Because he spills his seed."

3. The Medieval *Zohar*, or *Book of Splendor*, the guide to orthodox Jewish mysticism, defined a man's participation in a sexual act without the benefit of a woman as the penultimate no-no, citing wet dreams and **onanistic practices** as grave sins. Asking the question, "What brings man to grips with himself?" it answers, "The Devil made him do it!"

   The Devil indeed! According to the *Zohar* the evil spirits of the night encouraged such practices because every escaped seed provided one of them with bodily form. When a man finally died, all those midnight rides caught up with him. The little demonic bastards he had sired during his lifetime now swarm about him like wild bees, crying out, "You are our father!"—tugging and plucking at him, causing such pain as to remind both him and God of his sins. Clearly, we should all heed the chorus in Monty Python's *The Meaning of Life* (1983), "Every sperm is sacred / Every sperm is great / If a sperm is wasted / God is quite irate." The Moral: In a world perched at the brink of self-destruction and drowned in self-despair, man's individual woes are nothing but a drop in the bucket.

4. St. Thomas Aquinas helped matters by arranging his sins hierarchically, creating a "top forty" of sexuality, making a major distinction between **natural** and **unnatural vices**. The latter were the worst and included, in descending order of gravity: **sodomy, fellatio, cunnilingus, pederasty,** and finally, **masturbation.** Aquinas treated **masturbation** as **uncleanliness** or **effeminacy**, describing it as "procuring **pollution** without any **copulation** for the sake of **veneral pleasure**." He considered it the least grievous of all the **unnatural vices**, "as it merely omits connections with another." As usual, the Church was thinking babies and new customers; **sex** exclusively for pleasure was clearly unacceptable.

5. Krafft-Ebing (*Psychopathia Sexualis*, 1886) saw **the secret vice** as the essential cause of most sexual deviation. "It despoils the unyielding bud of perfume and beauty and leaves behind only the coarse, animal desire for sexual satisfaction."

   Paolo Mantegazza, the anthropologist, even went one better:

   > This nauseous stench of the solitary vice continues to contaminate every vein of our body social. It is an odor of moral decay, a moldy sexual smell on all sides with

thousands of young men and girls spilling in the sheets
or in dark passageways mankind's sovereign.

But for a Dr. Herbert (*Fundamentals in Sexual Ethics*, 1920) it was simply **the vice**, as if there were no others worthy of consideration. "It plucks the flower before the fruit has ripened, and when the true need comes, goes out empty."

Freud was also initially upset with the practice, but later took it somewhat less seriously, considering it infantile, likening it in seriousness as a habit to thumb-sucking.

6. Assisting her in her efforts was a best-seller, *Liberating Masturbation: A Meditation on Self-Love*, by Betty Dodson (1983). This underground classic sold more than 130,000 copies in one year, generating over a half-million dollars' worth of business. Eschewing the quickie, the author treats **masturbation** as a ritual of sorts. Towards this end, she has held countless workshops helping women "to claim their **orgasms**." ("That one over there...that's mine!"), thereby showing women everywhere the way from **self-abuse** to **self-love**. As an expression of their gratitude, many are now said to **do a Dodson**.

7. The **vibrator** gets very little respect nowadays. There was a time, however, when it was considered a legitimate medical device. According to historian Rachel Mannes (*The Technology of Orgasm: "Hysteria," the Vibrator, and Women's Sexual Satisfaction*) "...the **vibrator** was developed to perfect and automate a function that doctors had long performed for women: the relief of physical, emotional, and sexual tension through external pelvic massage, culminating in an orgasm." Eventually these devices became available for purchase and home use ; one such "portable **vibrator**" was advertised in the 1918 Sears and Roebuck catalogue as an "aid that very woman appreciates." The author incidentally chanced on the subject while researching the history of needlework, finding an advertisement for a **vibrator** while thumbing through a 1906 needlepoint magazine.

Act One

ow that we have properly named **it**, and also mastered the parts, it's time we finally got our act together. So let's **get it on** (c. 1970s, counterculture) or, as the British say, let's **have it off** (20thC). A bit of high drama and low comedy. We begin with the chief actors in the piece and the forces that move them, then on to the preliminaries, the act itself, variations thereof, and finally the results.

Thank Heaven for Little Girls

On center stage we have a **knock-out** (c. 1940s), the **sweet young thing**—a **real eyeful** (c. 1920s), an **armful** (c. 1930s), a **cutie** (c. 1919), a **real stunner** (c. 1862), and a **good looker** (c. 1894). She's got **bedroom eyes**, **plenty of dissa and datta**, and is just oozing **SA—sex appeal** (c. 1920–40s). The sounds you hear as she enters a room are: "**oomph**" (a sexual moan), "**unh, unh**" (Partridge suggests a bull's mating bellow), "**boing boing**" (ringing his bell), "**zing**" (go the strings of my heart) and "**va-va-va-voom!**" all courtesy of the forties. Or "**I say, what a smasher!**" (c. 1945, Eng.).

Some would simply suggest that she has plenty of **it**. **It** first caught the public's fancy during the twenties, when it was made popular by Clara Bow, the original **it** girl, star of the 1927 film *It*, based on a best-selling book of the same name by Elinor Glyn.

In short, she's a real **doll** (since c. 1904)—that is, if you don't care about her past. A **doll** was a common **harlot** through the seventeenth and early eighteenth centuries, and both **doll** and **dolly**

*'Tisn't beauty, so to speak, nor good talk
necessarily. It's just it. Some women'll stay in a
man's memory if they once walk down the street.*
        —*Rudyard Kipling,*
            Traffics and Discoveries, *1904*

occasionally served as a **mistress** and **slattern** right through the nineteenth century.

But don't get the wrong idea. This is a **nice girl**, one **so innocent that she thinks fucking is a town in China** (c. 1940). She's as pure as the driven snow, as **straight** (c. 1868) as they come, an **article of virtue** (c. 1850–1914), **a square Jane and no nonsense** (c. 1925, Aust.), **a proper bit of frock** (c. 1873–1910), who **draws the line at tick** (c. 1909, tick being the cloth casing of the mattress and the pillow). Self-control's her thing, and it's highly unlikely you'll ever find her ticked off. She's sui generis, the last of a vanishing species—the kind they just don't **make** anymore.

Mr. Everything

In this corner we have her male counterpart. Ideally, he's **tall, dark, and handsome** (late 1920s–50s), words that perfectly describe Caesar Romero, who starred in a film with that title in 1941 and who quickly became the standard by which teenage bobby-soxers judged their acned suitors. Earlier, the same words were used by female movie buffs when speaking of Rudolph Valentino, who was really short, dark, and handsome, but apparently ten feet tall to his admirers. More recently, he's a **hunk**, something akin to the female **piece**.

There's little else to say. As Stuart Berg Flexner noted in *I Hear America Talking*, women tend to talk much less about men than men do about women, unless the guy's an out-and-out **seducer**, of which we will say more later. So for now, let's simply write him off as **the boy next door**, popularized by Judy Garland who sang his praises in the 1947 film *Meet Me in St. Louis*. She's hoping he's **Mr. Right** (c. 1940), until his actions prove her wrong.

Nice is as Nice Does

Our young man doesn't want much—only a nice girl. But at times, he's not really sure. Prior to the eighteenth century, a "nice" girl was one who was foolish or stupid. Later, when irony was in vogue, she became a **good girl** (a **wanton** wench, late 17th–18thC), then a **perfect lady** (c. 1880, a **harlot**), or a **thorough good-natured wench** (19thC), which, according to Grose, meant "a female who being asked to sit down will lie down." "Nice" today means coy, shy, and Ivory-pure, generally considered good, except in the inner city, where she can also be **bad**. Every man would like to marry a "nice" girl; as far as the others are concerned, "**fuck** 'em!" The nice girl has only one thing in mind, wondering when **that certain someone** will pop the question.

Unfortunately, his only question is: Is she **easy** (since 17thC), **loose** (since 15thC), **fast** (18thC), **swift** (late 19th–20thC), **speedy**

(c. 1923), **light** (14thC), or **convenient** (19thC)? Does she **go all the way** (mid 20thC), **the whole route** (19th–20thC), or **the limit** (c. 1916)? Once we have the answer to those questions, we have established what is called a **reputation** (since 18thC).

Every girl has been warned to **watch out for her reputation** (19th–20thC). Traditional warnings include, "**Don't do anything I wouldn't do**," originally a farewell send-off in the armed services (c. 1939–45) for the man blessed with a pass and headed for a **dirty weekend**. Its impact, however, has been blunted when coming from a mother with a brood of five hanging on her arm. Well, there's always, "**Be good! If you can't be good, be careful**" (from the song of the same name, c. 1907), or **at least be sanitary**, **buy a pram**, **name it after me**, and **remember the date**.

One **slip-up** and it's all over. Once she's got a **rep**, forget it. Watch for her soon appearing on the wall of a bathroom stall near you. **For a good time call...**

Let's Fall in Love

But life has its peaks and valleys, love its **ups and downs** (19thC). Those who prematurely **scale the heights of connubial bliss** (19thC) often **tread the shoe awry** (16th–20thC), resulting in the inevitable **slip(-up)** (18thC).

Shakespeare's women were forever **tripping**, **stumbling**, and **tumbling**. In the nineteenth century a woman did a **flop** (from c. 1875) or a **turn on her back** (19thC). Men once **flopped a Judy** (c. 1874), Judy being a standard name for a woman, especially one of loose morals. Today women simply **go down** (19th–20thC). There's no mistaking the **fallen woman**. The next time you see one, pick her up.

Fallen women are **made**; they're not born that way. This is the story of one such unfortunate soul for whom **push came to shove** (19thC). **Did she fall or was she pushed** (19th–20thC)? An obvious **pushover** (c. 1925), some say. Draw your own conclusions.

I used to be Snow White but I drifted.
— Mae West

Julia: Wouldst thou counsel me to fall in love?
Lucetta: Ay Madam, so you stumble not unheedfully.
— *Shakespeare,* Two Gentlemen of Verona

Itching for it

Others think the problem begins with our young man. He suffers from a chronic affliction known as the **galloping gonads** or **blue balls**. A bad **case of the hots**, he's got **hot pants**, **rocks**, and **nuts** (all mid 20thC), leaving him **rooty** (mid 20thC), **randy** (since 18thC), **humpy** (mid 20thC), **juicy** (19thC), **itchy** (19thC), **hairy** (19thC), and **horny** (19th–20thC)—the seven dwarfs of lechdom.[1]

His **horniness** derives from the ancient horned gods of fertility and procreation, such as Pan and Dionysus, as well as the **instrument** itself on which he plays his tune. As for **hairy**, our locks have long been identified with virility and strength, as in the story

When I'm good, I'm very good, but when I'm bad,
I'm better.

—Mae West

of Samson. Hair has also been considered a highly erotic stimulant and, because of this, many cultures have taken great pains to cover the head. Others have adopted even more radical measures. Shaving of the head has often been linked to castration, and has symbolized control of libidinous desires, as with those who take an oath of chastity upon joining a religious order.

In language, **hair** was most active as a metaphor during the nineteenth century. We had men feeling **hairy** (c. 1860, **having a must**) and looking everywhere for **a bit of hair** or for a woman with **hair to sell**. All they wanted was to **take a turn in haircourt** or **get a haircut** so as to relieve the urgency. A crewcut? A little trim behind the ears? Take it all off? The Puritans introduced the modern short haircut to the world as well as their suffocating sexual strictures. Given the results, isn't it time we all let our hair down?[1]

That Certain Feeling

The answer to the question is obvious. She's also **amative** (early 17thC), **hot** (since 16thC), **hot and bothered** (20thC), **hot-assed** (since 19thC), **got hot pants** (since early 20thC), and **is hot in the biscuit** (early 20thC). You might also say she's **got peas in the pot** (late 19thC) or that she's **full of beans**. It was once thought that beans were an aphrodisiac, a theory which unfortunately proved to be so much hot air. But this time you can be sure: she's definitely **dripping for it** (c. 1910).

It was once considered unnatural for a woman to feel that way. In "The Merchant's Tale," Chaucer describes an aroused woman as **mannish**, as if being **amorous** were only for men. Henry Fielding, in *Tom Jones* (1750), however, saw her **coming**.

> I dare to swear the wench was willing as he, for she was not always a forward kind of body. And when wenches are so coming, young men are not so much to be blamed, neither for to be sure they do no more than what is natural.

So the feeling is mutual. They both have an **itch** (17th–20thC) and feel the **urge, accessus libidine**; they're definitely **sexually aroused** and know **lust** (since 19thC) in their heart.[2]

Galloping Gourmets

They are literally starved for affection. And what better way to manifest this lascivious craving than through a hearty **appetite**? **Appetite** derives from the Latin *appetere*, "to seek or desire eagerly." Man has been known to have both **raging appetites** (*Troilus and Cressida*) and **bestial appetites in charge of lust** (*Richard III*). His tastes are all-encompassing, pursuing woman as a **fine dinner** (jitterbug and student slang from the thirties for an attractive girl); a **picnic**, a peak sexual experience or one easily attained (from student and military use in the forties); or a **barbecue** (c. 1925), an exceptionally attractive female, from the black community, as in the song "Struttin' with Some Barbecue." In England, "**boys call meal after her**" (c. 1970–75, Liverpool), while in the States she's been **PEEP (perfectly elegant eating pussy** (mid 20thC).

Whatever form it took, the traditional meal was characterized by certain time-honored customs, grace being the standard ritual by which we gave thanks for what we were about to receive; hence, **grace before meat** (19th–20thC), a kiss or any other activity leading up to the main course. **Dinner without grace** (19thC) was **sex** without marriage—apparently a relationship without a prayer. There were always those without patience who wished to dispense with the preliminaries and have a **bit on the fork** (19thC) immediately. They often were sent home hungry. Those showing the proper etiquette, however, were always rewarded with a little something from the table.

'Tis not a year or two shows us a man;
They are all but stomach, and we all but food;
They eat us hungrily, and when they are full,
They belch us.
—Shakespeare, Othello

The Wayward Buss

It all begins with a **come-hither look** (c. 1920), then a friendly kiss, perhaps a **buss on the cheek**, or a **smack at her mums** (19thC)—nothing more than a **smooch** (since 19thC, also a **smoodge, smooge, smouch,** or **smouge**), or an innocent **peck**, an act of **osculation**, from *oscula*, Latin for "little mouth." What concerns us is what teenagers on the West Coast today call **sucking face**—a practice sure to leave its mark, a lasting impression known to kids as a **hickey** (c. 1930), a word derived from "doohickey," a whatchahmacallit of sorts.

Equally tasteless is the notorious **soul kiss** (20thC black U.S.) or **French kiss** (20thC), brought back by the American Expeditionary Force after World War I, an act so unspeakable as to leave one speechless. Leaving you tongue tied as well is the formal term for the act, **cataglottism** (c.1656) from an old French word meaning exactly what it says, "a kisse or kissing with the tongue." Writing in 1905, sexologist Havelock Ellis thought it both appoprriate and commonplace: "The kiss is not only an expression of feeling; it is a means of provoking it." **Cataglottism** is by no means confined to pigeons."

Nobody really knows why we began kissing. Some link kissing to food and nurturing or identify it with breathing and life itself, treating the commingling of lips as the joining of life forces. The word was first recorded in the language around the tenth century as *cosse*, close enough to both a "curse" and a "cuss" as to make us nervous. Most consider "kiss" to be onomatopoeic, since it sounds like the action it describes.

He was proper, tall, and handsome, and everything was right. He could lie with a pretty girl and kiss her twelve times a night.
—"You Remember the Nuts," Irish broadside ballad, 1870

In his work on the history of **sex**, Rabbi Brasch traces the **X** symbol for the kiss to the sign for two mouths kissing: >< going back to the time when illiterates signed legal documents with an X and then kissed the paper to lend it even greater veracity. It wasn't long before the kiss became fully identified with the mark.

In the fifties, we validated our affection by a string of **X**'s at the end of a letter, a stamp posted upside down on the envelope, and **SWAHAAK** ("sealed with a hug and a kiss") on the back.

Unbeknown to most, **kissing** is also an X-rated activity, having long stood for the **sexual favor** itself, especially in literature from the seventeenth to the nineteenth century. So the next time you're reading from that period and you come across a couple **kissing**, remember they're probably really not kissing but doing **you-know-what**. When the handsome lad **kyssed** the sweet young lass hello, she could probably kiss it all good-bye.[3]

Feeling Out the Situation

One thing quickly leads to another. In Colonial times, when privacy was hard to come by and warmth at a premium, there was a practice called **bundling**. The parties bedded down together fully clothed for some small talk and some sanctioned **hanky-panky** (originally some "sleight-of-hand"), but between them was inserted a "bedding board" to insure that most of the proprieties were met. In earlier times in Europe, they used a "chastity sword." More effective than the board, it guaranteed to keep cutting up to a minimum.

By the nineteenth century, all barriers had fallen, and a man and woman showed themselves to be **lovey-dovey** (c. 1870) by **spooning** (c. 1831)—engaging in silly and sentimental endearments leading to the couple resting comfortably in one another's arms like two spoons, an innocent enough practice, but one likely to end with her **on the old fork** (late 19thC). Many saw this as nothing more than **lally-gagging** (c. 1860, a *lally* being a tongue), an expression that also came to mean wasting one's time, which it no doubt was for some. But things heated up with some **sparking** (18th–19thC), **spunking up** (c. 1840), and **rotten-logging** (early 20thC). All deal with attempts to start a fire, "spunk" and "rotten logs" referring to the tinder and other materials necessary to get the fire going and the spark referring, of course, to that which sets it off, i.e., the right mix of **sweet talk**, a bit of **billing and cooing** (19thC), some **fumbling** (16th–20thC), **tickling** (16thC), **messing** (c. 1873) and **mucking about** (c. 1880), and some **fooling around** (c. 1880). Whatever, there'll be no **rushing up the petticoats straight** (c. 1850), at least not without the appropriate preliminary blandishments.

Drifting down the stream of izzen,
They were seated in the stern,
And she had her hand on hizzen,
And he had his hand on hern.
        —Anon., "Hizzen and Hern," 20thC

Ace Lamont (John Miljan): I'm just wild about you
Ruby Carter (Mae West): Some of the wildest men make the
best pets.

—*Belle of the Nineties*, 1934

Taking Hold of Things

The twentieth century featured **petting**, which was originally just a caress or two, and some **necking**. But the neck played only a minor part in the action, serving as a point of departure for more exotic parts. According to Groucho, whoever called it **necking** must have been a poor judge of anatomy. Both **necking** and **petting** entered the language around the same time (1905–10), with **necking** (also **giraffing**) becoming especially heavy during World Wars I and II. **Petting** was the more acceptable of the two and the one more publicly discussed, though in practice it was often difficult to distinguish from **necking**. Teenage practitioners often made arbitrary distinctions based on whether the action occurred above or below the waist and whether it happened clothed or unclothed.

Back to our young couple: He appears to be **making out** (mid 20thC), all right. He's now **practicing in the Milky Way** (19th–20thC), **getting a touch-up** (18thC), and **copping a cheap feel** (20thC). Next comes the realization of a boyhood dream: **getting bare tit** (mid 20thC) and living to tell about it, a feat writ even larger by having overcome the ultimate challenge—unlatching the demonic **bra**. That done, he's now **making time** (20thC), his ultimate goal being to **wind up the clock** (c. 1760).

Till that magic moment, he'll try his hand at some **canoodling** (mid 19th–20thC) or perhaps some **firkytoodling** (18th–19thC). **Canoodling?** According to George Sala (*Twice Around the Clock*, 1859), it's nothing more than "A sly kiss and a squeeze, and the pressure of the foot or so, and a variety of harmless endearing blandishments known to our American cousins (who are greater adepts at sweet-hearting)."[4]

Firkytoodling? "What do you think you're doing?" she might ask. "**Just diddling about**" (20thC), says he, indulging in some **foreplay** or **sexual expression** (20thC). Partridge would tell her that **firkytoddling** is simply "indulging in physically intimate endearments, especially in those provocative caresses which constitute the normal preliminaries to the **sexual congress**."[5] Put yet another way, he's **taking (manual) liberties, exploring her frilleries** (c. 1888–1914), **making free of the house** (20thC)—including **playing at stink-finger** (mid 19th–20thC), **tipping the long finger** (19thC), and **playing the harp**. He has now **felt her pulse** (c. 1648–50) and **tickled her fancy** (20thC), and they're

I like to wake up each morning feeling a new man.
—*Jean Harlow*

You're only as old as the woman you feel.
—*Groucho Marx*

"Stop, no you mustn't."
"Oh, come on baby, where've you been?"
"What do you take me for? I'm not that kind of girl."

—*Standard adolescent lines, 1950s*

going at it **hot and heavy** (20thC). Soon they have reached the highest stage of the **sensate-focus exercise** (c. 1982–83).

Getting Down to Basics

They have now shed their inhibitions and more. They've **peeled** (since late 18thC) and **disrobed** (since c. 1794). Consider them **bare** (before 10thC) or **naked**, though most would consider that indelicate. **Naked** is a good English word that's been around for quite a while. One of the earliest references to it can be found in *Beowulf* as **nacod** (c. 725). But somehow we prefer being **nude**, a relative newcomer (that's been with us only since 1873), derived from the Latin *nudus* and, ironically, a close cousin of **naked**.

Naked has always given moralists cause to shiver. In the Bible, when one saw another's **nakedness**, it meant to see their **privy parts**, as in Genesis 9:22, "And Ham saw the **nakedness** of his father." Stark as it is, **naked**'s definitely not for the squeamish.

An ancient Greek fable recounts how the goddesses Truth and Falsehood went for a swim. When they emerged from the water, Falsehood took Truth's garments, leaving Truth "you know what." But rather than don Falsehood's trappings, Truth went **naked**, and we know how dangerous the **naked** truth can be.

Naked or **bare**, the truth is never **nude**. Statues, on the other hand, are always **nude**, as are beaches where you leave your clothes and constraints behind. Both are considered quite harmless. Bodies that are fixed in position seldom if ever interact, making for little risk in being **nude**.[6] Robert Graves underscored the difference in his 1957 poem "The Naked and the Nude": "For me, the **naked** and the **nude** stand as wide apart / As love from lies, or truth from art."

If you still can't distinguish between **naked** and **nude**, try standing stark **nude** sometime.

A Winning Suit

There's an awful lot of euphemistic deception involved in going **bare-assed** (20thC). We speak of being **au naturel** (20thC) or **in the altogether** (since c. 1894) when we're really feeling unnatural in the untogether. Adding to the confusion is the rock group Bare Naked Ladies, which happens to be a group of fully clothed men.[7]

And though we are **without a stitch**, we like to cultivate the illusion of being dressed, like the Emperor with his new clothes. It began with Jonathan Swift and his **birthday gear** (c. 1731), inspiring the **birthday soot (suit)** as well as a host of lesser imitators including **birthday attire** (c. 1860), **nature's garb** (19thC), **Adam and Eve's togs** (c. 1909), and an **angel's suit** (19th–20thC). None

I went in the morning to a private place with the housemaid and we bathed in our birthday soot.

—*Tobias Smollet,* Humphrey Clinker, *1771*

of these, however, is to be confused with the original "birthday suit," the special splendid clothes ordered to be worn on a sovereign's birthday.

Today when we **air our pores** (20thC), we're mostly **in the buff** (19th–20thC), though we once **went in the buff** (17th–late 19thC) and **buffed it** (c. 1850). **Buff** derives from the buffalos and their treated hides. When we're **in the buff**, we're dressed in nothing but our own hide. Enthusiasts of a particular activity are also called "buffs" (c.1903), because uniforms of volunteer firemen in New York City at the time were buff-colored—making devotees of **nude** bathing, **buff-buffs**.

C'est la Guerre

Naked aggression soon makes itself felt. The unstable truce, the shaky cease-fire, collapses. Make no mistake about it—this is war!

Operations begin with reconnoitering by the **wandering-hand brigade** (**WHB**, late 19th–20thC), including foreign elements; **Russian hands and Roman fingers** (mid 20thC). He makes his advances. The **breastworks are assailed** (16thC) and **Fort Monjoy** comes under siege (16thC). The **encounter** (16thC) is brief. It is simply no contest. **Adam's arsenal** (late 19thC) proves too strong. He **batters down her portcullis** (17thC), a fortress or gateway, and **deals her** several **damaging blows**. He **invades** (17th–19thC) and **conquers** (16th–20thC). She **yields** or **surrenders**. This is followed by **possession** (17thC) and **occupation** (16th–early 19thC).

> Yet ever as he greedily asay'd
> To touch those dainties, she the harpy pla'd
> And every limb did as a soldier stout
> Defend the fort, and keep the foreman out.
>
> —Christopher Marlowe, *Hero and Leander*, 1598

Possession is thought by some to constitute nine-tenths of the law, a common male fallacy. **Occupying** a woman (16thC–early 19thC), though highly popular in practice, was considered obscene in both spoken and written form during the seventeenth and eighteenth centuries, and its absence from the language is noted in the OED. Better that they had sunk swords into ploughshares.

Coming Attractions

O-o-o-o-ps! You mean that's all there is to it, a **momentary trick** (Shakespeare)? He **discharged, let go** (19th–20thC), **shot his great stones** (c. 1604, Thomas Dekker), **his wad, his load** (both mid 20thC). Sometimes he just **shot** or **shot off**. He **came his cocoa** (20thC), **melted** (17thC), **dropped his load** (20thC), **gave**

Make love, not war.
—Gershon Legman, 1963

Fighting for peace is like fucking for virginity.
—Anon., 1983–84

Then off he earlier came
and blusht for shame so soon
that he had endit.
—"Walking in Meadow Green," in
Bishop Percy's Loose Songs, *1650*

The orgasm has replaced the cross as the focus of longing and the image of fulfillment.
—Malcolm Muggeridge

Nice Guys finish last.
—Leo Durocher

his gravy (19th–20thC), **jetted his juice** (19th–20thC), and just plain **ejaculated** (since c. 1578).

There's also the occasional malfunction, making it a **flash in the pan** (18th–20thC, **coition sans emission**). The English called it a **dry bob** (c. 1660–1930), the French, **avaler le poisson sans sauce** (19thC), "to devour the fish without sauce."

Sic transit gloria. Some men **come** (17th–20thC), others **go** (20thC). **Coming** or **going**, it's all the same. Of **come**, itself once a euphemism for **spend**, Partridge wrote, "how if the fact is to be expressed non-euphemistically, could one express it otherwise with such terse simplicity?"

> A Notorious harlot named Hearst
> In the pleasure of men is well-versed
>   Reads a sign o'er the head
>   Of her well-rumpled bed:
> "The Customer Always Comes First."
>
> —Anon, quoted in Gershon Legman, ed.,
> *The Limerick*, 1969

Some tried **getting it off** (10thC). While a British gent reduced the moment to a hygienic happening by **getting the dirty water off his chest** (early 20thC), coming clean, as it were, Americans were busily **getting their rocks** (or their **cookies**) **off** (mid 20thC).

Because the expenditure is generally considered worthwhile, most enjoy **spending it** (a favorite nineteenth-century term) though there are some who prefer putting something away for a rainy day. Grose wrote of those men "who made a coffeehouse of a woman's ****...go in and out and **spend** nothing." General Jack Ripper in *Dr. Strangelove* was so disposed: "I do not avoid women...but I deny them my life essence." You, too, might want to test your **mettle** (17th–20thC) or show no **spunk** (19thC) by exercising some self-discipline.

Coming Around.

And what of her? What's she doing while all this is going on? Not much, according to *The Erotic Tongue*. Man's interest in her end of things is evidenced by the paucity of phrases and expressions we have to describe her **orgasm** (early 19thC–20thC) or **climax** (20thC), apart from her **coming**, which she shares with him. Perhaps with your assistance we can do more than just:

Make her chimney smoke
Pop her cork
Flip her switch

_____ her _____
_____ her _____
_____ her _____

The Right Stuff

You could say she's **taken the starch out of him** (mid 19th–20thC), or, in a more exotic vein, taken some **thrice-decoted blood** (Marlowe), the **lewd infusion** (Rochester), or some **Cyprus sap** (c. 1611).[8]

The **oil's** especially important, but great care is required in its handling. As Rochester reminded us, "Too hasty zeal my hopes did spoil. Pressing to feed her lamp, I spilt my **oil**." (*The Imperfect Enjoyment*, 17thC). Not to worry. He has to get his **oil changed** (20thC) regularly to keep love's vehicle in good running condition, and a refill is in order. Even contemporary humorist, Lewis Grizzard, acknowledged its importance in his book entitled, *If Love Were Oil, I'd be About a Quart Low* (1983).

Popularly, we know it best as **come** or **cum** (c. 1923), **gism** or **jism** (20thC from **orgasm**); practically, **father-stuff** (Walt Whitman) and **baby juice** (19thC). **Pudding** is also nice, though Fletcher (*Beggar's Bush*, 1622) would "give her cold **jelly** to take up her belly." In Israel—where else?—they still **give milk for honey**. For those not lacteally challenged, we have **hot milk** (19th–20thC), **buttermilk**, and **seminal milk** (Whitman, c. 1860).

Most popular of all is **cream** (since 19thC). Traditionally, men would **dish out the cream** (19thC) while women **had a go at the creamstick** (18th–20thC). All quite titillating, it left teenage boys **creaming in their jeans** (20thC). And who of us was not once encouraged by the lady on TV calling out, "Come on and cream on me!" Or had his curiosity piqued by items such as the following?

> STRAWBERRIES and cream are a delectable dream for the true gormet [sic.]. I'm a yummy 29 yr 5 ft 11 strawberry blonde seeking generous gents to make a delicious tasteful memory with. P.O. box —, Salem, N.H. 03078. Can Travel.
> —*Boston Phoenix*, July 13, 1982

Against the Grain

Oats and **seed** (since the 13thC) have also been traditional synonyms for **semen**, while the **furrow** has long represented the female **genitalia**. Any wonder that young men enjoy **sowing their wild oats** (16thC), i.e., engaging in sexual promiscuity, the implication being that their seed could be put to better use, cultivating "good grain" on a family farm. Not every field, however, is worthy of consideration. Speaking of the barren Scottish queen in *Rob Roy* (1994): James Graham, Marquis of Montrose (John Hurt) remarked, " 'Aie, one might have hoped that a field so regularly plowed might have yielded one good crop. In truth I have seen healthier graveyards than that woman's womb." As to the more fertile terrain to which so many are drawn, best they remember, "Sow

Priapus squeez'd, one snowball did emit.
—*Rochester*, Works, *1718*

He rumbl'd and jumbl'd me o'er and o'er. Till I found he had almost wasted the store of his pudding.
—From "Twelve Years Old" in Wit and Mirth, *1682*

your wild oats on Saturday night, then on Sunday pray for crop failure (*Murphy's Laws on Sex*).

Cry Babies

Plaisir d'amour ne dure qu'un instant'
chagrin d'amour dure toute une vie.

The pleasure of love lasts no more than an instant;
the regret of love lasts a lifetime.
　　　　　　　　—*French epigram*

That's it! **It's** all over. But no tears, please. Apparently King David wept enough for all of us. According to a Talmudic interpretation of the Old Testament (Psalms 6:6), David found himself so extended by his eighteen wives that he tried **copulating** by day rather than by night in hopes of cutting down on his desires, but with only limited success:

> I am tired of my moaning; every night I flood my bed with tears. I soak my couch with my weeping. My strength is exhausted through my groaning all the day long; my moisture is dried up like the drought of summer. I am poured out like water; my moisture is evaporated as by the heat of the hot season; I am weary of my weeping.

Making Conversation

The job's complete but there's still more to talk about. If he's kind, literate, and subtle, he'll say he **took her** (C.P. Snow's favorite), **had her** (16th–20thC) and thoroughly **enjoyed her**; a **good time** (17thC) having been had by one and all.

From yet another perspective, he **saw her** (19thC) and **made eyes at her** (19thC), expressions that originated with the **ladies of the streets**. When a contemporary man and woman **make eyes at one another**, they invariably end up **seeing** each other. What we really mean to say is that they are **fucking**. Alan Sherman, for one, never understood how we managed to confuse **copulation** with vision, asking, "Have you ever heard of a **fucking**-eye dog?"

Only when man gets into the locker room does he see things clearly. There he **scored** (mid 20thC), **got into** (18th–20thC), **put in** (19thC), **put it in** and **had it in** (late 19thC). He also **made her** and **made it with her**, two expressions that seem as if they've been around forever, but in fact have been with us only since about 1918. They both helped make her what she is today—an **easy make**. More frequently he'll say, "**I laid her**" or "**I got laid**," also recent expressions that date from about 1930, though man has been **lying with a woman** for more than six hundred years.

High school students still find it difficult distinguishing between "lying down" "laying something down," and "laying someone." Dorothy Parker understood it properly, noting, "If all the girls at the Yale prom were laid end to end, I wouldn't be surprised." For men of the Land Down Under, it comes as no surprise. Hard times there are also good times. Unlike their American counterparts, men there look forward to a **lay-off** (20thC, Aust.).

"Well that's gone!" as the girl said to the sailor in the park when she lost her certificate from the Billerica Sunday School.
　　　　—*Anon.,* Pink 'Un and Pelican, *1898*

One Good Turn Deserves Another

Worst of all, he **screwed** her. To Alan Sherman, **screwing** created a mind-boggling image: "the man on top, revolving horizontally in a continuous spiral motion, with one Frankensteinian objective—to permanently attach the lady to the bed." **Screwing** her carries with it yet additional complications. Implicit in the process is that not only did he **fuck** her, but he also took advantage of her and cheated her. The challenge all women face is how to have **sexual intercourse** without also getting **screwed**.

Screw as a slang expression for **copulate** has been around only since the nineteenth century. But a century earlier, it could be found in Grose's Dictionary as a noun (**female screw**, or plain **screw**) for a **harlot**. The word itself is of Latin origin, from *scrofa*, "a sow" (the treads of a screw bearing marked similarity to a sow's tail), which in turn was influenced by *scrobis*, "a ditch" (*vulva* in Latin). Add the two together and what do you get but a sow's tail in a ditch. A truly romantic image.

A "screw" was also once slang for a skeleton key (c. 1795), perhaps the origin of its present usage as a "turnkey," a guard in a prison or jail. It took a turn for the better in England, around 1859, when it came to mean "wages" or "salary." According to Hugh Rawson, master of the euphemism, it was one of the few times when a person could openly proclaim, "I get a good weekly screw."

Would we could say the same today! As the Middle Ages featured the search for the Holy Grail, the twentieth century was noted for the pursuit of the ultimate **screw**.

Will you respect me in the morning?
—Anon.

"Years from now...when you talk about this...—and you will—...be kind." Gently she brings the boy's hands toward her opened blouse as the lights slowly dim out...and the curtain falls.
—Robert Anderson, Tea and Sympathy

Violators Will Be Towed

For her, it was quite another matter. She **did a backfall**, a **spread** (since late 17thC), **did** or **had a bottom-wetter** (19th–20thC), **got her leg lifted** and **lay with her feet uppermost** (19th–20thC).

At least it was fun, an **act of pleasure**, as when the Duchess of Marlborough recorded in her diary how the Duke "had **pleasured** me thrice in his boots." Then the feeling was mutual. There were times however when, the initiative and the pleasure was all his, as when she **succumbed to his blandishments** and **lost her honor**. Worse yet was when she was **ravished**, **defiled**, or **violated** (all since the 15thC).

To be **violated** was once considered pretty serious business—**a fate worse than death** (19thC). It's taken much more lightly today. Woody Allen once dreamt that his former wife had been arrested for **having sex** with another man, but that he had slept peacefully, knowing it could not have been a moving **violation**.

If I still had a cherry,
it would have been pushed
back so far I could use
it for a tail-light.
　　—*Nell Kimball, Nell Kimball:*
　　　　Her Life as an America Madam, 1970

She's got no cherry but that's no sin
She's got the box the cherry came in
　— *Redd Foxx, 1960s*

Man: Use it or lose it.
Woman: Use it and lose it.
　　—*Anon., 20thC*

Breaking Faith

Any way you put it, our young girl has **had it**. As a **first edition** (Oscar Wilde), her binding's been broken. Fresh fruit for the plucking, she's **lost her cherry** (20thC). Nothing new here; men have been **copping a cherry** since the early part of the twentieth century; having "copped" lots of things, meaning "to steal" them since the eighteenth.[9]

Her heart has been broken, and even more. There's **Judy's tea cup** (19th–20thC), her **pipkin** (17th–19thC), and her **ring. Her pitcher's cracked** (19thC) and there's no repairing her precious china. Still, things are not as bad as they're cracked up to be.

They might even be looking up. She's **gone star-gazing on her back** (mid 19thC). She's **seen the wolf** (Fr. *a vu le loup*) and even the **elephant** (c. 1875). The wolf is quite understandable. Ever since Red Riding Hood, young innocents have been warned not to **have eyes for** or **make eyes at the wolf**. As to the pachyderm sighting, God knows why anyone would have seen an elephant under the circumstances

Love in Full Bloom

Perhaps we should send some blossoms for the occasion. Having also been **deflowered** (since 14thC), she could surely use a few extra. Blooms have traditionally been the perfect symbol for blood, fertility, and delicacy, dating back to Greek mythology when Hades **seduced** Persephone as she gathered flowers, causing them to fall from her apron. Brides have traditionally tossed their bouquets away after the ceremony, and in the eighteenth century, when **virginity** was in flower, a favorite surgical operation of the time was called **rearranging the crumpled blossoms of the rose**. Reportedly, it was so popular a procedure, many women underwent several such floral arrangements.

Today, there is little need for it. Ours is a time when the bloom is definitely off the rose.

The Spirit of Compromise

At first glance, it appears that he got the best of it, and that **fucking** is a somewhat one-sided thing. To square matters somewhat you might want to **make a settlement in tail** (19thC).

He gets **a bit of snug for a bit of stiff** (19th–20thC, *stiff* also meaning "money")

She gives **mutton for beef** (19th–20thC)

She gives **juice for jelly** (19th–20thC)

He gives **a bit of hard for a bit of soft** (mid 19th–20thC)

Remember though—all trades are final.

Tips of the Tongue

1. Hair took on extra special meaning after the American Civil War when being a blonde became a fashion statement. Interest picked up further during the 20s and 30s with the emergence of the partying blonde chorus girl, encouraged by Anita Loos's novel: *Gentlemen Prefer Blondes* (1925). Enter also the **blonde bombshell**, "a real knockout," inspired by Jean Harlow, star of the 1933 film, *Bombshell*.

   Flash forward to the 1950s and Shirley Polykoff, an advertising copywriter for Clairol hair coloring, who asked "Is it true blondes have more fun?" This led to the question, **"Does she...or doesn't she?"** followed by, "Only her mother knows for sure." Not wanting to offend beauty salons, she later changed it to "Only her hairdresser knows for sure." *The Sensuous Woman* updated it in 1969: "Our world has changed. It's no longer a question of **Does she or doesn't she?** We all know she wants to, is about to, or does." New York graffiti further broadened its meaning with "Only *his* hairdresser knows for sure."

2. Graffiti reminds us, "Lead me not into temptation. I can find it myself." It's closer than you think. According to the Bible, Matthew (V.28), "Whoever looketh on a woman to lust after her, hath committed adultery with her already in his heart." In 1976, President Jimmy Carter admitted in an interview with *Playboy* magazine to looking on lots of women with **lust**, thus having "committed **adultery** in my heart many times." Not to worry, however, according to a 1984 ruling of the U.S. Court of Appeals which declared **lust** not to be **prurient interest** ("a shameful and morbid interest in **nudity**, **sex**, or **excretion**"), in striking down a Washington State law that declared as obscene that which "incited **lust**."

   > We do not think that Carter was describing a shameful or morbid interest; rather, he was obviously expressing a healthy, wholesome, human reaction common to millions of well-adjusted persons in our society. Certainly, we think it clear that this is how the country understood his remark, and how the term "lust" is generally perceived today... If the arousal of good, old-fashioned, healthy lust is equated with an appeal to "prurient interest," it might be necessary to hale into court our leading couturiers, perfumers, and manufacturers of soft drinks, soap suds, and automobiles, as well as mainstream stage, move and television producers. Only by distinguishing between the arousal of sexual instincts and the perversion of those instincts...can we ever hope to safeguard from state intrusion the already dim and uncertain boundary that surrounds \ expressions protected by the First Amendment.

3. There's similar confusion in French. The verb *baiser* means "to

kiss," but it's strictly for past literary use. Nowadays it primarily means "to **fuck**." Complicating matters, the noun, *le baiser* still means "the kiss." If you're looking to "kiss someone," use the verb *embrasser*. It alone should be employed in the act of kissing. Never say, *Je l'ai baisé* when you want to say, "I kissed her." Doing so, only **fucks** things up considerably.

4. Partridge finds **canoodling**'s origins in *cannie*, "gentle" and *noodle*, "to play the fool," leaving one "gently playing the fool." Others look to the canoe, from the shape of the **vulva** (Backed up by the infamous **little man in the boat** as the **clitoris**.) plus **doodle**, "to digitate," leaving the man **fingering the clit**. It's not a totally unreasonable premise, given how we also **talk to the canoe driver** (20thC for **cunnilingus**).

5. **Firkytoodling** supposedly derives from *firk*, to **fuck** and the *tootles*, a boy's **virilia**, hence simply **fucking** around with another's **privates**. What we today call **genital pleasuring**.

6. Not everyone, however, finds them benign. John Ashcroft, Attorney General in the administration of Bush the Younger, took the **nudity** of some of the statues at the Justice Department to be a form of **naked** aggression, and ordered them put under wraps.

7. We're talking the **full monty** here, "the whole shooting match." First formally recorded in 1986 as part of the jargon of a long running British soap opera, the term caught on in the early 1990s, achieving international recognition in 1997 from the film of the same name featuring male strippers who gave their all. There are many theories as to its source. The one which fits best finds its origins in Montague Burton, a noted British tailor from the North of England who featured a three piece suit replete with waist coat. How ironic that being fully clothed and properly decked out should end up being equated with being stark **naked**.

8. More old **stuff** (17th–20thC) of which dreams are made: **fetch** (late 19thC), **gravy** (mid 18th–20thC), **juice** (20thC), **letchwater** (18thC), **melted butter** (18th–20thC), **roe** (c. 1850), **seed** (since 13thC), **spermatic juice** (Rochester), **spume** (17thC), **starch** (19thC), **tail juice** (19thC), **tail water**, **tread**, and just plain **stuff** (17th–20thC). For the man who has everything: **love liquor**, **love's nectar**, **white honey**, and **baume de vie** (all 19thC). More recent samples are: **axle grease**, **bleach**, **charge**, **(dried)crud**, **fat**, **hockey/hookey**, **home brew**, **load**, **love juice**, **pecker tracks**, **prick juice**, **scum**, and **sugar**.

9. In current **gay** lingo, a **cherry picker** is one into **deflowering** young boys. We also have the **cherry orchard** (a girl's dormitory 20thC, with apologies to Chekhov) and a **virgin** Coke, "Coca-Cola with a dash of cherry in it."

Let Me Count the Ways

ex often takes a turn. It could be a slight turn from the norm, a diversion (from the Latin *di* and *vertere*), or a complete U-turn away from that which is normal, a **perversion** (from *per* and *vertere*).

According to Alfred Kinsey, a large number of people treat any kind of **sex** other than that involving a single man atop a single woman as abnormal. Other groups are less judgmental, considering such varied activity, creative and healthy.

Think you'd like **a spot of perving** (c. 1925, Aust.)? Fine. But only in moderation. As Voltaire reminded us upon declining a second invitation to an orgy, "Once a philosopher, twice a **pervert**."

Let Them Eat Cake

Everyone needs a break from the ordinary and the commonplace. An old blues song celebrated the wife who provided "**cornbread** for her husband and **biscuits** for her back-door man." According to J.L. Dillard (*American Talk*), both **cornbread** and **shortin' bread** were Southern black expressions for "coarse, undistinguished, and routine sex." It was what the French used to refer to as **le pain quotidien**, "the daily bread"—the **act of kind** done in a perfunctory manner, as in a longstanding marriage.[1] **Biscuits** stood for both worldly women and out-of-the-ordinary sexual activity, especially when **hot**. The **cold biscuit** (dull, perhaps unattractive, and only a leftover at that) was something else. When woman was serving, the **hot biscuit got it on** with the **biscuit roller**, one especially adept at the practice. More recently, Kinky Friedman of The Texas Jewboys took yet a different approach with "Get Your Biscuits in the Oven and Your Buns into Bed," (1992) thus incurring the wrath of Feminists who found his tastes all too stale. He and his male cohorts, however, can claim a higher motive, their predilection for **buns**, **biscuits**, and **muffins** clearly demonstrating that man cannot live by bread alone.

Suppose eating, not sex, were the taboo of our century? Suppose it was illegal for more than two people to eat together and suppose even they had to get a license for it and eat in secret while children were fed alone in dark closets? Suppose our billboards and newspaper ads, movies, and books and art devoted themselves to pictures of food—but never one glimpse of anyone eating?...Wouldn't it result in secret, general passions to try esoteric foods? And wouldn't people like to get together, law or none, and talk about the tabooed subject?

—Philip Wylie, Opus 21, 1949

Hot roll with cream?
—Cheeky lad asking a woman
to fuck,19th–20thC

Baker, not today.
—Housewife's reply to soldier paying
undesired court, (c. 1885–1915)

I like my women lying down.
I come from a long line of missionaries.
—David Addison (Bruce Willis),
Moonlighting, 1985

The Straight Up-and-Up

Tired of the daily **grind** (19th–20thC), bored with doing the **horizontalize** (c. 1845)? Not to worry. We've got more ways of **doing it** than Heinz has pickles; more flavors than Baskin-Robbins. Why settle for just **vanilla sex** (1990s)?

You can try it nestled together **spoon fashion** (19thC), or, if you're really game, attempt a **perpendicular** (mid 19thC), also known as an **upright grand** (c. 1925). It's nothing more than **the old three-penny bit** (late 18th–20thC)—what the girls on the corner once featured as their standing bargain.

Though a somewhat shaky proposition, your standard **knee-tembler** (c. 1860), otherwise known as a **quickie** (20thC), was the perfect answer to the man on the run. Ever a favorite of the pros, it has failed to catch on at home. According to Kinsey, only four percent of married woman say that they would stand for it.

Can You Top This?

In a world where everyone assumes that the best always come out on top, the favorite way of **doing it** has traditionally been with the man in the superior position, known as **figura veneris prima**, literally," the primary or essential position for making love."

Position and subjugation have always gone together. Parallel with the imperialism of the late nineteenth century by which the European powers extended their influence worldwide were the efforts of missionary societies, both Protestant and Catholic, to convert the "heathens." Their efforts embraced not only religious beliefs but cultural matters and societal practices as well. Finding the natives much more sexually open in ways they could never have imagined, the missionaries sought to get them to engage in more "civilized" behavior, emphasizing the only position with which they were familiar (from theory of course) — the **momma-poppa position**, long considered the **conjugal ordinary** (18th-19thC.). So associated did they become with the posture and its advocacy, it became known as the **missionary position**—in recognition of their good work and the **fucking** they gave the natives.

Why Don't We Do It in the Road?

Pet lovers, or those who are so inclined, generally enjoy **doing it dog-fashion** (Lassie-fashion, 20thC, U.S.), **dog-ways** (late 19thC), or **doggy style** (20thC). The French **baise en levrette** ("**fuck** like a greyhound bitch"). In medieval times, people knew it as **more canino**, a practice condemned by the Church because it was considered backward (**coiting a posteriori**) and way too pleasurable at that.

Impatient to get on with it? You might try **having a dog's marriage** (19thC) **or making a dog's match of it** (19th–20thC)—**doing it** by the wayside, down and dirty. **It**, however, just might take longer than you think. Dogs have been known to be linked together for hours on end after the **sexual act**. The **penis** swells, and the muscles of the female contract, locking the **penis** within; thus insuring that not till death will they part.

It's a tough act to follow, but you could possibly try **doing a dog's rig** (mid 18th–19thC), defined by Grose as "**sexual intercourse** to exhaustion followed by back-to-back indifference."

The only unnatural act is the one which you cannot perform.

—Alfred Kinsey

Chastity: the most unnatural of the sexual perversions.

—Aldous Huxley

You Animal, You!

Although the dog has a firm hold on man's loyalty, other animals also set a fine example. In ancient India, the Kamasutra (the laws of love) of Pandit Vatsyayana described 84 different postures (of which there were over 700 variations), all named after various animals such as cows, mules, donkeys, cats, dogs, tigers, and frogs. Couples were not only encouraged to try the different postures but to imitate the sound of the particular animal while **doing it**, to further enhance their pleasure.

"With a moo-moo here, a moo-moo there...everywhere a moo-moo."

Beastly Behavior

Some were inclined to take **it** literally, what we call **bestiality** or **zoophilia** (also **zooerasty** and **zoolagnia**, from the Greek *zoon* for "animal"). It was once a ceremonial part of religious worship in a number of cultures, including that of ancient Greece. Currently, it's practiced most in the countryside, where according to Kinsey as many as 17 percent of rural males have experienced **orgasm** at least once with an animal.

Though its meaning is eminently clear, **bestiality** has also on occasion been confused with other "unnatural" practices such as **buggery**. In the English town of Dunsberry, in 1642, a young servant named Thomas Granger was found guilty of committing **buggery** with a mare, a cow, two goats, five sheep, two calves, and a turkey. Someone (perhaps a pig) squealed, and although there were problems in making positive identifications, the animals were singled out and rounded up for execution, to be burned in a giant pit. When they finally got around to Granger, they found him well hung for his crimes.

Defining the practice continues to be a challenge. Witness the struggle of the Indiana Appellate Court on whether a chicken is a "beast" for purpose of interpreting Indiana's **bestiality** statute. Apparently they had not yet mastered the traditional distinction

Four legs good, two legs bad.

—George Orwell, Animal Farm (1945)

between **erotic** and **kinky**: "**Erotic** is when you use the feathers... **kinky**'s when you use the whole chicken."

Few look on **bestiality** kindly (except for **voyeurs**, when the animal's partner is a woman).[2] Generally, the act and its participants are treated with contempt and disdain. In parts of South America, calling someone a **sheep-fucker** or a **sheep-shagger** is pretty serious business, not unlike an allegation of **homosexuality** in Oscar Wilde's day.

Pardon Our French

According to surveys by Sandra Kahn and by *Playboy*, the practice which ranks most popular among men is **oral sex** (20thC). A favored activity through the ages, it was first heard of on American shores as an exotic Gallic sport brought home by our fighting men upon their return from World War I. They discovered it in France, and those good people, a pious and Puritanical folk, found themselves once more identified with things considered lewd, illicit, and downright naughty (as with the postcard and the kiss).

Because the practice often loses something in the translation, you'll probably need the services of a trained **linguist** (20thC), someone who really knows **French**, also **Frenching**, **French culture**, or the **French way**. If you don't know where to turn, the want ads offer all kinds of assistance:

> FR tutor. Beautiful blonde woman sks worthy gent 4 private lessons under my affluent [sic] tongue. SASE, Box 8154
>
> —*Grassroots*, March, 1978

In the United States, **French** traditionally was not spoken in the home, and men hoping to experience a foreign tongue had to look elsewhere. Fortunately, there were those who were quick to pick up on the demand. As the noted Detroit madam, Silver-Tongue Jean, remarked, "The **Johns** wanted it so we gave it to them. I think it also saved a lot of girls from contracting **VD**." Jean herself was a legend at the sport, openly boasting that there wasn't a man she couldn't lick.

Sex Rears Its Ugly Head

The professionals helped forge a common tongue. A man now had his **joint copped**, had some **derby**, or **had his hat nailed to the ceiling**. More frequently, men spoke of being **blown** or getting a **blow job** (all early 20thC).

Some find the **blow job's** origins in the **blow**, a shortened version of the cant **blowen** (17th–19thC), a **mistress**, **concubine**, or **prostitute**—arguing that it was just another job to her. It's a nice theory, but the **blow job** is a distinctly American phrase and didn't become part of our lingo until the twentieth century. A more likely

The French, they are a peculiar race
They fight with their feet and they fuck with their face.

—Anon., "Hinky Dinky Parley Vous,"
c. WWI

I say, hey lover, what're we gonna do?
An he jes look down.
I say, Yoo-hoo pretty baby, you wanna
French? Haff an'haff?
How bout jest a straight?
I say twenty berries an you alla roun'
the mothafuggin world.

—Robert Gover, Kitten *in* One Hundred
Dollar Misunderstanding, *1961*

source is the similarity between just putting your lips together and "blowing" and the pursing of one's lips when performing **oral sex**. Detailed instructions, including whether or not to inhale, were unfortunately not provided.

The **blow job** appears to have been most commonly offered initially not at home but in the **bawdy houses**. The girls who provided such services were known as **lick-spigots** (18thC), **mouth whores** (19thC), **suckstresses** (19thC), and **smokers** (20thC).

The pros were very responsive to the clients' requests. The girls stopped giving customers a piece of their mind and started **giving head** (since mid 20thC) instead. It was natural that the practice took root on our shores. America is after all about getting ahead; though **getting head** or **giving head** has never been treated with quite the same reverence.

Giving head, however, hasn't always been a clear signal for **oral sex**; some took it to also mean traditional **copulation**. Why **giving head** should also stand for **straight sex** is a cause of bewilderment. Psychologists tell us that it's a classic case of displacement of the birthplace, not a bad theory when you consider that Athena sprang full-blown from the brow of Zeus, and Rabelais's Gargantua emerged through his mother's ear. To the remnants of the counterculture it will forever remain a **mindfuck** of sorts.

Blow's just a figure of speech
—Anon., 20thC

Loose Lips

During the nineteenth century they preferred to **gamahuche** (also **gamaroosh** and **gamaruche**) or **gam**. Some think it derives from *Gamiani*, the heroine of a nineteenth-century erotic novel of the same name. Others theorize how it conjoined the Italian *gams*, for "legs" with the French *hucher*, "to purse one's lips."

These days psychologists, lawyers, journalists, educators, and talking heads on TV all like to clean up their language with Latin— a language noted for its remarkable cleansing power. When Latin's in, dirt's out, leaving filthy words sparkling clean.

The very same people who are shocked to hear of a woman **eating a man** (20thC) find it quite proper that she **fellate**.[4] They seem not at all disturbed by the fact that **fellatio** (also **fellation** and **fellatorism**) comes from the low Latin word for "suck" and was used by the Romans in the most obscene sense. Less familiar, and hence even less objectionable, are the **fellator** (male sucker) and the **fellatrice** (female sucker). They're really nothing more than your basic **cocksuckers** (since 19thC), known in more genteel quarters as **corksackers** (since mid 20thC).[5]

You'd have to go back to ancient Egypt to find the all-time great **fellatrice**, Cleopatra, who was referred to by the Greeks as "Merichane," or "gaper," the wide-mouthed one who allegedly gaped wide for some ten thousand men.

There was a young girl named Hornatio
Half the age of the Prez by ratio
*   As an intern unpaid*
*   She'd hoped to get laid*
But the Prez only wanted fellatio.[3]
*   —Anon., 1998*

"Eat me!"

"I want a meal, not a snack."

—Anon., mid 1950s

Katherina: *If I be waspish, best beware my sting.*

Petruchio: *My remedy is then to pluck it out.*

Katherina: *Ay, if the fool could find out where it lies.*

Petruchio: *Who knows not where a wasp does wear his sting?*

In his tail.

Katherina: *In his tongue.*

Petruchio: *Whose tongue?*

Katherina: *Yours, if you talk of tails; and so farewell.*

Petruchio: *What with my tongue in your tail? Nay, come again, good Kate; I am a gentleman.*

—Act 2, scene 1, Shakespeare,

The Taming of the Shrew

While some **fellate**, others get their licks in with **penilingus**, literally "tonguing the **penis**," a construction parallel to **cunnilingus**, its female equivalent. Most folks, though, prefer subsuming **cunnilingus** under **fellatio**, forgoing good grammar for good taste.[6]

Boy Eats Girl

There's yet another side to **oral sex**, one sure to bring men to their knees. A Chinese empress, Wu Hu of the T'ang dynasty, used to insist that all visitors to the royal court pay homage to her by an act known as the **licking of the lotus stamen**.

Westerners have been somewhat less poetic when **licking twat** (17thC), **tipping the velvet** (19th–20thC), or **muff-barking** (20thC).[7] Adding a playful dimension, the man can also **get a mustache** or **sneeze in the cabbage** (god bless!).

Today, it's primarily a matter of direction. Playing the active partner, the man **heads south** (also **Dixie**, early 20thC); finding himself **below C level**, he takes **a dip in the bush**. A myriad of other activities open up to him there, including **muff** or **pearl-diving**, **talking to the canoe driver**, or **yodeling in the gully** (all 20thC).

The man and the woman can extend the trip by heading **down highway 69 (soixante neuf** or just plain **69)** together for some reciprocal activity or having one partner **go around the world** (since mid 20thC), affording yet further opportunity to explore the international body politic.

Lickety-Split

Such a trip also presents an opportunity to partake in some novel culinary fare. The French toasted their own culture during the nineteenth century with **café au lait** (the female **pudendum**). **Aller au café**, "to go for coffee," and **prendre sa demitasse au café des deux colonnes**, "to have coffee at the café with two columns," meaning to place one's lips upon the **cup of pleasure** (18thC)—what to the uninitiated is known as **cunnilingus**.

Avaler les enfants des autres ("to swallow another's children") was to act as a **cunnilinctor** to a woman fresh from the embrace of another man, also described as to **gamahuche a buttered bun**. You don't have to go to France today to participate. It's but a short trip down **below 14th Street** (mid 20thC) to grab a bite.

Eating and **oral sex** are practiced by both sexes. The **face man** frequently **eats out**. Never averse to a bit of **cannibalism**, he **dines at the Y** with the **C-food Mama**. His favorite selections include a **box lunch**, a **furburger**, and a **tuna taco** (all **C-food** delicacies), topping it off with a slice of **fur** or **hair pie**.

Bottoming Out

In the 1811 *Dictionary of the Vulgar Tongue* under the heading "kiss mine **arse**" is the observation "An offer... very frequently made, but never ...literally accepted."

Not so. There are folks who enjoy **analingus**—oral stimulation of the **anus**, a practice popularly known as **rimming**. Food once more enters into the picture. Some **eat poundcake**; others, a **tossed salad** (**gay** usage, 1990s).

All forms of oral activity entail **going down** or **going South.**[7] This time, however, you'll have to modify your travel plans slightly, **going way down south in Dixie**. Care should always be exercised—never eat too fast on the way and be prepared for any exigency.

For the most part, however, eating at home is now an accepted and refined routine, giving one little reason to go out for exotic fare. This is not to say that there still aren't those who enjoy an occasional snack between meals. Many states still have laws on the books making it illegal to **eat** your own wife. Some folks adhere to the letter of the law. Others merely pay it lip service.

Swing Your Partners

We didn't take to a varied diet overnight, but once we developed a taste for it, we swung right in.

America first began to swing in the forties—to music. Swing was the big-band sound of the period, and when they told you to "Swing and sway with Sammy Kaye," you did so feeling comfortable that you were part of the current musical craze. After a while, swinging identified those who were knowledgeable and into the latest fads. It was the yardstick against which all things were measured. Duke Ellington reminded us, "It don't mean a thing if it ain't got that swing." It was left to Frank Sinatra, however, to point us in the right direction with his "Songs for Swinging Lovers" (1956), expanding upon a sexual theme just vaguely referred to earlier.[8]

Swinging and **sex** have always had a historical relationship reflecting the sexual fashions of the period: **fucking** (16th–17thC), **necking** and **petting** (early 20thC), and **homosexuality** (briefly, mid 20thC). Each had its moment to **swing**. Around 1953, a phenomenon called **wife swapping** was reported in the suburbs. During the early to mid sixties, **swinging couples** or **swingers** became the subject of serious study by sociologists, as well as a common male fantasy. But there was little need to limit **swinging** to married folks, and it expanded to include any kind of innovative sex with multiple partners, rendering all other definitions obsolete. The **swinging single** was now upon us.

We kiss so much ass ever day
We have to ice down our lips at night.
   —*Advisor to George W. Bush*
      on relationship with Congress, 2002.

There once was a pervert named Hoover
Who knew a sex fiend in Vancouver
  She was a lascivious young slut
  Plus she had a big butt
And she taught him the Hind-lick maneuver
   —*Kinky Friedman*, Steppin' on a
   Rainbow, *2001*

Non oscilarre, non tintinnabulare
If you don't swing, don't ring
   —*Legend affixed to plaque on*
    front door of the Playboy Mansion

Cast of Thousands

The kids also **swung** right in, joining in pursuit of their favorite rock stars, offering their bodies in service to the music. In tribute to their talents, Frank Zappa, of the Mothers of Invention, dubbed them **groupies**. But as Germaine Greer pointed out, the name had just the opposite effect from what was intended; in less than six months the term was considered an insult.

Of more lasting consequence was a specialized squad called the **plaster-casters**. Armed with an ample supply of plaster of Paris and nothing more than their nimble fingers to guide them, they made replicas of the **private parts** of the stars they had **fucked**. Their consummate skill and artistry earned them and the performers a permanent place in the history of sexual practices.

Stop It, I Love It

The beat continued with some **B/D** (mid 20thC)—a little **bondage and discipline**, courtesy of Ritter Leopold von Sacher-Masoch (1836–95), a man who put the **M** in **S and M** (sado-masochism).

A historian, dramatist, and novelist, Masoch loved children and cats, but his real penchant was for older and stronger women who could maltreat him physically and help scourge and subdue his animal lusts. Virtually all his books reflect this passion, and they always include a least one powerful and moving passage in which a woman in furs whips a pleasured male into a state of ecstasy.

"Wonderful woman!" I cried... "Whip me," I begged, "Whip me without pity."

It wasn't Masoch, however, who discovered sexual pleasure from self-inflicted pain. You'll find it in early pagan rites as well as in the Christian mysticism of suffering. Masoch merely captured it so well that he inspired Krafft-Ebing, in *Psychopathia Sexualis*, to name it after him.

Masochists today love being treated like slaves, little boys, animals, or lifeless objects such as doormats. A partner always helps. As Morticia (Anjelica Huston) reminded Gomez (Raul Julia) in *The Addams Family* (1991): " Don't torture yourself Gomez. That's my job."

Outside assistance can always be found in the personal columns under **English (also English guidance**, **acts**, or **culture)** from the British affection for the rod—spanking and flagellation long having been a staple of English sexual life. The French have always treated **masochism** as **le vice anglais**. Look for terms like **dominant**, **submissive**, **B/D**, and **S and M**. Furs are now out but leather is in, especially high boots, together with fishnet stockings and garter belts, the basic accoutrements of the practice. Whips, chains, and riding crops are optional.

Miss DuCane
Strict Governess
Corrective Training
   —*Window sign, Victorian England*

Mistress Blue
Imposing, Intelligent Goddess Offers skill and domination www.bluedungeon.com.
Discipline, bondage, medical, feminization, infant, and more. $200/hr. NO SEX.
   —*Seattle Weekly, April, 11, 2002*

The Whip, the Whip, Anything but...

Masochism is only one side of **algolagnia** (from the Greek *algos*, "pain," and *lagneia*, "voluptuousness"), the sexual urge tied to pain and that which causes it. **Sadism** is the other. But unlike **masochists**, **sadists** would rather give than receive, deriving their pleasure from humiliating or physically harming another or from merely watching another experience pain.

Sadism, of course, was inspired by the Count Donatien Alphonse François de Sade (1740–1814), one of the great philosophers and scientific minds of the eighteenth century. De Sade held God, virtue, and convention in equal contempt, spending much of his life in prison, twenty-seven years in eleven different institutions. De Sade had many passions and few inhibitions. His favorite activity was also his greatest hang-up—whipping a naked woman strung from the ceiling while being **masturbated** by his servant. **Sadism** today has fallen on bad times. The word simply connotes cruelty and abuse with none of the panache of the "Divine Marquis."

Those wanting to learn more about the topic might enjoy curling up with *The experimental lecture by Colonel Sparker on the exciting and voluptuous pleasures to be derived from crushing and humiliating the spirit of a beautiful and modest young lady; and delivered by him in the assembly room of the society of flagellants* (late 19thC). Providing, of course, you are able to get past the title.

"Why do you hang around with that sadist?*"*
"Beats me."
—B. Kliban, 1977

The Wild Bunch

If you can't beat 'em, you can always join 'em—in some **group sex**. What better way to meet new people and **make** new friends.

There's certainly no easier way to forge new relationships than through your neighborhood **daisy chain** (mid 20thC). We knew it once as a group of well-connected male **homosexuals** joined through **anal intercourse**, but over time, it's also come to represent **heterosexual** sport and to include oral activities as well. However, as Gershon Legman, "the high mathematician of **oral-genital sex**," pointed out, no **daisy chain**'s complete without some **homosexual** participation; otherwise it does not add up.

It's part of **Greek** and **Roman culture** (20thC), because of the Greek *orgia*, the secret rites of worship and the frolicsome and bawdy processions held in honor of Venus, Bacchus, Priapus, and the other good-time gods. The *bacchanalia*, or Roman **orgies** (since c. 1589), were especially noted for their sexual excesses, so much so they were finally halted by law. You don't have to be in Rome, however, to do as the Romans did. The Japanese also used to promote teamwork and interdependency in a game called **crossing the valley**. The girls would stretch out in line from one end of the

Male swingers who assert themselves through a polymorphic sexual abandon in which the line between the sexes dissolves, to the delight of all.
—Gore Vidal, Myra Breckinridge, 1968

If God had meant for us to have group sex, he'd have given us more organs.
  —Malcolm Bradbury

room to the other, while the boys would **fuck** each in turn, the object of the game being to cross the valley without **coming**.

Any Number Can Play

How do I love thee? Two's company, three's a **troilism**, where the third party functions either as a spectator or with specific **oral** or **genital** tasks to perform. One man by himself with two or more women was once considered as near heaven as he'd ever get, hence he was said to **lie in state** (c. 1780–1850); more discreet and personal arrangements created a **ménage à trois**, literally, "a family of three." The other way around, two guys and a gal, made a **cluster fuck** or a **club sandwich** (mid 20thC).

It was plain hard work for the lone gal having to pull her weight as well as that of her friends while **pulling the train** (mid 20thC), a succession of men who, like a string of boxcars, had to be coupled and uncoupled. Unfortunately, it was a **choo-choo** or **chuga-chuga** (20thC) that seldom put anyone back on track.

Most times, when it entailed one gal and more than two guys, it approached a **gang-bang** (or **shag**), also a rhythmic procession known as a **bunch punch** or a **team cream** (all 20thC), an act seldom voluntary on the female's part. Many considered it a case of **gang rape**, from the Latin *rapere*, "to seize or carry off."

That Special Something

If you'd rather just watch, you can be a **voyeur** and practice your **scopophilia**, the love of watching others undressing and engaging in sexual activity.

As a show-off of sorts, you stand exposed as an **exhibitionist**. The public, however, does not generally take kindly to the act. Displaying one's **genitals** publicly has been described by the clinical community as an act of degeneracy, neuropathy, psychosexual infantilism, and the expression of a pathological and perverted personality. **Exhibitionists** vary widely in their approach. **Flashers** (c. 1970), will stand for almost anything; while **streakers** (c. 1970) are always on the go.

Exhibitionism means literally "to hold forth or hold out" to someone (from the Latin *exhibere*: *ex*, "out," and *habere*, "to have or hold"). Though psychologists are unsettled by such behavior, they are also troubled by our more common "inhibitions" (holding things in). Perhaps it's time they made up their mind.

Still looking for the object of your affection? The **fetish** can be quite fashionable (its roots include the Latin *facticius* or *factitius*: "made by art"). The Latin became the Portuguese *fetico*, a word that Portuguese explorers used to describe amulets bought from

African natives with the added meaning of "a charm, sorcery, or something that works by a magical act." It passed into French as a *fetiche* on the way to the English **fetish**, a word we today identify with any item that generates irrational devotion. Sexual **fetishes** are legion. Enjoy certain parts of the body? **Shrimping** (1990s) is fun if you're into sucking toes. What have you? Fabric? High-heeled shoes? Hats? Bicycle seats? Cigars?

Tips of the Tongue

1. The French also say *avoir amour à la papa* for slow, conventional sex. Et à la Mama?

2. **Bestiality** isn't necessarily restricted to the barnyard. It hit Broadway in 2002 with Edward Albees's "The Goat, or Who Is Sylvia?" or as the headline in the *New York Times* headlined the play, "A secret **paramour**, one who nibbles tin cans." Its story line features an architect (with a **gay** teenage son) who cheats on his wife by **doing it** with a goat—an addiction which he acknowledges openly at an animal lovers' therapy group. The play's central question as articulated by its hero: "Is there anything anybody doesn't find arousing, whether we admit it or not, whether we know it or not?"— leaving us all on the horns of a dilemma. Where else?

3. They said it would only be a footnote in history and it is: November 15, 1995, a day that will live in infamy, or as one of his inquisitors described it, "The day, uh, of the first so-called salacious encounter..." The traumatic moment which brought an intern, a President, and a nation to their knees (in that order). It was the opening salvo of the national scandal known as **zippergate**. Language as we knew it would never again be the same. **Fellatio** became **head of state** and a **blow job** became a high crime or misdemeanor. Investigators called what happened "wholly unreciprocated sex." The President said he had only engaged in "improper intimate contact"

4. A subset of the activity is called **auto fellatio**. Contrary to popular belief, it does not occur in the back seat of your car. It's simply a person performing oral stimulation on his own **penis** or **vulva**. Not exactly a commonplace occurrence, approximately only two percent of males are actually able to do this—and that's stretching it some.

5. The Entertainment World has always been somewhat sensitive about **cocksuckers**. In a pivotal scene in *The Exorcist*, Linda Blair (via the voice of Mercedes McCambridge) demonically and virtually inaudibly announces, "Your mother **sucks cocks** in hell!" When the film was edited for TV, the censors

Said a President thought to get pecks
On areas other than necks
  "Although it's most sultry
  it isn't adultery
I'm not even sure that it's sex."
  —Anon., 1998

replaced her line with, "Your mother still rots in Hell!" In a later "Saturday Night Live" sketch with Richard Pryor, it ended up as "Your mother sews socks that smell!"

In 1971, Carl Reiner, director of the film *Where's Poppa?*, gave his son Rob the honor of being the first actor to clearly say **cocksucker** in a major film. This is not to be scoffed at. We are after all not talking your ordinary four-letter word. At last count, **cocksucker** was the second longest of the seven dirty words in the Supreme Court ruling (just behind **motherfucker**). Today, the expression is as repugnant as ever, but its use has been superceded by its abbreviated counterpart. In this form, it has become an integral part of every teenager's life. "Homework **sucks**." "Certain movies and CDs **suck**." All things considered—"life **sucks**." Graffiti takes it even further, "Gravity is a myth; the earth sucks." Seldom, though, is any mention made of the object being **sucked**.

...Make sure that no crooks, communists, or cocksucker get into this (community action programs).

—President Lydon Johnson to Sargent
Shriver, discussing the War on Poverty

Most have a good sense of it however. In the spring of 2002, a fan attending a Seattle Mariners–New York Yankees game, was forced by ballpark security to remove a T-shirt bearing the inscription, "Yankees **suck**." Others who tried to wear the shirts inside the ballpark were told to take them off, turn them inside out, or leave the stadium. A Mariners' spokesperson justified the action as consistent with the Safeco Field code of conduct regarding the ballpark's "family-friendly" atmosphere. The code states that Mariners' employees will "proactively intervene to support an environment where guests can enjoy the baseball experience free from the following behaviors," which include "obscene or indecent clothing."

Public protest, however, proved so embarrassing that the club was forced to revoke the ban, or as they say in the trade, "They sucked it up." There was no word, however, as to a second T-shirt carrying the legend, **Yankee my wankee**.

6. There are some common misconceptions about **cunnilingus**: (1) Though a flight of fancy in its own right, it has nothing to do with Aer Lingus; reservations not being required. (2) It makes the male who engages in the activity a **cunnilinctor**, but doesn't necessarily make an authority on **oral sex** into a "cunning linguist."

7. Alanis Morissettte's best-selling album of 1995, Jagged Little Pill, featured the song "You Oughta Know." Bemoaning her replacement by another, she asks her lover, "Is she **perverted** like me? Would she **go down on you** in a theater?"

8. Model Cindy Crawford later forged an even tighter link. Dismissing rumors she was **gay**, she joined Ellington with Mike Myers, " For me ...It don't mean a thing, if it ain't got that **schwing**."

One of a Kind

 n 1869 a Hungarian physician, Karoly Maria Benkert, coined the word **homosexual**.[1] It was a curious (dare we say "queer") blend of Greek (*homos*) and Latin (*sexus*), meaning "same sex." Lots of people were confused, thinking it meant "lover of men." Others were downright uncomfortable with the merger. Havelock Ellis was furious, calling it "a barbarously hybrid word." There have since been numerous attempts either to make the word philologically pure or to find substitutes for it.[2]

Scholars approached it from both sides, first creating the **homogenic**, the **homoerotic**, and the **homophile**; later, the **simulsexual** and the **isosexual**. Some made their feelings even clearer with the **controsexual**, or by cutting him down to size as a **homo** (also **homie**, c. 1925).

As the word became increasingly identified with men, it inspired the **feminosexual**, which created a new problem. If men were **homosexuals** and women **feminosexuals**, what were they collectively? From this dilemma there briefly emerged the **intersexual**.

Our most current entry is the proposed **herosexual**, who sounds as if he came out of a telephone booth rather than the closet. America, however, is not quite ready for that one.

Is it any wonder that we finally returned to the **homosexual**, the worst of all possible words—save all others.

Gentlemen will be Gentlemen
—Anita Loos

Q. Was your first sexual experience heterosexual or homosexual?
A. I was too polite to ask.
—Gore Vidal, replying to question by David Frost, 1971

Out of This World

It's not as if there weren't plenty of other options. **Urnings** may sound like something out of Dr. Seuss, but they really were the creation of Dr. Karl Heinrich Ulrichs (1825–1895), a nineteenth-century scientist. He was one of the first to try to explain and classify such behavior, calling it **uranism**, a condition he described as the female soul residing in a male body. **Urnings** and **uranism** came from the numerous references to Uranus in Plato's *Symposium*, which idealized **homosexual** activity. Like Plato, the good

Doctor always wrote on the topic with both sympathy and understanding.

Urnings, however, never caught on among Ulrichs's colleagues or within the lay community. And we are now the sadder for it, having lost a colorful and expressive term. Contemporary media would have simply adored it—what with some guy "**urning** a living" and two men "**urning** for each other." With several successful trips already to the moon, it would almost seem natural to also anticipate a trip to Uranus.

Gay Abandon

Most **urnings**, **homophiles**, and **isosexuals** made light of it all, choosing instead to be **gay**. "Gay" is a multi-faceted word. Apart from its primary definition of "bright" or "lively," its meaning as "sexually loose" and "dissipated" has been most popular and enduring. Being in the **gay life** once put you in the fast lane. Feeling **gay** left you **amorous**. The **gaying instrument** (19thC) was the **male member**, without which it wouldn't be possible to **gay it**. The **gay** woman was a major literary figure from Chaucer to Shakespeare and right on through the nineteenth century. She was **gay in the arse**, **groins**, or **legs** and spent much of her time in a **gay house**. Even today, in England, we have the **gay girl**, a hard-working **flat-backer** trying to turn an honest shilling (or is it a euro?).

Although there exists much controversy among scholars, the word most likely derives from the Old English *gal* for "lewd" and "lascivious" (which also gave us **quite a gal**, a nineteenth-century British term for a **prostitute**) rather than the more obvious *gai*, from Provence in southeastern France, a word which earlier referred to courtly love and its literature.

Gay did not become associated with **simulsex** (early 20thC) until the early part of the twentieth century, at first only as underground jargon. It went public with this meaning around 1903, with the **gay boy** in Australia, and 1935 in the United States in the film *Bringing Up Baby*, in which Cary Grant donned a dress and commented how he had **gone gay**. Between 1955 and 1960 the word captured everyone's fancy, culminating in the joyous outburst of the seventies.

And what a wide range of personalities emerged! Some were **gay as pink ink** (mid 1950s), or "overtly, obviously **homosexual**." Others were more restrained. They included the high achievers or **guppies**, "**gay** upwardly mobile professionals," the morally upright **gay Christians**; and the **gaybies**, "young gay males with a cute face, stylish clothes, and a warm personality"—the kind you'd bring home to mother.

Today, **gay**, or some word close to it, is used in more than a dozen countries in the same sense as in English. We have **gay** bars, **gay** boutiques, and **gay** publications. It's become all so respectable—a far cry from the days when proprietors handed out **gayola** (gay + payola, c.1960): "blackmail or extortion paid to police to protect a **homosexual** establishment."

Madison Avenue has at last awakened to the word's full commercial potential, and wordsmiths have begun to retool the language. It's probably only a matter of time before "the gay old dog" becomes an aged **homo**[3] and "the gay blade," a means of removing unwanted body hair.

Damned silly...A term which made us into frivolous Idiots—sort of bliss-ninnies.
—Christopher Isherwood

The Ins and the Outs

Initially, most **gays** were anything but **gay** while packed into crowded closets along with their hang-ups. Many had been **closeted** for years, "keeping their sexual preferences private". Among them were the **closet queer**, pretending to be straight, avoiding association with those who did not; the **closet case** or **closet queen**, one refusing to acknowledge his **gaiety** to others and struggling to keep it secret; and the **iron-closet** who wouldn't admit his sexual-orientation even to himself—truly the **queen of denial**.

Odd Man Out

The closet door slowly swung open. It started innocently enough when the first **gay** man **brought out** a putatively straight man—exposing him to his true nature and liberating his sublimated **gay** orientation. Help, however, was soon unnecessary. He first **came out** unassisted in 1941, "becoming progressively more and more exclusively **homosexual**." And in the sixties, he really **came out**, "publicly acknowledging his orientation or living it openly."

Over the next twenty years, scores of **gays** poured out of the closet, like a thousand clowns emerging from the tiny car at the circus. Others merely **dropped their hairpins** (1960s), admitting to having been **in the closet**.

Many hung back, but others, seeking to be helpful, **opened the closet** for them. Closet protocol is quite firm on this matter. **Outing**, "deliberately disclosing another's **homosexuality**," is a no-no. Under the **Absolute code**, aka **the golden rule**, you never expose a fellow **gay** publicly. An **outing** is not necessarily a pleasurable excursion and could have serious consequences, costing a person his job, his straight friends, or his family.

Coming out as an individual decision, however, is encouraged, as evidenced by the annual **National Coming Out Day**. No longer is there any stigma attached to it. **Being out** is now very much an in thing.

A Clothes Call

Gays may have been unnamed and unloved, but they were seldom unsightly. Many came out of the closet in high fashion. Clothes historically have made the man **one of those**, and special dress was at one time de rigueur. Henry III of France (1551–1589), probably the most notorious royal **homosexual** in history, loved to deck himself out in outrageous attire, transforming his royal majesty into what we would today call a **screaming queen** (20thC).

The **queen** has had a glorious and colorful career. She started as an **easy woman** and a **prostitute**, "a flaunting woman of loose morals if not practice" (Grose). During the nineteenth century she evolved into a man with girlish manners and carriage; and a century later, a highly conspicuous and garishly attired **homosexual**.[4] At his very best, her majesty is **flaming**—flaunting her effeminate traits in the most outrageous way.

> Even in the melee of queenfares, painted eyes, bodies in drag—even then she stood out from all the others...a queen perched on a stool like a startled white owl: a man with bleached, burned-out hair and a painted face dominated to the point of absolute impossibility by the largest, widest, darkest eyes I have ever seen, pointed into two enormous tadpoles, slanting to the very edges of her temples.
>
> ...Her dress, short, reaches her knees, the legs crossed so that the purple spike-heeled shoes coming to a long point; like those of a witch, protrude on either side of the stool: one foot swinging back and forth, impatiently, reckless, constantly like a pendulum.
>
> ...A queen.
>
> A flamboyant, flagrant, flashy queen. A queen in absurdly grotesque, clumsy drag.
>
> —John Rechy, *City of Night*

A Dressing Down

Drag (c. 1850) has long been the **queen**'s thing, from a long gown brushing or "dragging" against the floor, which also created the **swish** (also **swishy**, early 20thC), a man with an especially effeminate gait. During the second half of the nineteenth century he'd **go on drag** or **flash drag**. When it caught the attention of the authorities, they called it **doing** or **wearing the drag**, wearing women's clothes for "immoral" purposes, resulting in gaol time for the dresser.

Most today consider it all very **camp** (since c. 1920), from the Italian *campeggiare*, "to stand out from a background." They first began **camping**, "exaggerating feminine mannerisms," during the roaring twenties. By 1959, they were really **camping it up**, its meaning expanding to "engaging in any ostentatious or affected

display," or "acting coquettish and theatrical." Over time, however, such behavior simply became **campy**, "abrasive and wearisome." From this emerged **camp**, a form of humor popular in the **gay** community in which **gays** poke fun at themselves, a style that's highly satirical, often to the point of meanness.

Camp (1950s) was also once a **brothel** and a gathering place for **homosexual** males. Would you, we ask, still send this boy to **camp?**

Most **transvestites** (**cross-dressers** or **TVs**, mid 20thC) enjoy getting into a woman's pants—but prefer that the woman not be in them at the time. **Cross-dressing** has always been a kick for them as well as for the **TV** viewer. There's really nothing new here. According to Greek mythology, Achilles loved to deck himself out on occasion (what else but high heels?), and Hercules once dressed himself in the clothing of Queen Omphale. It was a tight fit. He squeezed into her girdle, splitting the sleeves of her gown, but the result proved so convincing that Pan tried to **put the make on** him. Hercules was so incensed that he threw Pan across the room—from which moment, Pan swore never again to have anything to do with clothes.

Getting to Know You

Drag can be—well—a drag. Part of the challenge of the **gay** life style is diplomatic recognition. As a rule, subtle is always better. In late nineteenth-century America, they simply **tied one on**. Havelock Ellis told of **inverts** of the time employing red neckties to identify themselves to fellow **fairies**, a practice especially favored by male **prostitutes** out for a **cruise** (early 20thC). More recently, **hanky codes** helped men recognize one another when they meet in public, the location and color of the handkerchief indicating the sexual interests of the potential sex partner.[5]

You could always ask. Are they **in the life?** (now used primarily within the black community). Are they **people like us?** Is he **family?** (the derogatory **Brown family** was popular during the 1940s). **Does he sing in the choir?** There is, after all, no need to preach to one already there.

Some favor the more direct approach. **Does he like boys? Is he a Streisand Ticket holder?** Or **a sister** or **a friend of Dorothy?** That's Dorothy from *The Wizard of Oz* as played by Judy Garland, one of the most beloved icons of the **gay** culture.[6]

Advance warning can be sounded with a **beep**, a signal used when one **gay** person sees someone they suspect is **gay**. It's been described by one wag as "the sound of their **gaydar** (**gay** radar) going off"—the uncanny ability **gays** have of detecting other **gay** people in their midst. Cute **buns?** ...Off the screen!

Still not sure? He could just be of the wrong **sexual orientation**.

There's really not much you can do about it. Why not just sit back and enjoy the **scenery** (1990s)?

Vice Versa

Not everyone liked what they saw. The public spoke in hushed whispers of **the love that dare not speak its name**, from the poem written by Alfred, Lord Douglas, to Oscar Wilde, introduced by the prosecution as prime evidence at Wilde's trial and the centerpiece of his eloquent and brilliant defense. However, few knew what else to call it, because of the general scarcity of euphemisms that existed at the time.

An early twentieth century euphemism popular in Great Britain was the **bachelor**. To avoid any confusion with the word's more traditional definition, The *Times* of London made a subtle distinction in its obituaries. The deceased **heterosexual** bachelor had **never married**. While the late **gay** gentleman had been a **confirmed bachelor**.

In private conversation, people had him doing a **detrimental** (early 20thC) or **the other** (c. 1925, from the criminal offense of **homosexuality** as opposed to **prostitution**). It was said **he didn't care much for members of the opposite sex** (c. 1925). He was **epicene** (early 20thC), a **member of the third sex** (20thC) or the **intermediate sex** (1890s). Today's he mostly **versatile**, of a **different sexual orientation**, or even **bisexual** (because it's more acceptable).

Stranger Than Life

Their hearts weren't always young and **gay**. Things got pretty heavy when the outside world described them as **deviants**, **degenerates** (both since late 19thC), **oddballs**, **weirdos**, **freaks** (all since mid 19thC), and **preverts** (*Dr. Strangelove*).

Most people believed that if you're not **straight**, you must be **bent** (19th–20thC, Eng.), **kinky** (c. 1920, for a **homosexual**; since c. 1960 for any kind of exotic, way-out sex), or **twisted** (mid 20thC).[7] Joe Sixpack wrote them all off as a bunch of **fuckin' queers, fruits, fairies**, and **faggots**.[8]

A **queer** (c. 1920) was once slang for counterfeit money. It didn't gain currency as a **homosexual** until 1925, when the connection was made public in *Variety*, the theatrical trade journal. Today, with both inflation and gaiety raging everywhere, being **as queer as a three-dollar bill** seems to have become an established fact. Some people think **queer** to be a polite term. Most consider it a curdling epithet, though many within the **gay** community have recently embraced it as their own.

If homosexuality were normal, God would have created Adam and Bruce.

—Anita Bryant, 1977

Fruit of the Loom

Some **fruit** is definitely forbidden. Both the U.S. **fruit** and the British **fruiterer** (also early 20thC, U.S.) derive from the youthful fruit dealers in fourteenth-century England and their predilection for **oral sex** and other sexual activity considered beyond the norm. Female **fruitesters** with similar tastes go back as far as Chaucer. Along the way, the **fruit** has had many identities, as a **loose** and **easy woman**, a man of similar morals, and even as a verb meaning to **fuck**. By the middle of the twentieth century, cool dudes in the inner-city were busy **fruiting—galavanting** about town, in search of a **piece of ass**.

Fruit is often depicted as ripe and easy for the picking. Like **gay**, **sucker**, and **dupe**, all of which have also been synonymous with **homosexuality**, he has been characterized as an unknowing tool—one easily influenced and often victimized.[9]

In 1912, the word began its stint as a weird and off-beat person. We later joined his promiscuous nature to his odd and eccentric character, producing the contemporary **fruit**. For the most part, however, **fruit**'s shelf life has expired. "Surely nobody has used the word 'fruit' to describe a **homosexual** since the thirties." (M. Korda, *New Yorker*, 1993).

A Grimm Reminder

If there's an air of unreality to it all, it must be the good **fairy**. Starting life around 1880 in the States as an attractive girl, the **fairy**, in early twentieth-century England, evolved into a debauched and hideous woman often reeling with drink, hitting rock bottom as a **lady of the night**. The **fairy**'s been **one of them** only since 1924 in England and 1949 in the U.S, though some spotted his presence as early as 1908. Teenagers still recount the classic **fairy** tale, which originated during the fifties of the lost tourist who inquired of a stranger, "Where can I find the Twelfth Street ferry?" And the famous response, done with a lisp and a flourish: "Thpeaking."

A Class Act

Like the **fairy**, the **faggot** (c. 1930, also **faggart**) has also done time as an old and dissipated woman (16th–19thC) as well as a **prostitute** (19th–20thC)—social outcasts all. The **faggot**'s origins were humble, beginning life as nothing more than "a bag of sticks" (14thC, Fr.), the small bundle of twigs and branches placed under the feet of the heretic to be burned at the stake. According to Bailey (1728), the faggot was once a proper symbol of recantation.

Who is that fruit?
   —*Ty Cobb on meeting Bill Tilden*

California: Home of Fruits and Nuts
   —*Bumper sticker, 1982*

In the beginning, God created fairies and they made men.
   —John Rechy, City of Night, *1963*

The heretic who escaped the stake was required either to actually bear one or wear its image on the sleeve as a badge of shame. This was a time when the Church often confused religious dissent with both social nonconformity and sexual deviance—a truly great bargain: three vices for the price of one. It was then but a simple leap of faith to identify the lost soul with the instrument by which he was put to death.

The Vatican no longer burns **faggots**. It encourages us instead to face **homosexuality** with the objectivity and understanding one would show such a "disorder."

Others find the **faggot**'s origin in the British public (what we call "private") schools. Boys from the upper forms traditionally forced weak and submissive underclassmen to perform mean and humiliating tasks. The work was so demanding as to leave them fatigued or "fagged," a complaint so frequently heard that the younger lads were transformed into **fags** or **faggots** in the eyes of their tormenters.

> Bob Trotter, the diminutive fag of the studio,...ran all the young men's errands and fetched them applies and oranges.
>
> —William Thackeray, *Newcomes*, 1855

The **faggot** made his first formal appearance in 1914 in *The Vocabulary of Criminal Slang* and shortly thereafter in abbreviated form. Though traditional sports were not his forte, many knew him as a **three-letter man**. **Fag** is still pejorative, but like "nigger" with black people, can be used affectionately within the community.[10]

Odd Man Out

They may not have been so crazy about **faggots**, but they were just wilde about Oscar, who in this case happens to be Oscar Wilde, British writer and wit (1854–1900), and the most celebrated **homosexual** of the nineteenth century. It was he who bequeathed us **Oscar** (late 19th–20thC) for males caught **oscarizing** or thought to be **on the Wilde side**.

People's names, both male and female, have always been favored. On the feminine side you might try **Nancy** (c. 1820), **Miss Nancy** (c. 1880), **Nance** (19th–20thC), **Molly** (18th–20thC), **Mary Anne** (c. 1890), **Alice, Flo, Sissie, Jesse, Margery** (c. 1850–1900), **Bessie, Beaulah** (both 20thC), and **John and Joan** (18th–mid 19thC). Currently, **Mary's** a grand old name, as is **Mable**, two stateside favorites, while **Mavis** does her thing in England.

You'd think the names normal enough, but in some quarters they still seem a strange bunch—of flowers: **daffodils** (England since c. 1945), **buttercups, lilies, ivies, roses, violets** (all 20thC), and of course everybody's favorite, **pansies** (since c. 1930)—making, we suppose, those who are slow to reveal themselves late bloomers of sorts.

Know what they call a Jewish fag? A Heblew.
Know what they call an Irish fag? A Gay-Lick.
    —Radano, Walking the Beat, *1968*

I want to live out my life as the one who wrote The Murder Game, *not as the faggot who killed his wife.*
    —The Deathtrap, *Ira Levin, 1980*

Now you see them; now you don't. In England, they've gone all **pouf**. A **pouf** (or **poufter**) was once a would-be actor or a silly fellow. No one's really sure of its origin. One can only surmise that the word is an affectation of sorts, a variation of "poof" or "pooh," as in "Pooh! I couldn't care less!"

Global Penetration

Thoroughly foreign to most, it's still probably **Greek** to you, as part of **Greek culture**, the **Greek way**, and the **Greek fashion** (all mid 20thC), or as the personal columns put it, just plain **Gr.** Those into that country's ancient architecture might also appreciate **Doric love** (1920s).

There is, however, nothing parochial about the practice. Its appeal is definitely global. Shakespeare named it the **Italian habit**. The French, ever appreciative of the Germans, came up with **le vice allemand**.

Shortly thereafter, the Christian world discovered a **Turkish culture** in which men **turked each other**. The Turks took the prize for their reputed excellence in the sport and for their invention of the fly, an open crotch in front of the pants, and a flap in the rear, allowing for ready access both fore and aft.

It was all part of the war of the words in which men shot off their mouths rather than their guns. Could it be that the United States passed up a potentially powerful new weapon in the Cold War when it failed to introduce the world to **commie culture**, losing one of those rare opportunities to truly stick it to the Russians? Fortunately, there's always another enemy on the horizon, "Islamic culture," in particular, offering intriguing possibilities.

Irish by birth
Greek by injection.
—Anon., 20thC

Tails of Two Cities

Talking turkey, you're also talking **sodomy**, from Sodom and Gomorrah, the twin-sin cities of the Old Testament (Genesis 19:24) with a reputation for abandoned sexuality and a special fondness for the practice of **coitus per anum**.[11]

Sodom's link with the **bum-fuck** (mid 20thC) comes directly from the Old Testament and the experience of the two angels whom God dispatched to the city. The decision had been made to destroy Sodom and Gomorrah for their wicked ways but, out of deference to Abraham, God agrees to spare the cities if ten good men can be found. The angels are sent to conduct the search. Upon their arrival, they secure lodging in Lot's house, but soon a mob of townsmen gather outside, demanding to know the strangers.

The entire story as well as the origin of **sodomy** turns on this incident and on the word "know." As noted earlier, in addition to

When lord St. Clancey became a nancy
It did not please his family fancy.
And so in order to protect him
They did inscribe upon his rectum:
All commoners must now drive steerage;
This asshole is reserved for peerage.
—Quoted by Leonard Ashley
in Maledicta, winter, 1980

its more innocent usage, to **know** someone in the Old Testament often meant to **fuck** them. What we don't know for sure is whether the Sodomites only wanted to get acquainted with the angels or had other things in mind. Philo of Alexandria took it in the worst possible way, and it was his interpretation that was later adopted by the Church fathers, firmly establishing the link between Sodom and the nasty act.

There are those scholars, however, who feel that the city's reputation has been unnecessarily sullied, and that charges of **anal intercourse** as a common practice there may be nothing more than—you should pardon the expression—a bum rap, pointing out that of the 943 recorded "knows" in the Old Testament, only 15 have any sexual meaning. But they fail to answer why the men of Sodom were so determined to **know** the strangers, and why Lot offered them instead a chance "to **know** his daughters who had not yet **known** any man." Also unanswered is what so angered a just and merciful God that He felt it necessary to strike them blind and destroy the city with fire and brimstone. It seems no one really knows the gospel truth.

Be that as it may, He finally did get the boys out of Sodom, though He never did quite get Sodom out of the boys, leaving us with a **ream of sodomists** (since c. 1785) as well as their abbreviated counterpart, the **sods** (late 19th–early 20thC).

Sodomy now serves as a general, catch-all term for any form of **non-orthogenic sex**, i.e., that of a non-procreative nature, encompassing everything from **anal copulation** to **lesbian acts, mutual masturbation, analingus, bestiality, exhibitionism**, and **taking indecent liberties with a minor**. In this country, most states still have laws on their books against **sodomy**—whatever it may mean. New York state's definition of the crime includes **oral copulation**, leading one critic to remark as to how its legislators apparently did not know heads from tails.

What's Buggin' You?

Sodomy, did, however make believers of some. Witness the Albigensians, a medieval religious sect with a reputation for abstaining from any sexual practices that might result in procreation. So repelled were they by **the act**, they not only avoided **it** but also shunned any food **it** engendered, including meat, eggs, cheese, and milk. Their beliefs not only limited their culinary options, but also forced them to seek new outlets for their sexuality, forging a lasting bond between them and the **unnatural vice** (19thC). Originating as they did in Bulgaria, they came to be known as **Bulgars** or **buggers** and their practice as **buggery** (16th–20thC).

There are some scholars, however, who discount the Bulgarian

Let me slip into something comfortable.
—*Gay graffiti, 1990s*

Mum, me bum's numb.
—*Anon., 20thC*

connection. They find **buggery**'s origins instead in Sir Robert LeBougre, the famous Inquisitor who gained unnatural pleasure from the suffering he inflicted upon his victims as well as the nature of the confessions he extracted—admission of both sexual and religious deviance, **buggery** being a common charge of the time.

Buggery's never been popularly received. British schoolboys once spoke of **the three B's** of public-school life: "birching, boredom, and **buggery**." It was once treated as an abominable crime and a gross indecency which, under England's Criminal Law Amendment Act of 1885, meant four years of hard labor for Oscar Wilde. Yet today we know its softer, gentler side as a term of surprise: "Well I'll be **buggered**!" as well as one of affection: "You little **bugger**, you!

Love means not having to say you're sore.
—Anon., 20th C.

Word of Mouth

Generally considered an acquired taste is the practice of one man **tonguing** another. Finding the right words, however, hasn't always been easy. In nineteenth-century America, they said a mouthful when practicing **orastupration**. Today, they have a **picnic** doing it.

Practitioners include not only the **tasters, munchers, noshers** (all 20thC), **nibblers** (early 20thC), and **gobblers** (19th–20thC) but also the more radical element known as **cannibals** and **man-eaters** (both 20thC). During the early 1900s, a **lick box** derisively referred to any **gay** man. More recently, he **gives cone** and **chews the goo**. Contemporary victuals include **bananas and cream** and a **basket lunch** (impromptu **fellatio**).

Some would rather turn it into a sporting proposition as **tonsil hockey**. What's good **sex**, however, without some feedback? The game then becomes **hoopsnake**, played for one's mutual satisfaction.

Today **oral sex** is quite commonplace and pretty much taken for granted. But it was once a special occasion, made festive by **wearing the kilts** (early 20thC) and **doing a bagpipe** (c. 1785), though even Grose considered that "a piece of bestiality too filthy for explanation."

It was music, however, to the ears of the **piccolo player** or **fluter** (early 20thC), one also known to **do a tune** (20thC). His graffiti proclaims: "I play the flute and swallow the music." It took years, however, for the world to finally grant him status as an artiste. No longer is he your ordinary **blow boy** (20thC), he's **Lord of the Flies** (1980s). You can recognize him by his T-shirt with the rooster-shaped lollipop on it or the inscription, "Have gums will travel."

Ne regrettez pas. If you've got it, **flute** it.

Oral sex: The taste of things to come.
—Anon., 1980s

Lick Dick in '72
—Bumper sticker, Presidential Election

André Gide lifted himself up by his own jockstrap so to speak—and one would like to see him hoisted on his own pederasty.

—F Scott Fitzgerald, Notebooks

Child's Play

"Kid stuff," you say! Not when it involves the young. We're then talking **child abuse** (1970s–80s). The Greeks called it **pedophilia** (from *pais*, "child," and *philos*, "loving"), describing the sexual attraction of an older person to a child. But as wordsmith William Safire points out, what about certain adults' passion for teenagers? Teens, after all, are not children. Thanks to a Pakistani scholar who found an earlier reference to it, we have **ephebophilia**, "the **lust** for postpubescent boys," from *ephebos*, an Athenian youth of about 18 who was in training for citizenship. All well and fine, but still no official word of the "lover of young girls."

Those who preferred sending a boy to do a man's job committed **pederasty** (since 14thC), an Anglicized version of the Greek **paiderasty**, again from *pais*, "boy" and *erastes*, "lover." The tradition created the **Ganymede** (16thC), the Trojan boy from Greek mythology who was so beautiful that Zeus, the father of the Gods, kidnapped him, making him his lover and cup bearer. Today, he's a young boy beloved by an older man or the younger partner in a **pederastic** relationship. In Latin, he became *catamitus*, our **catamite** (16th–20thC), currently defined as "any young boy used for immoral purposes." Latin would again come to the rescue when Pope John Paul II addressed the problem of priests engaging in the activity, citing "our brothers who had succumbed to *mysterium iniquitatis* ("the mystery of evil"). As noted by *New York Times* columnist Maureen Dowd, "There's nothing very mysterious about **pedophilia**. It's a crime."

Boys Will Be...

Socrates **had** his famous pupil Alcibiades. During the latter part of the nineteenth century, they used to say **se laisser Alcibiadiser**, to **play Alcibiades**, for one assuming the passive role in **pederasty**. A distinction soon arose between Socratic love (**amour socratique**) and that of a Platonic variety (**amour platonique**), though it's clear that when Plato wrote of human love in the *Phaedo*, he really meant **homosexual** love. This is further underscored in his other writings. In his *Symposium*, it's love between two men which he considered the noblest and most spiritual.

Henry III's favorite boys were called **mignons** (today, minions). A diarist at the court, Pierre de L'Estoile, described them thus:

> These pretty minions wore their hair pomaded, artificially curled and recurled, flowing back over their little velvet bonnets, like those of whores in a bordello, and the ruffs of their starched linen shirts were a half-foot long, so that seeing their heads above the ruffs was like seeing Saint John's head upon a platter. The rest of their clothes were made the same way.

Their exercises were playing, blaspheming, fencing, and whoring, and following their king everywhere.

Pederasty is still actively practiced today. It comes in the guise of the **chicken queen** and the **chicken hawk**, a.k.a. **Colonel Sanders** (all 20thC), **cruising** about, waiting for the right moment to swoop down from above and steal away a fresh young **chicken** (20thC) who may have strayed from the roost.[12]

Lady's Choice

The Criminal Law Amendment Act of 1885 under which Oscar Wilde was convicted made no mention of female **homosexuality** out of deference to the sensitivities of Her Majesty, Queen Victoria. Members of Parliament later sought to smuggle it in as part of the working definition of **gross indecency**, but it never made it past the House of Lords, primarily because the august gentlemen could not imagine what it was that two women might possibly be up to.

This same male vanity and ignorance, combined with male control of words, helps explain the current dearth of terms to describe members of the **sisterhood** (20thC) or their activities.

The one word which everyone knows, however, is **lesbian** (c. 1896) or one of its many variations: **Leslie, les, lez, lesbo**, and **lesbyterian**, to say nothing of those who have an irrational fear or hatred of them, the **lesbophobes**.[13] The **lesbian** and her friends all come from the Island of Lesbos, where the famed Greek poetess Sappho founded and directed her famous school for girls. Sappho's poetry was beautifully created and reveals a special depth of feeling and intimacy for women, much of it directed to her pupils. Because of that, she herself has also long been associated with the movement (**Sapphists**, 20thC).

There are historians, however, who are convinced that Sappho was **straight** and her school anything but a hotbed of carnal activity. It's hard to prove. Her work is difficult to translate and we have only fragments to work with, most of her writing having been destroyed by Christian zealots who feared its immoral character.

From what we know, the curriculum of the school featured dancing, singing, and instruction in musical instruments, with students also receiving lessons in grace, coquetry, and "womanly" skills. Fragments of lessons which survive show that the school stressed the passive and subordinate aspects of womanhood, with little or no emphasis on encouraging female independence. Students were taught how to lift their skirts in order to show a well-turned ankle, and much emphasis was placed on how a woman should not act proud while looking for a husband. Could these have been your original **lesbians?** Consistent with this, the term originally (17thC) mean "pliant and accommodating." Only during

Boys will be boys these days, and so, apparently, will girls.

—Jane Howard

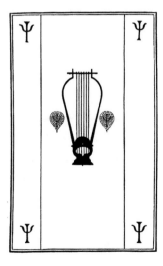

the nineteenth century did it begin to take on its present meaning and begin to connote more assertive if not militant behavior.

Les is More

Speaking of the **sorority**, we've got the **Daughters of Bilitis** (c. 1955), from the name of the **lesbian** poet in "Songs of Bilitis" by Pierre Louÿs. As for special words describing their activities, the best we can do is the somewhat stilted **tribadism** (16th–20thC), from the Greek for "to rub," describing sexual activity in which one woman rubs another's **pudenda** with her thigh or with a **dildo**. We have only a few phrases unique to the **lesbian** community, describing what goes on behind bedroom doors. Most have been borrowed from other parts of *The Erotic Tongue*. Some of the better ones are **flat fuck** or **Venus observa femina**, and **vice versa** for mutual **cunnilingus**.[14] There's really much more—lots of it being researched, much of it unrecorded, but for now, **Lesbian our way homo** (mid 20thC, U.S. teenage babble).

Guise and Gals

Men have not only been clumsy in treating the subject of **lesbianism** but also backward in their knowledge of the players. Among the types they spotted early on were the **Amy-Johns** (19thC pun on "Amazons"), who played the dominant role in a **lesbian** relationship, the **she-male** asserting herself in women's prisons, and the overbearing **sergeant** (1950s) who put everyone through their paces. She's known best today as a **dyke**, initially a derogatory reference, connoting masculine appearance or behavior. Her origins are unclear. Some trace her back to nineteenth-century British slang for male clothing. Others find her roots in the **morphadyte** or **morphadyke**, a Southern black folk term for a **hermaphrodite**, one having both male and female characteristics, applied first to a horse, then to a human being.

She's also a **diesel dike** (who'll drive right over you) and the **bull dyke** (or **bull dagger**). The **bull** is your sexual aggressor, who when joined with the **dyke** (also a nineteenth-century term for the female **genitalia**) created an "aggressive **hole**"—which is how some men saw her.

Dyke and her variants have now evolved from a stereotypical masculine, aggressive **lesbian** with an "attitude" into a strong independent person. In some quarters she's even become a **dykon**, a **lesbian** icon, such as KD Laing, Melissa Etheridge, or Ellen DeGeneres

The **dyke's** primary counterpart is the **butch** (20thC). Her masculine characteristic can make her **butch as Kong**—almost apelike. Her kinder, gentler side transforms her into a **baby butch**, a

I always get the feeling that when lesbians look at me, They're thinking "That's why I'm not a heterosexual."
—George Costanza (Jason Alexander),
Seinfeld

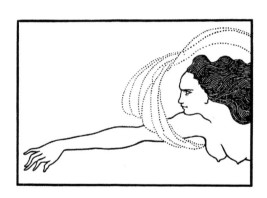

Angry young woman
They call me a dyke;
Don't know much about it
I just know what I like
—"Theme song" of the lesbian movement,
(c. 1982)

teenage **lesbian** (also a boyish adolescent) or a **soft butch**, featuring a warm demeanor.

Her origins are humble. A common nickname fathers once bestowed upon their sons, "Butch" told the whole world he was "all boy," like the firm handshake and eye contact, part of the requisite masculine style. The "butch" was also once your manly haircut, very short—the crewcut of the forties. All things "butch" originated with the "butcher," one who was never out of character as a man, making it quite clear where today's **butch** stands.

Cherchez la femme

Enter the **femme** (c.1972). During the 1940s, he was an effeminate male **homosexual**; but by 1972, he was a "she," transformed into a **lesbian** taking a passive role in sex or playing the stereotypical feminine role.

This was most often done in conjunction with the **butch** or the **dyke**, creating a relationship known as **Dyke/femme** or **butch/femme (B/F)**—a social structure prevalent in the working class **lesbian** bar scene through the early 1970s. Times changed, however and with the advent of **lesbian feminism** during the latter part of the decade, there was a backlash against this approach. Quicker than you could say A-OK!, **B/F** was no longer PC. As if from nowhere, there appeared the **andro** (androgynous) **dyke**, a **lesbian** whose sexual identity is unclear—neither very masculine nor very feminine in appearance or manner—and it was she who would become the model for the movement. Thanks to her the monolithic dyke finally burst.

B on B and **F on F** then took center stage, superceding **B/F**. It's not like **B/F** has been totally discredited; in some quarters it's even mustered a comeback. It's simply not applied as rigidly as it once was.

This war of words finally ended after a long and bitter struggle in which the participants had not always conducted themselves gracefully. Some found refuge in the **Boston Marriage**, "two single women living together in a romantic yet **asexual** long-term **lesbian** relationship." Others defined themselves in their own way, writing off the **B / F**, **B on B** and **F on F** brouhaha as so much BS.

What's the point of being a lesbian if a woman is going to look and act like an imitation man?
—Rita Mae Brown

The Sweet Bi and Bi

If you liked the **lesbian** and her friends, you'll flip over **twixters** and **tweenies** (c. 1909), boyish girls and girlish boys, **ambisexuals** (20thC for married men who have an occasional **homosexual** fling), and **bisexuals** who in addition to being just plain **bi** are **double-gated** and **bi-gated** (20thC), from horses that both trot and gallop. No need to be **uni-directional**, when the **two-way**

That the whole species or kinde should be bisexous
—Sir T. Browne, 1646

There are those who, like Dr. Reuben, cannot accept the following simple fact of so many lives (certainly my own): that it is possible to have a mature sexual relationship with a woman on Monday, and a mature sexual relationship with a man on Tuesday, and perhaps on Wednesday have both together (admittedly, you have to be in good condition for this).

—Gore Vidal *in rebuttal to Dr. David Reuben's review of* Myra Breckinridge *in* The New York Review of Books

boys and the **two-way Johnnies** are **going both ways** (all 1990s). Like **yo-yos** (1990s), they're making the best of life's **ups and downs**.

These are extraordinarily versatile people. Woody Allen considers them doubly fortunate, being twice as likely to be asked out on a Saturday night.

Such a talented group of performers! They're both **ambidextrous** (said primarily of women) and **bilingual**, as is your **preference**. They are **switch hitters** who can **bat from either side** or **go** and **swing both ways**. When singing the body electric, they're **AC/DC**, (all 20thC)—whatever or whichever turns you on. The French call it **marcher à la voile et à la vapeur**, literally "to function by sail and steam."

"Whatta trip!" you say. It's time to go **transsexual**. The word **transsexual**, like so many others in *The Erotic Tongue*, conveys special imagery—this one of rapid movement. Hugo Flesch suggests "a train that carries sexuals across the United States without any hassles." In 1952 the **transsexual** went trans-Atlantic when George (now Christine) Jorgenson underwent the first **sex change**, now called a **gender change**, making it into a grammatical exercise of sorts, ending with a large question mark.[15]

Revolting Matters

The legendary Mrs. Patrick Campbell had few questions or concerns about sexual behavior. She didn't care what we did as long as we didn't do it in the street and scared the horses.

What would Mrs. Campbell have said of today's goings on? We've not only taken to the streets but stormed the gates of constraint, torn down the pillars of convention and trampled the canons of morality underfoot. It's nothing short of a total upheaval in morals. We call it the **sexual revolution** (1960s). Critics describe it as "simply revolting."[16]

Tips of the Tongue

1. **Heterosexuality**, originating with the Greek *heteros*, "other," followed a different route, making its print debut in Richard Krafft-Ebbing's *Psychopathis Sexualis* in 1889. It's always been a volatile word. It made its first formal appearance in 1923, cited in Webster's Dictionary as "morbid sexual passion for one of the opposite sex." In 1979, Lilian Faderman raised questions about proclamations of **heterocentrism**, challenging some of the basic assumption of the **heterosexual** paradigm. *The Oxford Dictionary of New Words* later took things a step further, defining **heterosexism** as "Discrimination or prejudice in favor of **heterosexuals** (and by implication

against **homosexuals**); the view that **heterosexuality** is the only acceptable **sexual orientation**."

2. Because of what he considered the negative connotations associated with the word, **homosexual**, Kurt Hiller in 1946 suggested **androtrope** be used in reference to a **gay** man and **gynaeotrope** to a **lesbian** (from the Greek *tropos*, "turn or direction and *andros*, "man" and *gyne*, "woman"). As you may have already guessed, the only turn these neologisms took was for the worst.

3. As a card-carrying member of the **Geritol set**, he's now an **Aunt** or **Auntie**, a likeable older **gay** man. The term can be quite affectionate but also derogatory, underscoring his effeminate and gossipy nature. He's also **Grandma**, **Gray**, **Old girl**, a **goat**, and a **hen**. As **Abigail**, he's a middle age **gay** still **in the closet** or one simply with a conservative approach to life.

4. As befits their regal status, **queens** have their own unique way of presenting themselves to the world and indicating their preferences. Keeping with the original spirit of things, we have the **drag queen (DQ)** decked out in all her regal raiment, often the main attraction at **gay pride marches**. Close by, the **dangle queen**, an exhibitionist who favors long, dangling earrings. The **ace queen** appears as womanly as possible, with shaved legs, plucked eyebrows, etc. The **drama queen** tends to make an excessive fuss over a situation. The **éclair queen** is wealthy and not afraid to flaunt it.

    Attitude queens carry themselves with a snobbish air, as do the **piss elegant queens**, also noted for their holier-than-thou manner. Those somewhat less fashionable include the **hippy queens**, adopting the characteristic style of the 60s—long hair, tattered jeans, etc. Bringing up the rear, the more sedate **sweater queens**, **gay** men in nicely pressed sweaters and slacks, described by one lexicographer as "looking as if they are ready to head off to work at Macy's." The only question is who from this varied group will be the **main queen**, "one highly colorful or in demand sexually."

    Each has their own personal likes and dislikes. **Dairy queens** are black or Hispanic **gays** interested only in white men as sexual partners, especially favoring blonds or pale-skinned men. **Snow queens** date only white men. **Dinge queens** are attracted to black men, as is the **spade queen** (both terms also used for black **gays**, as is the **Egyptian queen**). The **Torah queen** digs Jews; the **rice queen**, who's Non-Asian, just loves Asian men.

    Other odds and ends of royalty include the **bog queen**, who frequents public toilets for sex and the **dirt queen** who trades gossip for sex. The **mitten queen** likes to **masturbate**

others, while the **size queen** bases his preference in partners on the size of their **penis**. The **theater queen**'s tastes are much more innocent. She just loves live stage productions, especially musical theater.

Queens just aren't what they used to be. That's what comes of democracy and broadening the franchise. Sheer numbers have diluted the impact of the original title, tarnishing much of her majesty's original flair. Their popularity, however, remains undiminished as noted by the graffiti, "**God save the queens!**"

5. Location is yet another issue. Options for recreational sex include **the French embassy**—any location, especially a gym or Y, where **gay** sex is readily available and where you may establish a **hydrogen bond**, a gay encounter in a locker room. There's also the **tea room**, a restroom used for hustling and **fellatio** which may or may not include a **glory hole**, carved in the partition between stalls used for **sexual liaisons**. Older **gays** favor the **cottage**, a passé term for a public toilet.

6. During the 50s and 60s, many a **drag queen** used to impersonate Garland, singing her signature song from that film, "Somewhere Over the Rainbow." It seemed only right that Friday night, June 17, 1969, the date that marked the birth of the **Gay and Lesbian liberation movement** with the Stonewall riots, was also the day of her funeral.

7. It's all an expression of **homophobia**, a term coined in 1972 by George Weinberg. In his work *Society and the Healthy Homosexual*, Weinberg defined it as the "irrational fear or hatred of **gay** people and **homosexuality**." We know it best today as **gay bashing**, "harassing or assaulting **homosexuals**, **bisexuals**, **transgendered persons**, and their allies either physically or verbally." Those engaged in such activity are of course **gay bashers**. The last time we employed **bashing** in this manner was during WWII when every good citizen was a "Japan basher." During the Cold War, we joined forces as "Commie bashers." Interesting how as a nation we have moved from bashing an external enemy to a home-grown minority.

8. The most cruel designations were those applied on **homosexual** inmates of Nazi concentration camps. **Homosexuals** were always marked with symbols, much like the Jews bearing the yellow star of David. Many were forced to wear a yellow band with an "A" on it, for **arschficker**, "**ass fucker**." Others had the number **176** on the back of their clothing, referring to paragraph 176 of the penal code under which they had been imprisoned. There was also an inverted pink triangle sewed on to clothing. Estimates are that between 500

thousand to 1 million **homosexuals** died in these camps.

9. **Fruiting** can be a selective endeavor. The **fruit fly** flits about in its varied manifestations: a **heterosexual** woman who hangs with **gays**, a **gay** male whose friends mainly consist of **lesbians**, or a woman who enjoys the company of **gay** men. The **fruit picker** is a **bisexual** male who occasionally seeks out **homosexual sex** partners.

10. Do we have **fags** or do we have **fags?** They come in a variety pack, everything from **cow fags**, **gays** working in ranching and farming, particularly in the Western plains of Canada to **fagateenies**, teenage **gays**. Not every **fag** carries the seal of authenticity. Some simply act **faggy**, like a stereotypical effeminate **gay** male. There's also the **token fag**, who wears many hats. He can be **gay** but denying it or simply too timid to participate in **gay sex**. The **token fag** can also be a **straight** who gave **gay** sex a try, one sympathetic to **gays**, someone who knows somebody who's **gay**, or, like the **fag stag**, a **heterosexual** male who enjoys the company of **gay** men.

The **fag** also has his feminine side. A **fag bag** is a woman married to a **gay** man, while the **fag hag** just likes to hang out with them. She's also a **Bette**. (Bette Middler is considered the ultimate **fag hag**). The term is most often applied to straight women but also applies to those who are **bi** or **lesbian**. All quite enough to leave one **fagged out**.

11. **Coitus per anum** has inspired all kinds of **back-door work** (19th–20thC), including a **behind the behind** (20thC), a **dip in the fudge pot** (mid 20thC), a **daub of the brush** (mid 20thC), **99** (20thC), a **keister-stab** or **bun-** or **butt-fuck** (20thC), some **pedication**, a **pig-sticking** (early 20thC), and a **ram rod** (mid 20thC).

Bee identified the practitioner as a **backgammoner** (mid 18th–early 19thC) or **backgammon player**: "a fellow whose propensities lie out of the natural order of things." We also knew him as a **gentleman of the back door** (18th–20thC). The active partner, or the **inserter** (or **insertee**), is also known as **birdie** (early–mid 20thC), a **bird-taker** (early 20thC), **brown-hatter** (early 20thC), **brownie** (mid 20thC), **brownie king or queen** (mid 20thC), **bugger** (14th–16thC), **burgler** (early 20thC), **cornholer** (20thC...Did they really used to clean the **anus** with corncobs?), **eye-opener** (20thC), **indorser** (late 18th–early 19thC), **ingler** (early 17thC), **inspector of manholes**, **jockey**, **reamer** (all early 20thC), and **stern chaser** (19thC). More recently, he's **biting the brown, doing the round eye, hosing or being hosed, doing a prat** (as in the "pratfall" from vaudeville), and **asking for the ring**.

Being the **top man** puts him on the ocean main, playing **anal buccaneer**, **ass pirate**, or **ass raider**, **riding the deck** in search of **booty**. It also made him into the non-too-pleasant **arse bandit**, **ass fucker**, and **ass leech**.

Occupational hazards of the activity include hemorrhoids, better known as **itchy eye** and **lilies of the valley**. Any wonder that graffiti has noted : "Homosexuality is a pain in the ass."

Looking for an alternative outlet? Some consider it the pits, but there are those who favor **axillary intercourse**, performed under the arm of a partner until ejaculation is reached, also called **huffling** or **bag-piping**. Latin lovers can opt for some **coitus interfemora**: where the male places his **penis** between the thighs of his partner, either female or male. When two men engage thus, it's commonly known as the **Princeton rub** or a **collegiate fuck**, both of which offer a variation in placement—between the partners' abdomens. The practice, however, remains somewhat obscure. Though an Ivy league education is not a prerequisite, the average person still can't stomach it.

12. The **chicken hawk** apparently suffers from the malady known as **chicken pox**, manifesting itself as the urge to **have sex** with a younger man. His search begins at a **chicken house**, a club or coffeehouse catering primarily to gays too young for the bar scene. He doesn't want much, only a **chicken dinner**, "sex with a teenager." **Chicken of the sea** would be nice, a young sailor, à la carte. He's not particular. Cock a doodle do is now **any cock'll do**. Easy prey is the **capon** who once gave his all in medieval Italy to keep his voice in the soprano range. He's ripe for the plucking today.

More fowl language along these lines includes the **gooser** (20thC, Can. for a **pederast**). No innocent bird here. The **goose** has seen it all, from a **finger thrust** to a **pederastic act** (earlier, in 19thC, it was a **prostitute**, and an act of **copulation**). Mencken defined the goose as "a most pugnacious bird often given to nipping the buttocks of humans who offend it." Where to locate the elusive bird? "Bend your knees and touch your toes, and I'll show you where the **wild goose** goes" (mid 20thC).

13. Men may not be able to distinguish between **lesbians**, but women certainly do. They offer a wide range of lifestyles to pick from. The **granola lesbian** is wholesome and health-conscious gal, also known as a **crunchy dyke**. **Lavender lesbians** are your earth mothers or hippies, often artists, usually espousing holistic medicine, herbal cures, health foods, or witchcraft. They often refer to the deity as "goddess" and participate in pagan rituals. Preferring the natural state, they

object to such practices as shaving armpits or legs. Georgia O'Keefe is considered their favorite artist. **Leather lesbians** are into **D&S** and **fetishes**; many are **dominatrixes**.

At the other extreme, we have the **lipstick lesbians** who favor fashionable clothes and make-up. They are also considered **ultra-feminine** or **femme**, the polar opposite of the **bull** or **butch dyke**. Trying out their wings for the first time are the **LUGs** ("**Lesbians** Until Graduation"), younger members of the sorority, adolescent **lesbians** who are also usually nonpolitical. The more sophisticated and experienced element includes the **Gertrude Stein lesbians**—intellectuals, usually middle-age or older, who tend to gravitate towards the arts. They usually have a perfect blend of ready wit, political outrage, and excellent schooling, and tend to dominate whatever field they're in.

There is also the more militant wing. Heading it up are the **gold star lesbians**, who have never had **intercourse** with a man. At its farthest pole, the **lesbian separatists**, frontline warriors in the battle of the sexes. Believing that women hold superior intuition and judgment, they shoot men down as "misogynous patriarchal bastards." Their opponents dub them **feminazis** (1970s), a fascist clique in unholy coalition with homosexuals, blacks, civil liberty groups, and environmental organizations arrayed against our way of life. That's another story altogether.

Professionally, we have the **chapstick lesbians** who are into sports, also called **sports dykes**, **jock lesbians**, and **jockettes**, a derisive term for women who win at sports whether **lesbian** or not. Favorites include Billy Jean King and Martina Navratilova.

Hollywood lesbians are best known for their film and TV exploits. Originally, their leadership consisted of just Lily Tomlin, who has since been joined by boisterous spokeswoman Sandra Bernhardt and the 70s film *Personal Best* star Mariel Hemingway, who, though not a **lesbian**, was the same actress who gave the first prime-time television kiss—on an episode of "Roseanne," where else? **Music lesbians** even have their own organization, "Strong Women in Music" (SWIM), which includes not just big stars but famous nonmembers as well. Prominent among them is Melissa Etheridge, who, when she announced her girlfriend was pregnant, quipped, "that will put an end to the rumor that I'm impotent."

14. Her oral predisposition made her into a **carpet muncher**, the activity itself being called **carpet munching** or **licking rug**. Because her culinary preferences excluded "meat," she was also dubbed a **vagitarian**.

15. Christine's legacy lives on through the phrase **Danish pastry**, in honor of her country of rebirth. This sweet treat is synonymous with the contemporary **transsexual** or **trannie**, clearly more substantial fare than the **twinkie**, who's just another young **gay** male.

16. Many are confused by all this exotic terminology. In his senatorial race against Claude Pepper in 1950, George Smathers ran a particularly brutal campaign. The annals of political history include this especially memorable charge leveled against his opponent—geared to the uneducated voters of rural Florida.

> Are you aware that Claude Pepper is known all over Washington as a shameless extrovert? Not only that, but this man is reliably reported to practice nepotism with his sister-in-law, and he has a sister who was once a thespian in wicked New York. Worst of all, it is an established fact that Mr. Pepper before his marriage habitually practiced celibacy.

It was an amusing low point in American politics and a classic study of the campaign smear. Evidence, however, points to Smathers never having made the remarks, that it was rather a spoof put together by reporters to amuse themselves. Be that as it may, it serves to further confirm the need of the public to better master *The Erotic Tongue*.

The Dynamic Duo

ex as the world's greatest act makes for fine theater, but most people still consider it a game in which competitors with finely honed skills are pitted against each other. The stakes are high, the action fast-paced. A program is essential: you can't tell the players without one.

How you play the game depends largely on how you look at it. Seasoned male practitioners see as its primary objective **getting into her pants** (mid 20thC), a challenge made all the more difficult by her being in them at the same time. Once in there, i.e., having **got it on** successfully, he is said to have **scored**. Points are awarded for both technical proficiency and artistic impression.

We all are mortal men and frail,
And oft are guided by the tail.
    —*Bridge,* Burlesque Humor, *1774*

Your One and Only

It's all in the approach. We once knew it as the **three F's** (19thC): **fuck, fun, and a footrace**, referring both to a wild time and a **lewd** person. More recently it's been **the four-F method** (c. 1890): **find, feel, fuck, and forget**, though we later thoughtfully added "'em" to the expression. Hoping to avoid any controversy, the editors of *The American Thesaurus of Slang* (1953) coyly recorded the expression as **find 'em, feel 'em, frig 'em, and forget 'em**.

The game's leading scorer is the legendary **assman** (mid 20thC). The **assman** cometh but saith little. A deep conversation consists primarily of "**getting much?**" or "**getting any?**" His reputation speaks for itself. His credo: "**I've seen more ass than a toilet seat.**"

Here's Looking at You!

That man has a limited perspective is obvious. It comes from **looking at every woman through the hole in his prick** (late 19th–20thC). He used to look for a **fast filly** (early 17thC); today it's the **fox** (1960s, U.S. black slang) he's after. More likely he'll

Put a bag over her head
You don't have to fuck the bag.
    —*Anon., 20thC*

come home with a **dog** or a **bow-wow** (mid 20thC) on his arm.
Even a **pig** (mid 20thC) isn't out of the question. Though he makes
such distinctions, in practice he's quite democratic: **"All petticoats are sisters in the dark"** (18thC). An equal-opportunity
employer, he's not concerned with age. As for older women: **"They
don't swell, won't tell, and are as grateful as hell"** (20thC). His
general assessment of most females: **"I wouldn't kick her out of
bed for eating crackers"** (mid 20thC).

Mr. Everything

There's no avoiding the **assman**. He's everywhere—perched on
street corners or just strolling down the highways and byways of
life. Today, he frequents the singles bar. Years ago he slithered
about as a **parlor snake** (c. 1915) and a **lounge-lizard** (c. 1912).
Leching always brings out the animal in him, several, in fact: **the
young stud** (19thC), **the old goat**, **the town bull** (both 16thC),
the game-cock (19thC), **the gay dog** (1920s), and **the tomcat**
(19thC), just to name a few.[1] But let's not forget the **wolf** who first
entered the lexicon as a **homosexual** around World War I,
quickly established his manhood, and emerged from World War II
as a **WFC** ("wolf, first class"). He's your classic **lech** (c. 1918),
always **on the prowl** (17th–20thC).

For many years we thought him **gallant**, polite and attentive to
women. His roots (*galer*), however, show him also simply having a
good time. *Galer* comes from the old High German *geil*, "wanton,"
with ties to the Anglo-Saxon *gal*, the source of "gay" (as in "joyous"), making for a "gala" occasion at that.

French **gallants** were reputed to be extraordinary lovers,
though not everyone was impressed by their sexual prowess. During the Franco-Prussian War (1870–71), an English **demimondaine** visiting Paris had her own gut reaction to them: "The
tripe-colored mousquetaires who infest this capital are not capable
of making anything heave except my stomach."

The Man for All Seasons

In a short time he had made a legitimate name for himself as a
philanderer (17thC), originally a female lover of men, later simply
a lover, and finally a male flirt; a **libertine** (16thC), from the
Roman deity Liber, a god of fertility whose annual celebration featured a giant wooden **phallus** carted about the countryside, followed by a crowd of drunken revelers who later crowned it with a
wreath); and a **rake** (16thC—"you'd have to rake hell to find
another like him").

He was now an integral part of the Western literary tradition and a major cultural icon. This isn't just your average Romeo we're talking about.[2]

Faint Preys

In striking contrast to his female counterpart, the **assman** has had few harsh words said about him. Most thought the **lecher** (since 12thC) pretty bad, but nonetheless found him acceptable. Unlike the vile **rapist**, no matter how despicable his crime his name has never been considered obscene.

The closest we've come is the **gigolo**, a **kept man** (c.1685), "one maintained or supported financially by an older woman in return for his affection." Tempting as it is to make the connection, he has nothing to do with the **gig** or **giggie**, "the **cunt**," or even the "gig" (c.1928), "a job or a musical engagement." His roots instead can be traced to the late fourteenth century and the Middle English *gigolette*, a "dancing girl" or **prostitute**, and *giglot*, "a villainous man."

The first modern day definition we have of him appears in 1922 in, of all places, *The Woman's Home Companion*: "A **gigolo**…one of the incredibly pathetic creatures…who for ten francs…would dance with any woman wishing to dance in the cafes, hotels, and restaurants of France." As pathetic as the **gigolo** is, however, he is seldom treated with the contempt or disdain shown his female counterpart.

This is not to say we haven't kidded him or his fellow **assman** on occasion. **The answer to a maiden's prayer** (19th–20thC), they used to say, **God's gift to women** (20thC), satisfaction guaranteed. Simply return the unused portion for a full refund. Establishing his value has always been somewhat of a challenge. Some say he's not worth a **pendejo**—a "pubic hair" in Spanish.

Vanessa (Elizabeth Hurley): Mr. Powers, I would never have sex with you, ever! If you were the last man on earth and I was the last woman on earth, and the future of the human race depended on our having sex, simply for procreation, I still would not have sex with you.
Austin Powers (Mike Meyers): What's your point, Vanessa?
— Austin Powers, International Man of Mystery, *1997*

So's Your Father

The day of the **assman** is now over. We no longer consider him **gallant**, not even a **smooth article** (c. 1913), or a **smoothie** (c. 1915). He's still **macho**, however, from the Spanish *machismo* for exaggerated masculine pride, and there's none more **macho** than the **dude**. Entering the language in 1883 as a term of ridicule for a dandy or a swell, he brought with him his entire entourage: **dudedom**, **dudeness**, **dudery**, and **dudism**: the state, style, character, and manners of a **dude**, as well as the **dudine**, the **dudess**, and the **dudette** (1984), his female counterparts. Though now a **real cool dude** (mid 20thC), he's the same person he was in the year of his coming out, "one of those creatures which are perfectly harmless and a necessary evil to civilization." (*Prince Albert Times,*

He's so tough they have to take a wrench to loosen his nuts at night so he can sleep.
—Anon., 20thC

Macho does not prove mucho.
—Zsa Zsa Gabor

Saskatchewan). Today he is everyman—one common, ordinary, and ugly **dude** among many.

What in Creation?

The **assman**'s not just anybody's fool. He's primarily woman's. She's his chief competitor and arch foe, and every bit as good at playing the game.

The contest goes back to Year One, to the world's first woman, and a **fallen woman** at that. Her name was **Lilith**. "What of Eve?" one might ask. Contrary to conventional wisdom, Eve, Adam's helpmate, was but a poor second—falsely represented as number one by the same folks who brought you the rest of the Western intellectual tradition. But because few males celebrate **Lilith** as an ideal type of womanhood, she has been successfully exorcised from scripture and erased from consciousness of contemporary men and women.

You won't find her story in the Old Testament despite what appear to be two conflicting accounts of the creation of woman. The popular version can be found in Chapter 2 of Genesis— woman as sparerib. It is a humiliating story in which she is fashioned almost as a divine afterthought out of an insignificant portion of the masculine frame in order to comply with Adam's need for amusement. This account is the one that has some to be accepted as gospel. Less well known, however, is the untold story referred to in Chapter 1 of Genesis, in which Woman is created simultaneously with Man, each reflecting in equal measure the glory of the divine original. It's a tale that appears to have gotten lost in the telling, and it's time to set the record straight.

Medieval scholars used **Lilith** to help reconcile the apparent contradiction to citing her as the first woman in Adam's life, the woman mentioned in Chapter 1. **Lilith** and Adam—a match made in heaven. Though literally created for each other, they're in trouble from the outset. Adam insists on exercising his male prerogative and tries to dominate the household. **Lilith** refuses to be subservient, believing herself Adam's equal, since they have been created in the same manner.

Angry and hurt, Adam is beside himself. Things come to a head when she refuses to lie beneath him—to assume the recumbent or passive posture during **intercourse**. This really gets his back up and sets the stage for a confrontation between the first male chauvinist pig and the first liberated woman. Adam has had it, and he cries out to God in his agony. **Lilith** simply packs up and leaves. She declines paradise and a subordinate role for the right to assert her own identity and establish a life of her own. **Lilith** thus bears witness for all womanhood and its future burdens of submission.

But an uppity woman is a **fallen woman**. It's only a matter of

So God created man in His own image, in the image of God created He him; male and female created He them.

—Genesis 1:17

And Adam said, This is now bone of my bones and flesh of my flesh.

—Adam, on seeing Eve, Genesis 2:23

time before **Lilith** becomes history's first **good-time girl**. She settles down in the notorious Red Sea region, an area populated by evil spirits and other devilish creatures. There her passion for equality blossoms into a full-blown demonic career. She consorts with various and sundry lascivious spirits of the night and generates "lillum," ass-haunched devil-children, at the prodigious rate of one hundred per day.

At Adam's request, God dispatches a trio of angels to bring her back. He strikes dead a number of her progeny and threatens worse. But **Lilith** is adamant and refuses to return. Why trade her exciting new life by the Red Sea for a mundane role as an honest housewife? God finally gives up, and the angels return empty-handed, but God pacifies Adam by creating Eve as a proper stay-at-home mate.

Rabbinical tradition has **Lilith** consorting again with Adam—returning to him both during the period of 130 years when he is separated from Eve following the expulsion from the Garden of Eden, and also during the time when, after Abel was murdered, Adam decides to have no further relations with Eve. From Adam's and **Lilith**'s unholy **union**, in which it is said that Adam's "generative powers were misused and misdirected," comes a variety of demons, or *Shedim*, who rove about the world plaguing mankind.

As time goes on the **Lilith** myth becomes even more elaborately embroidered, and **Lilith**, the forerunner of equal rights, is eclipsed completely by **Lilith**, Queen of the Underworld. What ensues is the most sweeping and devastating character assassination in history. Aspersions begin to be circulated as to her origin. It is said by some that she was created not from pure dust, as was Adam, but from filth and sediment. Others identify her as one of the wives of Sammaell, or Satan; being of a wild and passionate nature, she had deserted her demonic spouse in order to take up with Adam.

She is depicted as heading up a retinue of evil spirits and destroying angels—taking to the skies each night, screeching her hatred of mankind and vowing vengeance for the contemptible manner in which she was and continues to be treated by the Adams of the world. She terrifies households and poses a special threat to children therein. She is further charged with provoking men to commit the gravest of sins—participation in a sexual act without benefit of a woman. (Would you have it **nocturnal pollution**?) As the quintessential **other woman**, she's your original home-wrecker, actively working to destroy the family unit of which she cannot be a part.

So there's your **Lilith**: Everyman's fantasy. Woman as Man would like her—but totally out of his reach and class.

Isn't it time that her name was cleared and that she was returned to the language, synonymous with the independence of spirit, intelligence, and free will that she represents?

God created woman. And boredom did indeed cease from that moment—but many other things ceased as well! Woman was God's second mistake.
—*Friedrich Nietzsche (1844–1900)*

Women! What can you say? Who made them? God must have been a fucking genius.
— *Frank Slade (Al Pacino),*
Scent of a Woman, *1993*

We've already made a good start in that direction, elevating her from a no-name to a feminist icon. There's now a **Lilith** magazine, a **Lilith** music festival, an orchestral piece based on her story, and countless associations, groups, and web sites which carry her name. Clearly, if you don't make it in one life, there's always the next.

Who Was That Lady?

Lilith was only the first in a long line of historical figures whose names have become synonymous with the highest virtues of the oldest vice. The Old Testament provided us with the deceitful **Delilah** as well as the utterly shameless **Jezebel** (II Kings 9:33): "And he said, throw her down. So they threw her down." Ancient Greece and Rome likewise made significant contributions.

She was at her very best as a **hetaera** (literally, "companion or woman friend") and considered among the most treasured assets of the Athenian city-state. Renowned for their beauty, many **hetaerae** were also famous for their intellectual capabilities, their quick wit and repartee, and the considerable political and economic influence they wielded. Relationships with **hetaerae** were often lasting, and **liaisons** were not merely sexual.

The most famous include **Thäis**, the Athenian **courtesan** and **mistress** of Alexander the Great and Ptolemy; **Aspasia**, mistress of Pericles; and **Phryne**, who was charged with impiety by the state and was defended by one of her lovers, the orator Hyperides, who secured her acquittal by exhibiting her partially in the **nude**, the **naked** truth ultimately winning out.

They continued their activity in one form or another through the centuries. One born of sufficiently high social class who was also discriminating about whom she bedded down with was likely to be viewed with envy and grudging respect. People spoke of her as **a woman of the world**, **a woman of pleasure**, or, at the very worst, an **adventuress**. A favorite of the nineteenth **century** was the **demimondaine** (sometimes shortened to just **mondaine** or **demi**), a phrase invented by Alexandre Dumas the Younger to refer to a woman of doubtful reputation and social standing who occupied the half-world or half-society on the outskirts of the established order. Though many were uncomfortable with her uncertain status, others took to her for her services, believing half aloof better than none.

Fallout

In Adam's fall we all took quite a tumble, but women fell hardest. The aforementioned ladies lost society's respect in the process, leaving them all **promiscuous**. **Promiscuous** comes from the Latin *pro* and *miscere*, "in favor of mixing it up." Both men and

Phryne had talents for mankind;
Open she was and unconfined,
Like some free port of trade:
Merchants unloaded here their freight,
And agents from each foreign state
here first their entry made.
    —Alexander Pope, *Phryne, early 18thC*

Wives for child-bearing,
Hetaerae for companionship,
Slaves for lust.
    —Demosthenes

The tree of knowledge stood—ah! yes, it stood.
Past tense, you see—and while the past was good,
The present need was great, without a doubt
And pretty Eve began to fret and pout.
She wept and sighed and said, "I see it all,
For here was life and there, alas! The fall."
    —Anon., *"The Fall of Man"*

women mix well, but only women are thought **promiscuous**—for doing what men do all the time.

The Broad-based Experience

A woman without respect is just another **broad** (c. 1925). "**Have you ever been abroad?**" (mid 20thC, teenage boy struggling to make conversation). Originally a term for a **mistress** or a **prostitute**, **broad** is now a catch-all term of contempt. We're not terribly sure about her origins. Much speculation centers on the **bawd** (14th–17thC, "**procurer**," 18thC, "**procuresss**"), who made her way up through the ranks. Partridge found her "broad in the beams," i.e., "broad where a **broad** should be broad" ("Honey Bun" in *South Pacific*). **Broad** also implies a certain latitude in matters personal. After all, she was once a **lady of expansive sensibilities** (19thC).

Making Do

This girl has definitely **been there** (19th–20thC). She's **on the make** and **puts out** (both 20thC, U.S.)—though the British had a better sense of direction as a **put-in** (19thC). The lass is **merry-legged** (19thC), **nimble-hipped** (19th–20thC), **on the flutter** (c. 1875), and **willing to pay a bill on sight** (c. 1820–1910). **Easy** (17thC) does it. She's an **easy lay** (17thC), and an **easy make** (20thC). She's got **the rabbit habit** and is **hopping for it** (both 20thC). A college education always helps. As members of a notable seven sisters' institution once proudly proclaimed,

When better men are made,
Vassar women will make them.

—Wall hanging, Vassar College, 1960s

Let us eat, drink, and make merry
for tomorrow Mary may reform.
—Anon., 1920's

The Heat of the Moment

The **heat is on** (19th–20thC, said of a woman who is sexually excited), and some like it hot. The **fire-box** (c. 1900–15, a "man of unceasing passion") is a **fiery lot** (c. 1840–1900, "a fast man"), and there's simply no cooling his ardor. This **broad** is **as warm as they make them** (c. 1909); in fact, **there's a fire down below** (mid 20thC). She's got **a bad case of the hots** (20thC), **a hot back, hot pants,** and **a hot-bot.** Call her **Miss Hotbot** or **Lady Hotbot** (c. 1920). She's a **hot sketch, hot stuff** (20thC), **a hot biscuit** (1930s), **hotter than a red firewagon, hotter'n a Fourth-of-July hoedown** (both 20thC), **hot as a firecracker** (c. 1910), to the point of being downright explosive, a regular **bangster** (19thC)—she's your **blonde bombshell** with the great **gams** (1940s).[3]

When Gods have hot backs,
What shall poor men do?
      —Shakespeare, The Merry Wives of
      Windsor

An itching cunt feels no shame.
      —Anon., mid 18th–20thC

Do You Take This Man?

Out of the novice category and fast approaching professional status, she's now a full-fledged **nympho**, a truncated **nymphomaniac**, suffering from an insatiable **sex drive**, formally known as **erotomania** or **furor feminus**. The original **nymphs** of Greek mythology were the eternal brides of the streams and forests known to cavort with **satyrs**. Latin assisted us with the word *nubilis*, which is related to **nymph**, giving us not only our **nubile** maiden, but also making her ripe for the **nuptials**.

Nymphomaniacs are not always born that way; they're often the product of circumstances. On April 29, 1970, a jury awarded $50,000 to a woman who claimed a San Francisco cable car accident had made her a **nymphomaniac**—giving whole new meaning to "riding for a fall!"

Their Finest Hour

The **town bull** (17thC) and the **common cow** (19th–20thC) are destined for each other. **She's got an itch in her belly to play with the scarlet hue** (c. 1720, D'Urfey), and he's just dying to **get it on**. Their last words? **"Don't fight it, it's bigger than both of us"** (mid 20thC).

The dénouement? Faster than a speeding bullet: **"Wham-bam-thank-you-ma'am"** (20thC), a phrase which began life in the black community around 1895 as **bip-bam**, from a popular song of the times. Once considered a descriptive term expressing gratitude after **lovemaking**, it now connotes a rapid and uninvolved **sexual encounter**—a fine thank-you if ever you heard one.

Bits and Pieces

Man has always had difficulty dealing with women as a total entity, choosing instead to pursue her a little at a time. This has forever made her attractive to him as **bits**, **pieces**, **chippies**, and **hunks** (20thC, also used by a woman speaking of a man).

In Victorian times, they made every little bit count, including **a fresh bit** (c. 1840, a beginner or a new mistress), **a bit of crumb** (c. 1880, a pretty, plump girl, similar to the Yiddish **zaftig**, 20thC), as well as **a bit of skin, stuff** (mid 19th–20thC), or **goods** (c. 1860)—which they hoped would also be a **bit of all right** (20thC, one who was both attractive and obliging).

Settling for relatively modest increments, they only wanted **to tear off a piece** (19thC). Who or what wasn't material. It could be **a fine piece of dry goods**, some **fluff** (20thC), **a bit of frock** (c. 1875–1910, attractive and well-dressed), or **as pretty a piece of**

muslin as you'd wish to see (19thC). In the eighteenth century, they **labored leather** (18thC, one very young), after which they pursued **calico** (1880–1920, U.S.).

Men today continue to **chase skirt**, but a piece of dacron or polyester just doesn't have quite the same feel to it.

Riding for a Fall

Women have also long been considered **fair game** (late 17th–early 19thC collective term for **harlots**): **moose** (20thC), **badgers** (19thC), and **squirrels** (late 18th–mid 19thC), because, as Grose said, a squirrel "covers its back with its tail."

Students of **horsemanship** (16th-17thC., **copulation**) favored the **pretty filly,** turf talk for a pert young lass. Captain Bee (*Sportsman's Slang*) further delineated the species as "**fillies, running fillies** and **entered fillies** which express the condition of town-girls — usually such as attend at races and parts adjacent.".

They were not, however, to be confused with **trots** (16th–17thC), **hobby-horses** (16th–17thC), and **bob-tails** (17th–18thC)—experienced carriers, ready to be mounted for the right price; or **mares**, a general term for a woman or a wife (16th–17thC). Especially to be avoided were the **jades**—workhorses, worn out and long past their prime who by the sixteenth century had been transformed into contemptible women and **whores**.

You have sent me a Flanders mare.
—Henry VIII (1491–1547) on meeting his fourth wife, Anne of Cleves

Winging It

Taking flight from the stable, man found solace in the roost, using **chick and chick-a-biddy** (c. 1795) as innocent terms of endearment for a young girl. One hundred and fifty years later, he still favored **chicks**, especially when they were "slick," and accompanied by cats such as himself, deemed "hip" and "cool" (1940s). Such talk is now considered for the birds—passé and sexist. No one calls a woman a **chick** today, there being no surer way to ruffle her feathers.[4]

Long gone is the **chicken fancier** or **pullet-squeezer looking to strop his beak** (c. 1830). As a **womanizer** who "likes 'em young," he had his eye on the **virgin pullet**, "a young woman, though often **trod**, has never **laid**" (Bee, c. 1820–70). In fact, any **game pullet** (late 18th–19thC), one guaranteeing a **good lay**, would do.

Quail (17thC) was also a prime bird—a **covey** of same (late 17th–early 19thC) referring to a well-filled **bawdy house**. **San Quentin quail** (mid 20thC) was **jail bait**, "one under age," whose pursuit was not without risk, often landing not the bird, but the fancier, in the cage.

It takes a tough man to make a tender chicken.
—Frank Perdue, TV commercial, c. 1976

With several coated quails and laced muttons waggishly singing.
—Rabelais, Peter Motteux, trans., 1708

Down and Dirty

Language describing woman has also traditionally joined dirtiness with sex. Words describing her as slovenly and untidy made her immoral as well, inferring that sloppy women were as derelict in their morals as they were in appearance. Man meanwhile **got off** clean.

A case in point is the evolution of the **slut** (14thC) or **slattern** (17thC). She started life innocently enough as a slovenly woman, speaking more to her messiness than her morals. But she soon developed a playful side. Samuel Pepys wrote in his diary: "Our little girl Susan is a most advanced **slut** and pleases us mightily." It was then but a short jump to impudence and then to you know what. As Henry Fielding noted, "I never knew any of these forward **sluts** to come to good." Indeed. A hundred years later Dickens told us exactly what she had become, "a **slut**, a **hussy**."

So too with the **draggle-tail** (16thC) or the **dabble-tail** (19thC, literally "one who dirties the hem of her skirt"). She quickly became synonymous with the **bob-tail** (17th–18thC, Grose, "one who plays with her tail"), and the **cock-tail** (19th–20thC) who put it to professional use.

It's not like there aren't occasional opportunities for redemption, however, as with our **floosie** (also **floosey**, or **floozie**, c. 1940). Her origins go back to her proper name, "Florence" (17th–early 19thC) meaning "a girl who had been tousled and ruffled" or just sloppily dressed. But around 1935 she began to clean up her act, when her nickname "flossy" entered the language as one "dressed up or refurbished." This led to the new and improved **floosie**—one finely decked out and ready to party. Word then spread quickly from the popular song, "The Flat-Foot Floogie with the Floy-Floy" (c. 1938). Her popularity among navy men helped things further, establishing **floosie**'s reputation as a bubble-headed, fun-loving, and **accessible** simp.

A Class by Herself

Her reputation was further suspect as **a woman of a certain class** (19thC).[5] **Bunters** (18th–19thC) picked up the rags from the streets, **scrubbers** (early 20thC) cleaned and washed, and **doxies** (16th–18thC, from the Dutch *docke*, a "**doll** or **dolly**, a **mistress** or **prostitute**") accompanied those who begged for a living. The **trollop** (17th–19thC) was a coarse and vulgar street person. Everyone knew the **tramp** and her friends for what they were. Class distinctions always made it easy to identify them, though the **hoity-toity wench** (late 17th–early 19thC) didn't know her place.

Not only was it traditional to treat lower-class women like dirt, but to further characterize them as **lewd**. **Lewd** once referred to anyone not belonging to the holy orders, hence unlearned and unteachable. Being **lewd** made a woman rude and artless, which some deemed characteristic of the lower classes. Her ignorance and rude manners were then accepted as conclusive evidence of **lascivious** and **unchaste** behavior, the meaning which we associate with being **lewd** today.

The language claimed many an innocent victim in this fashion. The **hussy** (early 16thC) started life as a simple phonetic reduction of "housewife." Over time, it soon came to mean a "country woman," then a "lower-class bumpkin," and finally (19th–20thC), a "temptress" and "seductress," which, when preceded by "brazen" or "shameless," made this housewife a threat to families everywhere.

Is You Is or Is You Ain't...

Her innocence also contributed further to her fall. **Wanton** (c.1300) originally described "undisciplined and rebellious" children. By 1393 it meant **lascivious**, **unchaste**, and **lewd**, and was applied primarily to women. A **wench** (c 1300) was a female child, in 1300, but by 1362, had grown into a **wanton** woman, creating the **light wench**, **wanton wench**, and **wench of the stews**. She later served a term of endearment for a daughter, wife or sweetheart, but by the end of the nineteenth century, reverted to a girl of rustic or working class origin, hence a **woman of loose** (or **questionable) morals**.

The **bimbo** (c.1918-19) also began life as a "young child" or "baby," from the Italian *bambino*. It then followed the same path trod by the **harlot**, the **trollop**, and the **slattern**, first describing a man, an ordinary chap; then a stupid, inconsequential or contemptuous fellow; and finally, a **woman of ill repute**.

Women should be obscene and not heard.
—John Lennon

The male **bimbo** still makes an infrequent appearance. P.G. Wodehouse wrote in 1947 of " **Bimbos** ... making passes at innocent girls after discarding their wives." More recently, Phil Donahue called Vice President Dan Quayle "the stereotypical **bimbo**." (NBC-TV, 1990). For the most part, however, **bimbo**'s a she—a **promiscuous** female airhead.

Smile When You Say That

Her attitude didn't help things either. The **minx** (16thC) was pert and cheeky, but men interpreted that to mean she was **wanton**. **Wanton** (13thC) always implied a certain lack of discipline, but by the sixteenth century, described any lewd and immoral person, especially a woman.

A woman's place is at her husband's feet.
—Pope Pius XIII

"When I use a word," Humpty Dumpty said in a rather scornful tone, "it means just what I choose it to mean. Neither more nor less." "The question is," said Alice, "whether you can make words mean so many different things." "The question is," said Humpty Dumpty, "who is to be master. That is all."
—Lewis Carroll, Alice in Wonderland

The **chippy** (also **chippie**, 1880s) should have seen it coming. Beginning life as an impudent lass with a shortness of temper, she quickly began her descent. We soon knew her as a **dance-hall girl**, then one given to **amorous dalliance**, and finally as a **semi-pro**, "one who would just as soon give it away as charge for it." Her origins may come from the chirping sound she made to attract passing males, or from the treatment of her as just another piece—a small chip(py) off the old block. This, however, could all be nothing more than folk etymology. According to Gershon Legman (*Maledicta*, VIII, 1985), "Every French slang dictionary for two centuries back...and every French speaking person today, is aware of the common French word **chippie** (or **chipie**) for an evil-tempered (formerly immoral) woman."

There they are—**les girls** (**lay girls**, mid 20thC). Becoming part of this group was not difficult. You were simply selected for it. Any female who made men uncomfortable, either by appearance or manners, was eligible. Our condolences to the poor lass who was ill kempt, doing menial work, and known to be high spirited and independent—all of which established her as an **easy mark**.

Tips of the Tongue

1. The **assman's** many aliases over the years include:

Amorist (16thC)	**Gap stopper** (late 18thC)
Ballocker (19thC)	**Gay man** (19thC)
Basher (20thC)	**Gully raker** (19thC)
Bed-presser (17thC)	**Holer** (18thC)
Belly-bumper (late 17thC)	**Ladykiller** (20thC)
Bird's nester (19thC)	**Lover boy** (20thC)
Carnalite (late 16thC)	**Make-out artist** (mid 20thC)
Chimney Sweep (19thC)	**Mutton monger** (c. 1580)
Cocksmith (20thC)	**Passionate Pilgrim** (18thC)
Dolly mopper (19thC)	**Poopster** (19thC)
Faggoteer (19thC)	**Sexpert** (1940s)
Faggot master (19thC)	**Skirt chaser** (20thC)
Fishmonger (19thC)	**Top diver** (late 17th–late 18thC)
Fleece Hunter (19thC)	**Wencher** (since 16thC)
Forbidden fruit eater (20thC)	**Whisker splitter** (c. 1785–1840)

2. **Lothario, Don Juan,** and **Casanova** are the big three of **libertinism. Lothario** was the **lech** in *The Fair Penitent*, a play by Nicholas Rowe (1703). **Don Juan** made his debut in the *Rake of Seville*, and quickly became the dominant **sex symbol** of his age. We also know him from the works of Molière, Corneille, Dumas, Balzac, and Flaubert. He was immortalized

by Mozart in the opera *Don Giovanni* (libretto by Lorenzo da Ponte) and came to be most prominently associated with **libertinism** through Lord Byron's *Don Juan*. His figure in fiction proved so popular that it soon overtook reality, helping transform seduction and desertion from malicious sport into an admired and exalted activity. His spirit lives on.

Giovanni Jacopo **Casanova** de Seingalt (1725–1798) was an Italian of Spanish descent who found his calling in life quite early. He was expelled from the University of Padua at fifteen for gambling and at sixteen for immoral conduct. His first recorded sexual experience was with two young sisters in one bed. An inveterate **fuckster**, he listed 116 **mistresses** by name, claiming hundreds of seductions, from noblewomen to chambermaids, done standing, lying down, sitting, in bed, on couches, on boats, on floors, and in alleyways. His conquests included his own daughter, a nine-year-old child, and a seventy-year-old woman. As he lay on his deathbed awaiting his maker, his last words were "I regret nothing. I have lived and died a Christian." Indeed.

3.   Checking out the **lay of the land** (20thC), we find:
The low road (Shakespeare): "trodden by many feet as a hen may be trodden by many cocks."

The common shore (Haywood and Massinger, "The Honest Whore"): "Your body is like the common shore that still receives all the town's filth. The sin of many men is with you!"

A hay bag (19th–20thC): something to lie upon

A hat rack (20thC): receiving all sizes and shapes

An easy mark (20thC): frequently punctuated

The town bike, omnibus (c. 1920, Aust., and 20thC, Eng.): ridden by all

The public ledger (19thC): hundreds of entries

As discriminating as she was democratic, she only **fucks her friends**, and she **doesn't have an enemy in the world** (mid 20thC). More currently, "We call her "Turnpike," because you got to pay to get on and pay to get off," (*Truck Turner* (1974). There's also the classic line spoken by Rita Hayworth in the title role in *Gilda* (1946), "If I had been a ranch, they would have called me The Bar-Nothing."

4.   Those known best for their inconstancy were the **fly-by-nights** (19th–20thC); they included **canaries** (18th–early 19thC), **nightingales** (c. 1840), **soiled doves** (late 17th–mid 18thC), **wrens** (c. 1869), **plovers** (early 17thC), **pheasants** (17thC), and **partridges** (early 17th–mid 18thC)—not all **spring chickens**, but **pigeons** all. This is to say nothing of an occasional **bat** (17th–early 19thC) or **moth** (c. 1876).

Not all **birds** (**harlots** from c. 1900), however, were **high**

See the mort and the cull at clicket in the dyke.

*(Look at the broad and the guy getting it on in the
    ditch.)*

The cull wapt the mort's bite.

(The fellow enjoyed the wench heartily.)

      —Captain Bee, 1823

fliers—fashionable **prostitutes**, "women about town who would job a coach or keep a couple of saddle horses." (**Bee**). We also had **coquettes**, literally "little cocks," noted for their flirtatious manner and **lady birds** who expressed affection and were often described as life-long companions, as with President Lyndon Johnson's one and only.

5.   The poor had their own inimitable way of describing things, derived from the cant and criminal jargon of the English underclass of the seventeenth and eighteenth centuries. Theirs was a world peopled by **morts, dells,** and **culls. Morts** were the more experienced females. **Dells**, according to Bee, were "young **buxom** wenches, ripe and prone to **venery** but who have not lost their **virginity**," which the upright man (one of the more powerful men in the criminal hierarchy) had first claim to by virtue of his prerogative, after which they were then fair game for any of the fraternity.

The Sporting Life

 er fee tells you that she means business. It places her clearly **on the batter** (c. 1830), **on the grind** (19thC), **on the loose, on the business** (c. 1921), or **into the trade.**

What else would she be doing? Maybe **peddling her hips, fluttering her skirt** (c. 1850), **trading on her bottom, selling custom-house goods** (mid 18th–early 19thC), and **hawking her meat** (19th–20thC). "Get it while it's hot!"

As a **well-rigged frigate**, she could be found **carrying the broom up** (c. 1820–90), from the time when it was customary to attach a broom to the masthead of a ship that was up for sale.

Some still missed the boat. When a judge asked the prisoner standing before him, "What are you, young lady?" she replied, "I am **in the way of life**, your honor" (c. 1823, Grose). Once she was **on the game** (17thC) or **in a mode of living** (movie newsreel: *News of the World*). Today, she's **in the life** or **into the game.** Don't trivialize it. Just because it's a **game** doesn't mean it's not a serious matter. As a distinguished **pimp** once put it, "man, the **game** is deep!"

Ho, ho, ho!

'Tis a pity she's a **whore**, but them's the breaks of the **game**. She's been one since before the twelfth century (Old English **hore**). We once considered the word polite, a euphemism for another expression long since forgotten. In fact, it's a relative of the Latin *carus* for "dear." But like all good euphemisms, it would in time become common, vulgar, and unacceptable.[1]

Many were uncomfortable in her presence. In 1833, Noah Webster sounded an uncertain **strumpet** (c. 1327, from the Latin *strumpum*, "dishonor"), bowdlerizing the Old Testament by driving all **whores** to cover. **Hoores** had been present in the first English edition of the Bible in the fourteenth century, but Webster thought it best to replace them with **lewd women** and **harlots.**

169

Now that we have agreed on the principle, we must merely be haggling over the price.
—George Bernard Shaw

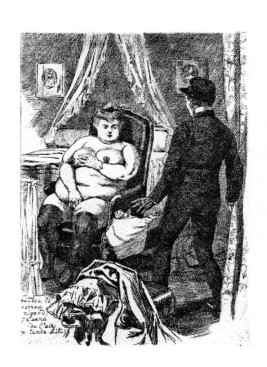

If you've got the money, honey, I've got the time.
—Popular song, 1940s

Sing whore, sing whore
Behind and before.
Her price is a shilling
She never gets more.

      —*Song in Farmer and Henley,*
       Slang and Its Analogues

You can lead a horticulture, but you can't make her think

    —*Dorothy Parker*

More recently, we'd rather not speak of her at all. In 1934, H. L. Mencken noted how New York newspapers reviewing the play *Within the Gates* handled the part of the Young **Whore**. One newspaper referred to her as the Young **Prostitute**; a second, as the Young **Harlot**; the third, as a girl who had **gone astray**. The fourth simply avoided any mention of her at all by ignoring the entire cast.

We've tried to cushion her impact, promoting the British pronunciation **hoor** and the inner-city **ho**, and disguising her in rhyming slang with **Jane Shore, sloop of war** (19thC), and **two-by-four** (early 20thC, U.S.). But nothing seems to work. In England, you'll still find her blatantly **whoring along the dilly** (Picadilly Circus). In the States we still have **the hard-leg whore**, street-hardened and used up "with millions of miles on her." Tuned up for yet another trip around the square.[2]

Courtesy Pays

The **courtesan**, like the **whore**, lost her dignity and standing over time. Originally, **courtesans** were ladies of the court. Modeled after the *hetaerae*, they read and composed poetry and were noted for their fine minds as well as their bodies. By the sixteenth century, however, they also had a clear-cut reputation, as recorded by traveler Thomas Coryat in his *Credities*:

> As for the number of these Venetian courtezans, it is very great…at the least 20,000, whereof many are esteemed so loose that they are said to open their quiver to every arrow.

The Victorian era elevated the **courtesans'** status slightly, several notches above your ordinary **streetwalker**. Not everyone, however, was impressed. When someone asked Nell Kimball, the noted **madam**, about the **courtesan**, she testily replied, "I knew what a **courtesan** was; it was a high-class, high-kicking **harr!**" Currently she's a high-priced **call girl** with a few "select" customers.

An Oft-repeated Tail

The **harlot**'s quite another story. This one takes place in the sixteenth-century French countryside and features the beautiful Arlette, or *Heleva*, daughter of Falbert, a tanner of Falaise. Physically mature beyond her years, but innocence personified, our young maiden made the tragic error of washing her clothes outdoors while **naked**. Chance had the handsome Robert LeDiable, Duck of Normandy, riding by. Their eyes met, and the rest is history—the birth of William the Conqueror, known to his contemporaries as "The Bastard." For her **wanton** behavior, all women so disposed in the future were to carry her name—Arlette, or **harlot**.

Would it were true. Unfortunately, the first recorded **harlot** was not a woman but a man. Chaucer, in fact, treated him as a good fellow and a decent chap. Many knew him later as a jester, a traveling showman, or a buffoon. But between the thirteenth and the fifteenth-centuries, his disposition took a turn for the worst, turning him into a rascal, a knave, a **fornicator,** and a general rogue of sorts, closer to his original roots, the Old French *herlot,* "rogue, beggar, or vagabond." It wasn't until the fifteenth century (about the same time that **Arlette** came into vogue) that the word was applied to a woman, and then only in reference to show-biz types such as jugglers and dancers, a group always deemed suspect by ordinary citizens. Shortly thereafter the **harlot** became **unchaste**, transforming her into a **prostitute** or a **strumpet**. In the lower-archy of loose women, however, she had yet to hit rock bottom, the sixteenth- century version of the Bible using **harlot** as a euphemism for **hoore.**

A harlot with sincerity and a square egg:
They both do not exist.
—Japanese proverb

Part and Parcel

Many such women went on to become war beggars and **camp followers.** The latter were standard equipment of a medieval army. Charles the Bald of France had more than two thousand such pieces in his entourage, one for every four of his soldiers.

Women knew their place in this man's army. The officers' ladies traveled by carriage while the common foot solders and **camp followers** brought up the rear with the supplies and the baggage, from which they became virtually indistinguishable.

We first used **baggage** (16thC) to refer to personal belongings that were portable. Later it became synonymous with trash, refuse, or dirt, the meaning of which was then transferred to **women of a disreputable** or **immoral life**; perhaps related to the French *bagasse,* a **slut**. According to the OED, men employed the term mostly in a "playful" sense (17th–19thC), often prefacing it with "artful," "cunning," "sly," "pert," and "silly." Though they avoided **heavy baggage (**18thC, women and children), many found themselves holding the **bag** (19thC) with an old **prostitute**. It was enough to drive a man **satchel-crazy** (20thC, from **satchel,** an old Ozark term for the female **genitalia**) from all these carryings-on.

I believe the baggage loves me.
—William Congreve, The Old Bachelor,
1693

By Hook or by Crook

The meanings of most words change frequently, but one has always stood firm. The **prostitute** (c. 1613) early on took her stance from *pro-statuere* and her willingness to come forward, to stand before her place of business and put herself out for her clients. Her meaning is still intact today.

But in today's hurry-up world you have to do more than just

stand there and wait for business to come to you. You have to be a **hustler** or a **hooker** to make it. Some align her with "Fighting Joe" Hooker, the famous Civil War general and onetime commander of the Union Army. Allegedly, in tribute to his reputation as a **ladies' man** and a notorious **quiff hunter**, his soldiers named the camp followers of the Union Army quartered on Pennsylvania Avenue "Hooker's Division" and "Hooker's Brigade," making the girls themselves into **hookers**.

It makes for a good story, but the first **hooker** appeared on our streets some twenty years before the Civil War, sighted around Corlear's Hook, a notorious section of New York City.

Some also find her origins in the Old English *hok*, a long instrument with a hook at the end used for thieving items out of stores and home windows. It's the origin of the word "to hook," as in "to steal," as well as the "hock shop" where pilfered goods were sold. It also gave us the **hooker**, the thief who was adept at using the instrument. Given both the **whore**'s penchant for petty thievery and her efforts to sink her hooks into prospective customers, calling her a **hooker** looks to be right. How does that grab you?

Moving Right Along

The **hooker**'s also a real **hustler** (same roots, *hokster* or *hochster*) who's always on the move. She has to be, with all that heavy **traffic** (late 16th–early 17thC, from the large amount of business she plies) out there. The **stroll** (20thC, the beat she walks) is crowded with **streetwalkers** (c. 1592), **nymphs de pave**, **pavement pretties**, **pavement pounders**, and **cruisers** (19th–20thC, also U.S. homosexual lingo, 20thC). It takes all kinds, from all walks of life: not only the **infantry**, your common foot soldier, but also a **princess of the pavement** (20thC, Aust.) and even an occasional **queen** or two.

Ladies of the street always had to be a few steps ahead of the competition. In ancient Athens, they adopted the practice of placing nails on the soles of their shoes, forming the words "follow me" on the soft streets as they strolled about in search of customers, thereby establishing advertising as the **world's oldest profession**.

Some of the **hetaerae**, the highest class of **prostitutes** in the ancient world, worked the cemeteries, inscribing on the tombstones with eyebrow makeup the names of men in whom they were interested. Prospective patrons would, in turn, write down the names of those who attracted them. Slave girls would then carry word back and forth, the final negotiations to be consummated in the cemeteries.

The Romans had more than a dozen different designations for the **prostitute**, depending on her class, location, and the nature of

What's the difference between a prostitute, a mistress, and a wife?

—*Prostitute: "That'll be $100."*

—*Mistress: "Do you have to go already?"*

—*Wife: "Beige...we really ought to paint the ceiling beige."*

    —*Anon., 20thC.*

the services provided. Some favored the time of day between the afternoon meal and four or five o'clock in the afternoon. This interlude was known as a *merando*, "a time well earned" (from *mereo*, "I earn"). People dedicated that part of the day to themselves as a reward for a hard morning's work. It also named the woman most active during that time who merited the designation **meretrix**, (pl.: *meretrices*). Because many thought the **meretrix** cheap and tawdry, she gave us the word "meretricious," which we now use to describe items of little value. Not all were experienced thus. The **lupae** (female wolves) prowled the parks and gardens of the city, attracting customers with their distinctive cry.

Girls Will Be Girls

The girls' feet carried them everywhere—from the church towers during the fourteenth century to the theaters of Restoration England. There they were known as the **orange girls**, who walked among the spectators hawking fresh fruit, playbills, and other assorted odds and ends. They also sold themselves, helping turn theaters into commodious **brothels** where they play on the stage was only incidental to the acts taking place in the wings.

What's a Girl to do?

Through the years, they've been **business girls** (c. 1921), **good-time girls**, **company girls**, and **sporting girls**. The **party girl** (c. 1910) made special appearances at private gatherings, often popping out of cakes and bathing in champagne, and was once considered a sine qua non of every **bachelor** or **stag party** (c. 1859), or just plain **stag** (c. 1900), a sure bet to **make** both your party and your party-goers. During the twenties, her meaning shifted, and she gained a degree of respectability, indistinguishable from the **flapper** who loved nothing more than partying about. But in the 1950s things changed once more. She was now any young actress or model who was introduced to a client by a third party who set the fee. The fact that she retained the prerogative of whether or not to sleep with him was now the only thing setting her apart from ordinary **working girls**.

Today, **working girls** mostly work the streets, unlike the **call girls** (19th–20thC) who let their fingers do the walking. We once knew them from the **call house** (18th–19thC), where all the girls were on call. The **call house** is now a distant memory, but the days of the house call are still with us. To receive such service, call an **escort service** direct and ask if they make **out-calls**. The internet makes it even easier. Thanks to the marvel of modern telecommunications, you're but a touch stroke away.

What's a nice girl like you doing in a place like this?

—Anon., 1930s-50s

I tried to have cybersex once, but I kept getting a busy signal.

—Birdie (Jean Stapleton) in
You've Got Mail, *1999*

A woman that will be drunk
Will easily play the punk;
For when her wits are sunk
All keys will fit her trunk.
   —"Cuckold's Haven" in
      Roxburghe Ballads, 1871

The serving man has his punk, the student his
nun...the puritan his sister.
   —*Dekker,* Westward Ho, *1607*

Summer songs for me and my aunts
While we lie tumbling in the hay.
   —*Shakespeare,* The Winter's Tale

Tout de Suite

The girls are at their best during periods of great adversity. World War I had its **charity girls** (also **dames** and **molls**) and World War II, its **victory** or **V-girls**, who began as amateurs with a particular fondness for boys in khaki and who then drifted into **prostitution**. They were generally found around army bases, giving their all for the war effort. Unstinting in their devotion to duty, they were considered by many to be our first real **patriotutes** (c. 1940s). Inadvertently, they may also have contributed a colorful new suffix to the language. Examples of its use include:

Astrotutes	First in space
Celebratutes	Catering to the very famous
Flute and tutes	Favoring the woodwind section
Root 'n' tutes	Ride 'em cowboy!
Verisimilitutes	Two for the price of one
No regretatutes	Without guilt

You too can tute your own:

_____   _____

_____   _____

The Lay of the Land

Once a woman turned professional, she no longer had to travel as an **incognita** (19thC), an **anonyma** (c. 1860–77), or **just one of them** (19th–20thC). She could now proudly hang out her shingle: "**Ammunition Wife** (c. 1820–1870), More Bang for the Buck," or any of the more than five hundred other terms we have to describe her.

Some call her after the hole she dug for herself and the use to which she put it. Any of the words describing her **genitals** may be used for her as well, including **punk** (late 16th–18thC), from *punctum*, Latin for "a small opening or crack." The **bimbo**'s (early 20thC) there as well, from *bumbo* (18thC), a word once used for the female **genitals** via the **bum**. Both the **bimbo** and the **punk** went on to become terms of insult; the **bimbo** as a simple minded twit, often preceded by "blonde," the **punk** as a nasty urchin, and a young **catamite** in the **gay** lexicon—its most redeeming moments coming as a genre of music noted for its antisocial bent.

Her work also named her a **put** (18thC), as in **to do a put**, **put it in**, and to **play at two-handed put**, all perhaps a shortened version of the French *putain*. But if a **put**, why not also a **shake** (18th–19thC), a **flatbacker**, or a **horizontal** (c. 1886) as she was prone to be? The nighttime being the right time, she was the **nocturnal**, the **nightingale**, the **bat**, or a **lady of the evening**.

Often considered **frail**, **unfortunate**, and **impure** (as opposed to a **pure**, "a proper **mistress**"), she always kept her sunny side up as a **joy girl**, **fille de joie**, **good-time girl**, and **lady of pleasure**. She further enhanced her surroundings as a **scarlet lady** and a **painted lady**—introducing some color to an otherwise drab scene. Never difficult to deal with, she was always a **lady of easy virtue** (c. 1780–20thC).

Kissing Cousins

A closely knit group, hers was a **family of love** (17th–20thC), including several sisters: the **speedy sister**, **erring sister**, **burlap sister**, **frail sister**, **scarlet sister**, and **street sister**, as well as **one of my cousins** (late 17th–early 19thC) and **my** or **mine aunt** (16th–19thC)—making activity with such women morally relative.

Trick or Treat

The **game**'s not only relatively deep but tricky. **Trick** as a bout of **lovemaking** has been part of our vocabulary for more than four hundred years. During that time folks have both **turned a trick** and **done the trick** (also a term for a turn of duty aboard a ship). Most **relationships** were also based on some form of trickery. As one nineteenth-century **wench** put it, "If the little 'un don't **do the trick**, me an' him'll fall out (*Derby Day*, 1864).

How's tricks? Most are pretty good. The ultimate **trick** is the one the **whore** plays on her customer. She **fucks** for money and pretends to **come**. As **tricks** go, it really isn't much, but those who know it's a **trick** still love being deceived. As Nell Kimball explained, "It isn't just **nookie**—what a girl really sells is an illusion, the idea that the **John** is some guy and she's crackers about his kind of **kip work**."

Occasionally, fate plays a cruel trick, leaving her with a **trick-baby**, one fathered by a client. There are even rare instances when a **prostitute** gets personally involved, **getting down** (doing it for real) while **doing the trick**. But as one Kitty reminded her colleagues in *Gentlemen of Leisure*, "**Tricks** are **tricks**—that's how they got their name. When they turn around and satisfy you, you're a **trick**, and **tricks** ain't **shit**."

A Real Tough Customer

This is a **trick**. His name is **John**. **John** was once a **sugar daddy** (early 20thC, sugar meaning "money") and represented a long-term commitment. Today he's just a customer and strictly a one-

"Did you see the score on the blackboard this morning?"
"Sure I did—87 tricks in one week. Let Jenny and the Nigger match that when there ain't no holidays."
　　　　—*Jubilation at Faye's*, John Steinbeck, East of Eden

It was a Saturday night around ten. The vice section was overrun with Johns. It seemed that every white man in town was over there, scratch in one hand and rod in the other ripping and running after the black whores with the wildest, blackest asses.
　　　　—*Iceberg Slim: The Story of My Life*, 1967

shot proposition. **John** is a popular name for the male organ with which he is closely identified. It also speaks to the anonymity he seeks—"John Doe"—as well as his commonality, his sameness, and his generally undistinguished character.

On first sighting, **John** appears a **deadhead** or a **sightseer**, perhaps one with only **Georgia** on his mind. **Georgia**'s long been a freebie in the trade. For a professional to be **georgia'd** meant she was taken advantage of sexually without receiving any money—the ultimate disgrace befalling a pro. If he's a **live one**, he's right on target as a **mark** or a potential **score**, a simple transaction as **trade**, or just so much meat waiting to be ground—a **beefburger** (all 20thC).

John's always been a topic of speculation. In the eighteenth century they asked of him, "Is he foolish or is he **flash**?" (c. 1788, Grose, flash, meaning" being into the underworld life"). Today, we all know that he's simply foolish. As one madam duly noted, "anyone who spends money on **it** must be out of his mind."

John could care less what others think. Most **Johns** come from business and industry, with politics and theater a secondary source. The cream of our country's leadership, they know what our nation needs most and will do everything in their power to see that we get it.

The Crack Salesman

John often loses his way off the straight and narrow. It's then he'll turn anywhere for help, even to a known scoundrel. In this case it's the Old French *pimpreneau*, source of the notorious **pimp** (17th–20thC), one known to never miss a **trick**. In eighteenth-century London, the **pimp** introduced the wood to the fire. We still know him best for making introductions. It's a dirty job, but somebody has to do it.

Currently, he's fancier than ever as a **mack** (or **mac**, c. 1870–90) from the Standard English *mackarel*, from the French *maquereau*, "a **pimp**"—a real **player** who's deep into the life with style.[3]

As seen by his naming, every ethnic and racial group has taken a turn at it. At the turn of the twentieth century we knew him as **Max** and **Hymie**; during the twenties and thirties, as **Tony** and **Carlo**; in the thirties and forties, **Louis** and **Jacques**; more recently he answers to **Red Devil** and **Blue Snapper**. You can't miss him. He's the one decked out in a white mink jacket and matching cap, turtleneck, and red and blue boots, cruising about town in his baby-blue hog.

The **pimp** plays an important role.[4] He's the girl's **sweet man** or just **her man**, and looking after her is a full-time job. As noted in

Gentlemen of Leisure, "It's almost inevitable that a **prostitute** ends up with a **player**. It's hand in glove. Birds of a feather. The two just go together." But it's no walk in the park. As one New York **mack** commented: "You think I take it easy? I have to take care of my **hole**, keep her away from other guys, get her welfare check on 'Mother's Day' and take care of myself. It's a tough life." He's also has to replenish his stock, **cop a new hole or two** ("induce new girls to join the **family**"), and move a **hard leg** ("one with 50,000 miles on her") out to pasture.

Every major **pimp** has a **stable**, a group of **whores** belonging to him, referred to in more intimate terms as **family**. As head of the **family**, much of his time goes into maintaining peace between his **wives-in-law**. This is no easy task and may require an occasional **gorilla** ("a beating"). The **wife** he favors most is his **bottom woman**, his **number-one-woman**, or his **main lady**, who coincidentally happens to be his bread and butter (or his brie and chablis). She's a rare commodity. Iceberg Slim tells us "ain't more than three or four good **bottom women** promised a **pimp** in his lifetime."

The **pimp** himself is unique, one of a few non-obscene words in *The Erotic Tongue* that is insulting to man. And that is only because he lives off the earnings of women. We despise him so much for this that a **mack** was once synonymous with a **bastard**. Yet it is the **pimp** and his trade who have helped make this country what it is today. They're an integral element of the economy. As one **whore** noted in Susan Hall's *Ladies of the Night*, "Business would crumble without us. We consummate deals. We're like a barter system. In fact we're like money. Our backs are the bridges which link business deals." But they are simply the commodities. It's the **pimp** who makes it all possible. **Pimping** remains one of the few democratic callings available in our society: from the lowly bellhop with his famous line, "The package you ordered has arrived," to the middle-level junior executive entertaining clients and lobbyists in Congress who trade **favors** for favors. **Pimping** is democracy in action.

Food for Thought

John is famished. He's **suffering from the night starvation** (19thC). The mere thought of a **saucy** or **spicy** female is enough to cause him to **have the fever**. A little **cooking** (20thC, "stirring and teasing") only encourages his appetite further.

He's hardly a fussy eater. If she's not **properly tasty** (c. 1890s, "sexually alluring"), all it takes is an extra pinch of **salt** to enhance things. **Salt** as an adjective meaning **lewd, amorous,** or **obscene** dates back to Elizabethan times.

Man rules woman. In being a mack you acknowledge this fact. You put yourself in a superior position and you don't let a woman put you in no position. Most women are very tricky. They like to have their own way. But "women of the night" don't look up to a man—they can do anything they want to. He's a john then. Just a trick.

—Susan Hall, Gentlemen of Leisure, 1972

He will to his Egyptian dish again.
—*Shakespeare, Enobarbus speaking of Antony in* Antony and Cleopatra

...As prime as goats
as hot as monkeys
As salt as wolves in pride.
　　　　　　　—Shakespeare, *Othello*

Salt (mid 17th–early 18thC) also served as a noun for **sexual intercourse** and as a verb, meaning to **coit**. A spicy liaison didn't stop there, however. At her best the woman was **hot mustard** (19thC). **Cutting the mustard**, however, was up to him, referring to his **virility** and **potency**. **Relish** in Shakespeare only added extra flavor, but by the nineteenth century described **the act** itself, lending a whole new meaning to the phrase, "mustard and relish to go." Even today, sexual partners both bring something to the table. The message from the past is as relevant as ever: Practice safe sex—use condiments.

How Sweet It Is!

Till the main meal arrives, a brief snack might hold him—a **crumpet** (woman as an item of sexual pleasure, c. 1880), perhaps, or a **buttered bun**. A **buttered bun** (c. 1670–90) was once a **mistress**, later (19thC) a **harlot** who offered herself to several men in repeated succession. **Pastry** (19th–20thC) also traditionally served as a collective term for young and attractive women, the **French** and **Danish** (both 20thC) varieties being most **accessible**.

Among our more outstanding **pastries** we have the **tart**, though it's gone through some tortuous turns, derived as it was from the Latin *tortus*, meaning "twisted." Originally a term of endearment, like "honey" or "sweetheart," for an innocent young girl, by the beginning of the twentieth century we had distorted her into a **fast** or **immoral** woman. By 1908 she had become a hardened **prostitute**, the adjective **tarty** (c. 1920) describing her behavior. The **jam tart** (c. 1804) remained constant as a **mistress** or **harlot**.

If the **tart**'s not to your taste, would you prefer a **cookie**? It's been a **prostitute** and her **genitalia** in such disparate areas as nineteenth-century Scotland and the black community of the Southern United States, there being numerous references to it both in plantation literature and the lyrics of jazz and the blues. **Tarts** and even **pie** (especially **custard pie** among Southern blacks) have also traditionally been open to the suggestion. All are variations on a single theme—women as a piece of cake.

Pleased to Meat You

Dinner's on, and there's much to choose from. John's particularly **fond of meat**, as befits one who's over-amorous and prone to **wenching**. His taste extends especially to **sweet meat**, "a kept **mistress** of tender years," and to her **tender parts**.

If the Lord had not wanted us to be tempted by the flesh, why did he make us of flesh—why not burlap or Jell-O?

　　　—Marty Feldman, In God We Trust, *1980*

A fine palate, though, is not always adequate to the task: "Is she man's meat?" he asks. As Falkland in *Marriage Night* observed, "I have a tender appetite and can scarcely digest one in her teens" (1664). We are also reminded in Bailey's *English Dictionary* that "After sweet meat comes sour sauce,...an excellent monitor to temperance and sobriety" (1726).

Throwing caution to the winds, he's off for a wild **evening of meat and drink** (19th–20thC), making the rounds of the **brothels** and the bars, ending up at the **meat house**—often confused with the **meat market** itself (female **pudendum** and **breasts**)—where the **meat merchant** displays his merchandise (all 19thC).

His tastes generally run to **fresh meat** (one new at plying her trade or a non-**prostitute**, 19thC), **meaty** (c. 1820, sexually enjoyable), **white** or **dark** (20thC, U.S.), **hot** and **well done over** (said of a woman with whom one has had **intercourse**, 19thC). He even dreams of thin: "The nearer the bone, the sweeter the meat." What he more than likely settles for, however, is **dead** or **frozen meat** (an aged **prostitute**) served **raw** (**naked** in the act, also inexpert and inexperienced), or even just a **bit of fat** (a stout woman—all 19thC). It matters little to **John**. Meat is meat; he's happy whether **in a woman's beef** (18th–mid 19thC) or **in her mutton** (19th–20thC).

An angry woman might tell him to simply **beat it**—his **meat**, that is. Any further objectification of women in such a fashion only serves to confirm she has—ahem—legitimate beefs.

House Calls

The street is neat, but there's nothing like a place of your own. In ancient Greece the girls had the **porneia** (which, when joined with the graphic descriptions on the walls therein, gave us our first glimpse of **pornography**) and in Rome the **lupinari** (home of she-wolves). In 1347, Giovanna I, Queen of Naples, made it official when she took the girls off the streets and legalized the first **houses of sin** in the Christian world. Her intent was to provide a source of taxable income for the State, security for the "girls" by giving them a home, and safe conduct for females everywhere by deflecting overtures aimed at "respectable" women.

French kings had other goals in mind, using the **bordello** (late 16th–18thC, "a little house") to discourage **homosexuality** and other behavior deemed aberrant. These abodes were also known as **brothels** (c. 1593) from the word for a "good-for-nothing man," a "wretch of sorts" (15thC), and, later, the **prostitute** whose services he was known to frequent. The **brothel house** (16thC) soon became a place in which you might find them both. It was then just a matter of time before we dropped the "house," leaving us with the plain old **brothel**.

It took a heap o'lovin' to make a home a **house**, but there was soon one for every taste and mood, over one hundred at last count. Those most frequented include the **bawdy house** (c. 1552), **call house, can house** (early 1930s), **cathouse** (c. 1925), **fancy house, garden house, gay house** (19th–20thC), **grinding house, hothouse, house of civil reception** (mid 18th–early 19thC), **house of ill delight, ill fame,** and **ill repute, naughty house, parlor house** (c. 1867), **slaughterhouse, sporting house** (c. 1890), **vaulting house** (17thC), and **whorehouse** (16thC). And that's just for openers. Best, however, that you not settle in. As former Madam Polly Adler reminded us in the title of her memoir, "A House is not a Home."

Learn, Baby, Learn

A vaulting house...Where I used to spend my afternoons among superb she-gamesters...I have cracked a ring or two there.

—Massinger, Unnatural Combat, *1639*

No ordinary houses, these. Many were centers for higher learning known as the **pushing** (17th–19thC), **vaulting,** or **finishing school** or **academy** (c. 1760–1820). As the **Ladies' College** (18th–early 19thC) or the **School of Venus** (17th–19thC) it was the school of hard knocks where the **rule of three** (18th–20thC) for the **penis** and **testes** was practiced daily. More serious students of the craft studied under **academicians** (c. 1760–1820) known for their strict discipline ("If you don't get it the first time, we'll do it again and again, until you get it right"). The quest for knowledge continued during Victorian times when the **mottes** placed cards in their tenement windows announcing, "Foreign language school featuring **French** (what else?) **lessons.**"

If you're looking to pursue some form of cultural enrichment today you might try a **library,** often advertised as "well stacked, with **librarians** ready to meet your every need."

For Heaven's Sake

Those three nymphs...are three nuns, and the plump female is of great notoriety and generally designated the abbess.

—Pierce Egan, Life in London, *1821*

Others sought spiritual uplift through visits to a **nunnery** (late 16th–20thC). Because nunneries in general never enjoyed a good reputation, and all kinds of venal activity was imagined to occur in them, they soon became a code word for a **brothel.** Hamlet's injunction to Ophelia, "Get thee to a **nunnery,**" was penned by one who knew the slang of his day. Several years ago, the *New York Daily News,* in one of its better gaffes, ran a feature story using that as its headline. The story was a somewhat maudlin account of a middle-aged woman's decision to join a religious order. But this was one **nunnery** in which a devout woman in her middle years didn't have a prayer. Behind the walls of this institution the **nuns** (18th–19thC) were **punchable** (18th–19thC, "ripe for a man") and **punctured, praying with their knees upward,** working diligently at **putting the devil into hell** (18th–20thC).

Home Free

The eighteenth-century European model introduced elaborate rituals and extravaganzas as well as finely dressed and specially selected girls, carefully chosen, closely supervised, and under close medical scrutiny. These classy houses were known as **seraglios** (late 17th–early 19thC) from *serai*, the Turkish palace where the women were kept. Girls were pre-selected and sent for in sedan chairs.

The less exotic and less exclusive sites were known as **kips** (c. 1766, from the cant word for "sleep") or likened to other business establishments: the **hook shop, flesh** or **meat market, button-hole factory, bum shop, chamber of commerce, moll shop, bread-and-butter warehouse**, and the **body shop**.

Special needs were also accommodated. During the late nineteenth and early twentieth centuries we also had **houses of assignation** for couples looking for a secluded rendezvous and a place where lower-class **prostitutes** and shop girls might supplement their incomes. The better **houses of assignation** catered to a more select clientele, offering food, servants, and posh surroundings, and were generally open only till five o'clock in the afternoon.

Cribs were a twentieth-century invention in the U.S., small cramped areas (roughly four by six feet) not unlike the Midwestern corncribs from which they got their name. Often they were nothing but mean shacks with a display room in front and a work area in the rear. The earliest **cribs** could be found on the Barbary Coast and were worked primarily by Chinese slave girls who used to hang out the windows negotiating the fees. A **lookee** was free, a **feelie** or **touchee** went for ten cents, and a **doee**, twenty-five or fifty cents.

We later had the **cowyard,** a three-or-four-floor building with long hallways of small closet-like rooms and two to three hundred **whores** hard at work milking every customer for all he was worth.

Fighting for Piece

Housing starts have been down in the U.S. since World War II, but they had a brief revival during the Vietnam War with the **boum-boum parlors** of Ankhe, captured so vividly by an American soldier on his visit to the rest and recreation center, also known as **Disneyland East:**

> Before I got a pass, I had to pick up a rubber and pass an exam on how to use it. I went to a native barber shop where I got a great haircut, manicure, some great pot and a blow job. I relaxed for a few hours with the pot and then went out to Disneyland and went to one of the houses. I had a drink and the Mama San told me I could get a boum-boum for 300 piastres or a sop-sop (fellatio) for 500. I got a boum-boum. Not bad,

though it only took a few minutes. When I left the compound, the MP at the gate told me to wash myself to avoid clap or syphilis. I went back to the company and got a pro-treatment. The whole deal had cost me about seven bucks, and I had enough pot to last for a couple of weeks.

—Charles Winick and Paul Kinsie,
The Lively Commerce, 1971

Signs of the Times

It was easy to stray from the beaten path, so to keep a customer from losing his way, houses were marked by large bold numbers, had colored lampshades in the windows, or featured large translucent globes hanging over the sidewalks or doorways—often showing a red light. When we put enough of these together, we had a **red-light district** (late 19thC).

One version has it that in the early days of the railroad in Kansas City, during the night when freight trains were made up, brakemen would often pass the time with trips to **whorehouses** near the yards, carrying with them their red signal lamps, which they would hang outside the tents or houses to which they were paying a visit. When trains were ready to pull out, the dispatcher would send young boys to retrieve the brakemen, locating them by the red lanterns hanging outside the **bordellos.**

It's a story worth sharing, but it doesn't shed much light on the notorious **district de lampe rouge** which flourished around the Palais Royal in Paris some 150 years before the first railroad.

The French were there first. But for the most impressive **red-light district** in history you'd have to go to New Orleans. The area was known as **Storyville** (1897–1917), after Alderman Sidney Story, the creative force who legitimized overt **prostitution** in a thirty-six-square-mile area of the French Quarter. It has no parallel in human history. At its peak, the district housed some 230 **brothels**, 30 **houses of assignation**, and thousands of **prostitutes**— making for what some today might call "Super Ball XXXXXX."

Alas, nothing is forever. **Storyville** closed its doors at the beginning of World War I, victim of a concerted drive by authorities looking to protect our boys in uniform from the vagaries of sin. This led critics to protest that our young men might die for their country but not get **laid** for it.

An area less grand in scope, but also well-known, was the **Tenderloin** (c. 1887) or **loin**. It hosted a substantial amount of activity, but never in as concentrated a form as the **red-light district**. The first **Tenderloin** of note was an area of New York ridden with **prostitutes**. The name was coined by one of New York's finest, from one of the more expensive cuts of meat or, as some think, the meaty payoffs to the police who protected the operation.

Honi Soit Qui Mal Y Pense.
Evil to him who evil thinks.
— *Motto, Order of the Garter, and*
introduction to The Blue Book, *the*
directory of prostitutes in New
Orleans, 19thC

Call Me Madam

Upon arrival at such an establishment, your first question might be, "Is the **madam** of the house in?"

Madam(e) (18th–20thC) has long been the owner or manager of a **brothel**. Speculation has her originating in the court of Louis XV, a monarch noted for his sexual appetite. His royal harem was called *le parc aux cerfs* ("the park of stags"). The one who managed it, kept the girls happy, oversaw the expenses, and maintained order was called the *surintendante*. She was an elderly woman who allegedly came from one of the best families in Burgundy and worked hard to keep her identity a secret. At the *parc* they knew her only as "Madame"; none dared call her by any other name.

It was the **madam** who made any **house** work. Everything revolved around her. Experienced, cynical, and intelligent, she ruled with an iron fist. Adept at recruiting and training, she was also skilled in providing amusement for her charges and attracting new customers, ever sensitive to the needs of her clients. Her forte was collecting, managing, and spending the money as well as dealing with the law. The more famous American **madams** include Polly Adler (*A House Is Not A Home*), Nell Kimball, Jew Jenny of Salt Lake City, Silver-Tongue Jean of Detroit, and Mother Lena Hyman of Toledo, noted for her chicken dinners, which she served the police with an accompanying payoff under each plate.

I Remember Mama

Madam has long been a term of respect and, in this instance, is well deserved. No one would dream of detracting from her stature. But "what is a home without **Mother**?"—a common homily you might find over the credenza of a Victorian home or on the wall of a **crib**. **Mother** (19th–20thC), also **mother of the maids** or **mammy**, was a designation frequently applied to the central figure of the household. It was she who clothed, fed, and comforted the girls—tending to their every need, in loco parentis. As one Victorian **motte** reminisced about the famed Mother Willit of London's Gerrard Street:

> So help her kindness, she al'us turned her gals out with a clean arse and a good tog; and as she turned 'em out, she didn't care who turned 'em up, cause 'em vos as clean as a smelt and as fresh as a daisy.

Mom's status was elevated further as a **mother superior** and an **abbess** (late 18th–19thC), the ultimate authority in a **nunnery**. When **flagellation brothels** later came into vogue, adding to her duties, she became the **governess**, noted for her ability to maintain discipline, whipping both her charges and her customers into line.

Mother, how many tails have you in your cab? How many girls do you have in your bawdy house?
      —Lexicon Balantronicum, *1811*

So an old abbess, for the rattling rakes, A tempting dish of human nature makes And dresses up a luscious maid.
      —Peter Pindar, *1819*

There's the Rub

Though they were now off the streets, many of the girls still found themselves in hot water. Many were in the **stews**, a throwback to the old Roman baths where folks used to "stew" themselves in hot air or steam, a practice reintroduced to Europe by the Crusaders on their return from the Middle East.

A **stew** had several large tubs, each of which held five or six people at a time, as well as smaller ones allowing for greater intimacy. They started off innocently enough, but when gambling, food, drink, and other services were added, together with female camaraderie and associated goings-on, they soon became hotbeds of illicit activity.

Bathing and cleanliness had never been favored by the Christian world, but with the public baths, cleansing of the body took on new popularity. The **stews** flourished until the 1530s and '40s, when authorities closed them down because of an outbreak of **syphilis**. However, we continued to use the word **stews**, both as **brothels** and for those who worked there, through the nineteenth century. Some also knew them as **bagnios** (17th–18thC), the Turkish baths of Elizabethan times, from the Italian word *bagno* for "bath."

Sound familiar? It's all akin to today's **physical culture** and **health establishments**, **relaxation clubs** or **parlors**, **steambaths**, **saunas** (in England), and, of course, the ever-popular **massage parlors**, which date back to just before World War I. **Massage parlors** have in fact become so closely identified with sexual services that in Las Vegas, city officials tried unsuccessfully to close down two which apparently rubbed customers the wrong way—by offering only legitimate massages. City authorities took them to court claiming misrepresentation.

Personal Best

Not everyone fancied such public activity. Those looking for a quieter and more discreet game tried the **personal columns**, also known as the plain old **personals** that have flourished since the late 1970s. Players generally present themselves in abbreviated form as SWM, DWM, SWF, DWF, GWF, GWM, SBM, DBM, SBF, DBF, GBF, GBM, BI-F, BI-M, depending on whether they are male, female, black, white, single, divorced, **gay**, or **bisexual**. Women most often are "in search of" a **relationship**, represented as ISO. Men are looking to **get laid** and seldom make mention of it. **Relationships** often prove as abbreviated as the ads themselves.

A late nineteenth-century precursor to the practice was known as the **personal bureau**. One such enterprise could be found in New York City above a quiet, modest-looking stationery store on

I do feel rather strongly that an institution [a sauna] associated with fitness, cold water, steam and deep breathing should not suffer the indignity of having to go under the same name as one in which the object is a commercial exercise in sexual stimulation carried out by grim harridans on unhappy men in the shabby back rooms of garishly lit premises in the less pleasant areas of our larger cities.

—Bernard Levin, London Times, 1980

one of the uptown streets near Broadway, convenient to the better class of **demimondaines** who patronized it. Upstairs, atop a counter, sat a large book open to a page on which a lady might write down her name, address, and interests. Men would go through the book, selecting women consistent with their fantasies. A sample entry was:

> Miss Lavinia, 15 years of age, beautiful brunette; she likes an old man, blind preferred; must have teeth and money.

Tips of the Tongue

1. No one likes being called a **whore**. In San Francisco a judge ruled that a street preacher has free-speech rights to call working women **whores,** suggesting that a woman who had the preacher arrested should just have punched him instead. The woman testified that she was walking across the Civic Center Plaza when the preacher followed her, pointing her out and saying that women who leave their homes and go out to work and carry briefcases and wear suits think they are liberated, and liberated women are **whores.**

   The preacher denied the woman's allegations after the judge acquitted him. "The only thing I ever told Mrs. Golden was that Jesus loves her," he said. (AP, December 2, 1983)

2. There are worse things than being called a **whore**. "I may be a **whore**, but I can't be a **bitch**!" was a cry often heard from the mouth of an irate lower-class woman of the late eighteenth or mid nineteenth century. It's a word Grose cited as the "most offensive appellation that can be given to an English woman, even more provoking than that of **whore**."

   The **bitch** has been a **lewd** woman since the fifteenth century and it still has that meaning in England today. **Bitch** has also served as a verb, "to complain or to make disparaging and sarcastic remarks." Since Restoration times, it's also meant to go **whoring**. An interesting trade-off in that it gave both men and women something to **bitch** about.

   Today, your favorite **bitch** is multi-faceted, representing anything from a **gay** lover or a subservient girl friend to an ill tempered, malicious person, or a situation that is large and unmanageable. As the Cat Woman (Michelle Pfeiffer) told Batman (Michael Keaton) in *Batman Returns* (1992), " I'm a woman and can't be taken for granted. Life's a **bitch**; now so am I."

   It can even be the reverse of its traditional meaning— "something remarkable or surprising or otherwise extraordinary" ("That tune is a **bitch**.") or a person with truly remarkable skills ("He's a real **bitch** on the piano."). Mostly, however, it's the province of angry women who pride them-selves on their sharp tongue and spiteful manner, i.e., their **bitchiness**: "That's Mrs. **Bitch** to you," they like to say. Though others are uncomfortable with it, they themselves see nothing wrong with their demeanor: "You say I'm a **bitch** like it's a bad thing."

3. Something fishy about the **maquereau?** The French also know him as *un hareng*, "a "herring." Both go back to what they're selling; a **cunt** in France being known both as *la maquerelle*, a "mackerel" and *la morue*, "a cod," both with roots once more to the alleged "fishy" odor of the **vagina**.

4. In England they once distinguished between the **pounce** and the **pimp**. The **pounce** (did he pounce on her, or come from Alphonse?) ran the girl's life while the **pimp solicited** (16thC) for her. In America he's always been an all-service provider. As her **solicitor** he (or she) has been a **bawd** (c. 1362), a **panderer** (c. 1450), **procurer** or **procuress** (c. 1632), a **go-between, buttock-broker (**17th–early 19thC), **flesh-peddler, middleman**, and **holesaler** (all 20thC).

As the lady's **protector**, he was her **Louis** (c. 1935), her **bully**, her **fancy Joseph** (19thC), or just her **fancy man** (c. 1821). In this category we also have the classic **souteneur** (c. 1906), with his broad-striped jersey, red waistband, apache cap tilted jauntily on his head, and tightly curled lips from which dangled a cigarette.

The Wages of Sin

The experienced sexual athlete knows enough to shield himself from some of life's contingencies. For short-term protection he favors the **condom**.[1]

The device is said to draw its name from the mysterious Dr. Condom or Conton, a physician at the court of Charles II (c. 1660–1685) who allegedly created the item to help put a cap on His Majesty's growing number of illegitimate children. Students of that period, though, have been unable to locate the good Doctor, and they're not even sure he really existed.

Other theories regarding the origin of the word range from a Colonel Condum in the Royal Guard to Condom, a town in Germany recorded as a fortress of considerable strength, to an oilskin case that held the colors of the regiment (18th–early 19thC). Some think the word may even be a unique blend of *cunnus* (for the female **pudenda**) and "dum" or "dumb"—together rendering the organ incapable of functioning.

Another claim regarding the invention of the **condom**, and its first published description, was made by Gabriello Fallopio (1523–1562)—whose name is most closely associated with the **Fallopian tubes**—in *De Morbo Gallico*, published two years after his death, in which he encouraged use of linen sheets as **condoms**.

It must have been great **between the sheets**. From what we know, however, the **condom** actually originated long before, in the slaughterhouses of medieval Europe where lamb intestines and the membranes of other animals were dried and then well lubricated to make them soft and pliant. In those days it apparently took guts to **have sex**.

Letter Perfect

The **condom** achieved its greatest popularity during the seventeenth and eighteenth centuries, often appearing in print as **c-d-m** and frequently spoken of as a **letter** (**French, Italian,** or **Spanish,**

It is said that President Carter is considering changing the Democratic party emblem from the jackass to a condom, because it stands for inflation, protects a bunch of pricks, halts production, and gives a false sense of security while one is being screwed.
—Anon., reported by Reinhold Aman, Maledicta, 1978

the letter and envelope being virtually one), a form of correspondence which absolutely, positively, had to be there overnight.

Its ability to deliver the goods was dramatically extolled in a pamphlet coauthored by the Earl of Rochester in 1667, "A Panegyric Upon **Cundum**," in which he wrote: "Happy the man who in his pocket keeps, whether with green or scarlet riband bound, a well-made **cundum**." Not everyone agreed. In 1862, Pope Leo XII damned the use of the discovery "because it hindered the arrangements of providence"—a statement received in many quarters as so much papal bull.

Steel Yourself

Town blades continued to encourage their cohorts to "take a **letter!**" in spite of the church's attitude. One noted lady of the court, however, found it nothing to write home about, noting how it was "gossamer against infection, steel against love." Other critics described it as **armor**, mocking those who donned the raiment as **pot valiant** (both 18thC). The **condom** had tried to prove its mettle but was found failing.

New and dramatic developments, however, brought the skeptics around. The vulcanization of the rubber sheath in 1876 lent it newfound flexibility and favor. We appropriately named it a **rubber** (20thC).[2] It wasn't completely foolproof, however. In England an eraser is also called a "rubber," causing untold confusion whenever an Englishman in an American office asks to borrow one.

Wash 'n' Wear

You wouldn't go wrong, however, treating it as an extra garment of sorts, something for the head, perhaps—**la capote anglaise**, **la capote allemande** ("an English or German hood") or a **French cap**, depending on your national origin and which enemy is in vogue at the time. Casanova often came with cap in hand and a dozen on call. Though personally favoring such headgear, his friend the **nun** seemed less than pleased with their aesthetics: "There you are hooded like a mother abbess, but in spite of the fineness of the sheath I like the little fellow better quite **naked**. I think that this covering degrades us both."

Casanova dubbed it a **redingote d'Angleterre**, an "English riding coat." Today, it's a plain old **overcoat**; though those into formal dress, don a **rented tux** (1990s). Others consider it an article to help brave the elements—a **diving suit**, a **shower cap** (both mid 20thC), and a **raincoat**. Not everyone was comfortable with the coverage however. Critics likened its use to **taking a shower with a raincoat on**. Yet what better precaution for an evening of stormy **love-making**?

A Tip of the Cap

A final tribute: It's easy to write the **condom** off as a mere **plumbing fixture** (1990s) or a **disposable sanitary device** (early 20thC). But it has truly worked hard on man's behalf—some say like a **Trojan** (one of the more popular twentieth-century brand names, after a people noted for laboring energetically and doggedly). Many now use it on every conceivable occasion. It has also served them well as a **prophylactic** (20thC, from *pro*, "in favor of," and *phylaxis*, "watching or being on one's guard"), forging an effective advance guard whose job it is to keep all infections out.[3]

This fear of infection—safety first—rather than concern for making the woman **with child** has always been uppermost in man's thoughts, turning the **condom** into an **instrument of safety** (early 20thC) and also giving us the twentieth-century favorite, a **safety**, furthering the illusion that **sex** could really be made safe.

Catch-As-Catch-Can

For those who failed to take cautionary measures came the moment of reckoning—the time for the final payment, the **wages of sin**.

Remember the **pleasure boat**, the one with the **finely trimmed sails, high in the bows** and **wide in the beams**? At bottom she was nothing but a **fire ship** (c. 1670–1850). She caught the last guy **napping** (nap: to catch VD—"you have **napt it**") and **tipped him the token** (c. 1780, **token**: "a blotch or discoloration," Standard English for the plague). He was really taken in. What he thought a token of her affection turned out to be nothing but a real **pip** (late 16th–17thC), and is he **burnt** (16th–17thC) up!

When You Care Enough to Send the Very Best

Abandon ship! It's **Venus's curse**, the **garden gout**, and the **forget-me-not**. Or it might be the **pox**, with which it was often confused, because the facial disfigurement that resulted bore similarities to that caused by smallpox. Most think it was Columbus and his crew who first discovered this **pox**, having received it from Indian givers and then carried it back to Europe along with other treasures from the New World. However, physical anthropologists who have studied bone lesions from that time, determined that **syphilis** existed in Europe long before Columbus, and that the more likely scenario has Columbus and his men as the bearers of this gift.

There's no denying, however, that it did catch on during this time. Two years later, when Charles VIII of France invaded Italy, he got extra support from Ferdinand and Isabella, who sent Spanish

Grandmother makes cheap prophylactics,
She punctures the end with a pin;
Grandfather performs the abortions.
My God, how the money rolls in.
—Anon., Sung to the tune of "My Bonnie Lies over the Ocean," 20thC

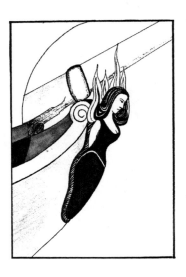

She seemed a stately pleasure boat
with tempting good attire;
But little knew that (underdeck)
her Gun-Room was on Fire.
—From a popular Elizabethan broadside

Ay, she quickly poopt him:
She made him roast-meat with worms.
—Shakespeare, Pericles

These London wenches are so stout,
They care not what they do;
They will not let you have a bout,
Without a crown or two.
They double their chops and curl their locks
Their breaths perfume they do;
Their tails are pepper'd with the pox.
And that you're welcome to.
                              —English ballad, c. 1719

troops that brought with them these same glad tidings. By the time the French had captured Naples, all of Italy had fallen to the **pox**. The **Neapolitan bone ache** then spread throughout all of Europe, and intrepid sea-going explorers—those folks we learned about in seventh-grade history—soon carried it together with civilization's other blessings, around the world. As noted by Professor Abraham Van Helsing (Anthony Hopkins) in Bram Stoker's *Dracula* (1993), "Civilization and syphilisation have advanced together." Vasco da Gama's crew left it in India, and in 1505 it landed in China. It was truly **the gift that goes on giving** (20thC).

The French Connection

Who was the original **gift giver** (1990s)? No one knew for sure. Everyone picked on the French, identified by the whole world as the wellspring of degeneracy (**morbus Gallicus**: the **French disease**, the **French gout**, the **French pox**, the **French measles**). A man was said to wear a **French crown**, a baldness associated with the disease; and an infected wench was described as **Frenchified**. Disfigured **testicles** came to be called **French marbles**—though logic, based on an early "cure" which involved submerging the afflicted party in hot oil, would dictate "Frenchified potatoes."

He suffered by a blow over the snout with a French faggot. He lost his nose by the pox.
                              —Grose

Other nations soon got into the act, including the Spanish, the Italians, and the Germans, giving us the **Spanish gout**, **German scabies**, and dozens of other permutations. The Spanish even gave the **needle** (c. 1611) to the Americans. There appeared to be no end to it, until the Turks settled such parochial squabbling, treating it collectively as the **Christian disease**.

Love-struck

It was a poet, however, who had the last word on the subject. The word was **syphilis**, first appearing in 1530 in a poem by Girolamo Fracastoro called "Syphilis sive morbus gallicus" ("**Syphilis, or the French disease**"), a tract which purported to show both the symptoms and possible treatment of the dreaded malady.

O, Harvard is run by Princeton,
  And Princeton is run by Yale,
And Yale is run by Vassar,
  And Vassar's run by tail;
But Stanford's run by stud-horse juice,
  They say it's made by hand,
It's the house of clap and syph,
  It's the asshole of the land.
            —Anon., Univ. of Cal. at Berkeley

The hero of the piece is a handsome young herdsman named Syphilis, who loses his cattle because of an extended drought. Angry and hurt, he lashes out at the Sun God, blaming him for his misfortune. Apollo, however, does not take kindly to such impiety and afflicts Syphilis with the disease that is soon to bear his name. Miserable and alone, Syphilis is forced to wander the earth's substrata. There he discovers the marvels of the element mercury, with which he treats the disease and cures himself. Humbled by his experience and made wiser by it all, he then dedicates his life to Diana, goddess of chastity.

Many found it so compelling a tale that they adopted its hero's name as an internationally neutral term for the disease. After having known it on more intimate terms, they reduced it to **syph** (mid 20thC) and **phylis** (early 20thC). The disease proved so popular in this form that there still are folks who have not yet received full word of it.

Two for the Money

Syphilis made sex a gamble—what some called "the Russian roulette of the **gay** (as in "fast-living") set. But as one Victorian wag put it, "The revolver held not one but two bullets." Those fortunate enough to dodge the bullet at the **big casino (syphilis)**, still had to duck another at **the little casino (gonorrhea)**. Either way they stood a good chance of cashing in their chips.

Gonorrhea comes from *gonos*, "**semen**" and *rhein*, "flow"—"running or flowing **semen**," named for the discharge identified with the disease, mistakenly thought to be the fluid produced by the male reproductive organ. Men so afflicted were said to **piss pins and needles** (c. 1780) from the accompanying discomfort and to **piss pure cream** (19th–20thC), from the look of the discharge. No mere also-ran, **gonorrhea** is one of our more popular infectious diseases. It is second only to the common cold and nothing to sneeze at.

For the longest time **syphilis** and **gonorrhea** were thought to be different stages of the same disease. It wasn't until 1793 that researchers established **gonorrhea** as separate and distinct. Scientists everywhere applauded the discovery. The rest of the civilized world simply **clapped** approvingly (**clap**, from the French *clapoir*—Standard English, late 16th–20thC).

Diseased Minds

There was no applauding the use of these words. Neither **syphilis** nor **gonorrhea** was deemed verbally proper or permissible in the United States through the 1930s.

The medical fraternity felt especially uncomfortable in their presence. Rather than speak directly of them they made reference to **a certain illness, a bad disease, a blood disease, a preventable disease, a secret disease**, and **a vice disease**. If you think they're vague, you might enjoy Mencken's accounts of doctors treating patients with **specific stomachs** or **specific ulcers**.

Newspapers were equally stiff-necked on the topic, refusing to carry any advertisements or copy making reference to it until the outbreak of World War II.[4] Mencken recounts how efforts to alert us to the danger (of **VD**, not the war) and to encourage use of **prophylactics** by the U.S. War Advertising Council were protested by the National Commander of Catholic War Veterans, who argued

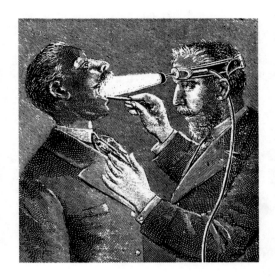

The Virgin she did prove
a trap, a trap;
The end of all her love
the clap, the clap.
            —Anon., 18thC

He went out by Had 'em and came around by
    Clapham home.
He went out wenching and got a clap.
            —Grose

It was evening, I lay dying
Spirit wandering, flame reposing,
But one though would never leave me
Till poetic form it bore;
Though to you it may appear, Sir,
For a poet rather queer, Sir,
That I'd caught a week before, Sir.
It was about the gonorrhea, Sir,
That I'd caught a week before.
And I wrote these warning stanzas,
As I trickled down before,
Trickle, trickle, evermore!
        —Victorian parody of Poe's The Raven

that publication of such information would "weaken the sense of decency in the American people,...increase immorality by promising to make **promiscuity** safe, and ignore the fundamental fact of human conduct, that shame and embarrassment are among the strongest deterrents to the sins that spread **VD**."

Venereal disease entered the language in 1658, an innocent enough expression for a discomfort associated with Venus's type of activities, a euphemism for an expression we no longer remember. But people in the States never took kindly to **venereal disease** or its abbreviated successor, **VD**, avoiding both like the plague. They finally agreed upon **social disease**, an all-inclusive term so general and inoffensive as to embrace everything from bad breath to publicly **breaking wind** and **humping the hostess**.

Germs of Endearment

Times change. Students of the game no longer speak of **VD**, opting instead for **STD** (1980s, **sexually transmitted disease**). **Syph** and **clap** have fallen into disuse—lucky to receive even an honorable mention. **Herpes** (Greek for "to spread or to creep") had its moment of glory when it was briefly considered by connoisseurs of the traffic as the "in" disease and the favorite item of discussion at singles bars everywhere. Some couldn't even distinguish **herpes** from true love. The difference, we were told, was that **herpes** is forever.

The new Russian roulette of sexual encounter blows the competition away. It's the only game in town—one so devastating, few dare call it by name, reducing it instead to **the A word** (1990s, **gay** community usage).[5] There are still some who continue playing this high stakes game. Some do so but cautiously, hedging their bets by practicing **safe sex** (c.1989); others have just stopped playing all together, considering all such gaming high risk.[6]

Tips of the Tongue

1. Not everyone is so disposed. There are those to whom the **condom** will always be a conundrum. Count Rocky among them. In the third segment of his film epic, his financial advisor asked of our champ, "would you be interested in investing in condominiums?" Rocky turns brusquely away mumbling, "Never use 'em."

    Also a conundrum is the late pop star Lisa Lopes of the R&B trio TLC, who commonly attached **condoms** to her eyeglasses during concerts. Confusing **copulation** with vision is a frequent error nowadays. See the discussion on this in *Act One, Making Conversation.*

2. Rubber didn't prove flexible to all. Anthony Comstock, Spe-

cial Agent and Secretary of the New Society for the Suppression of Vice, had his own take on the subject. If open sex was public enemy number one, why arm the enemy, encouraging it in its activities? He successfully lobbied Congress to pass a bill branding **contraceptives** obscene and prohibiting their distribution across state lines or through the mails. Similar legislation was soon enacted in 24 states. But manufacturers always had a market for their wares, selling them under the counter, advertising them euphemistically as "**rubber goods for gents**, 25 cents each," and **married women's friends**. Today, they no longer travel incognito and are as close as your nearest **bubble gum machine** ("**condom** vending unit," **gay** lingo, 1990s). One can only imagine Comstock's reaction; if not angered by it, it certainly would have given him something to chew on.

There's a new medical crisis. Doctors are reporting that many men are having allergic reactions to latex condoms. They say they cause severe swelling. So what's the problem?
—Dustin Hoffman

3. In 1918, amid wartime concerns about **venereal disease**, Judge Frederick Crane in a case brought to his New York Appeals Court found **contraceptives** legal as instruments for the maintenance of health. The decision transformed the **birth control** industry, allowing **condoms** to be sold openly, though they marked the packages, "for the prevention of disease only." That same role is emphasized today. Those who think of sex as their life work risk an **occupational hazard** (**AIDS** and other **STDs**), especially when they **rough it** or **bare it all**, making the **condom** a potential **life saver** (all **gay** lingo, 1990s). Those who consider the campaign against **AIDS** a war should, as combatants have always done, **take cover** (1990s).

4. There was one exception. In 1912–13 Margaret Sanger published her first major document on sex and reproduction, "What Every Girl Should Know," in serialized form in the socialist newspaper *The Call*. The article on **gonorrhea** ran without incident. But inspired by Anthony Comstock, the Postal Service threatened to revoke the newspaper's mailing permit if the second article on **syphilis** were to appear, citing its authority to bar **lewd** and **lascivious** materials from the mails. Reluctantly, *The Call* bowed to the demand, but not without a protest. The column appeared under the headline, "What Every Girl Should Know," and was totally blank, except for one word where the text would be, and that was the word "Nothing."

Ironically, the text was later reprinted in full and distributed by the United States government to its troops during World War II. It would have been a rather nice, if belated, tribute to Miss Sanger if someone had remembered to credit her as its author.

5. In the summer of 1981, doctors in several large American

cities observed the genesis of a new disease. Because it was first detected in homosexual males, it was initially called **The gay plague**, **gay cancer**, or **GRID** ("**gay**-related immune disorder") and largely dismissed because gay men were deemed dispensable. A year later the syndrome was renamed because it was clear that it did not affect just **gay** men. The Centers for Disease Control linked the new disease to blood and sexual transmission, calling it **Acquired Immune Deficiency Syndrome** or **AIDS**. The word "acquired" was used because unlike other immune deficiency illnesses, this one was acquired from someone else as opposed to being something that happened to you. It was caused by infection from another by the **human immune deficiency virus (HIV)** which attacked selected cells in the immune system.

In 1986, its presence was noted in Africa, where it was called **the slim disease**, from the emaciated state it left its victims in its final stages. Many still cannot find the words to describe the growing plague, badly neglected both by both government and science.

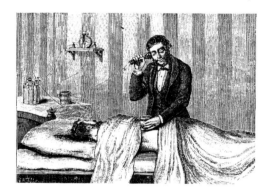

6. By 1989, in a belated response to the **AIDS** epidemic, Americans sought protection through incantation, encouraging the population to say **safe sex**. The phrase was doomed at the outset. Meant to encourage responsible behavior, the campaign on its behalf was itself irresponsible, never really addressing the role that **sex** plays in our lives. It instead passed judgment, cultivating guilt and shame in anyone unable to achieve a "zero-risk sexual life style."

The Final Act

ex cannot continue in this wild and abandoned manner. Invariably it settles down into a **relationship**, occasionally stormy, but hopefully **meaningful**. The word **meaningful** lends the requisite legitimacy to all matters sexual. It makes even the **one-night stand** (mid 20thC, a brief **encounter**, 19thC, an **erection**, i.e., one that is very brief) **relevant** as a **meaningful quickie** (c. 1980s).

A **meaningful quickie** may appear to be a contradiction in terms but as the product of fast-food technology and the sexual revolution, it must be considered **relevant**. All the best things in life are **relevant**. **Relevant** adds yet another dimension to **meaningful**. You can't do much better than a **relationship** that is both **relevant** and **meaningful**.

It was once considered **relevant** to live together **without benefit of clergy** (19thC, a term which originally described denial of the last rites to one who had committed suicide), though it was less so when you were **shacking up** (c. 1940s). We no longer do that kind of thing. Today, we enter into a **primary relationship** with a **significant other** (both c. 1980s).

Strangers in the Night

For one so significant, however, the **other** remains somewhat vague and nondescript. We know him/her only as **partner, friend, roommate, live-in, lover,** or **cohabitor**. But politics (in this case the U.S. Census Bureau) makes the strangest bedfellow of all—the **posslq**, "the person of the opposite sex sharing living quarters." Paeans of praise have already been sung on his/her behalf:

> There's nothing that I wouldn't do
> If you would be my posslq.
> You live with me and I live with you
> Please, dear, be my posslq.
>
> —Charles Osgood, CBS Radio, 1982

A relationship is a fine place to sleep
But you wouldn't want to live there.
      —Elie (Kevin Pollak) The Opposite
      Sex and How to Live with Them, *1993*

She clung about his neck, gave
him ten kisses.
Toyed with his locks, looked
babies in his eyes.
  —*Thomas Heywood,* Love's Maistresse,
  1633

You've Got to Be Kidding

Sex with each other leaves nothing—save children—to be desired. The man and woman involved **look babies in one another's eyes** (17thC, "seeing cupids therein"), but they prefer not to think of it as **the work of increase** (18th–19thC). **The divine work of fatherhood** (Walt Whitman) is totally inconceivable to them. Rather than **making faces** (mid 18th–early 19thC) or **making feet for children's shoes** (late 18th–mid 19thC), he's getting cold feet and making steps.

> But don't forget folks
> That's what you get, folks,
> For makin' whoopee!
>
> —Kahn and Donaldson
> "Makin' Whoopee," 1928

Lady's Choice

Sometimes in the heat of passion, the little head
tells the big head what to do and the big head
should think twice about it.
  — *Lorenzo (Robert De Niro),* A Bronx
  Tale, *1993*

See the problem is that God gave men a brain
and a penis, and only enough blood to run one at
a time.
  —*Robin Williams*

There are steps, however, that he can take—by donning a **contraceptive** or an **anticonceptive** (early 20thC, they're both "against" **conception**). Most times, however, he'll hop right on, **riding bareback** (19thC) **without a saddle** (20thC, U.S. black usage for **sex** without a **condom**).

Fearful that she's the one riding for a fall, the woman has traditionally taken such matters on herself. In ancient Egypt, they used pulverized crocodile dung combined with honey and sodium carbonate; since then they've tried a variety of other herbs and other nostrums.

Catholics, as everyone knows, have **rhythm** (20thC)...and blues. The results notwithstanding, some still consider it an interesting gamble, a game of **Vatican roulette** (20thC), but with ten out of every hundred women who play ending up **you-know-how**, it appears that all bets are off.

It was left to Margaret Sanger, founder of **Planned Parenthood** (c. 1920), to take the chance out of it, but it wasn't easy to find the right name for it. She tried everything from **Malthusianism** (from Reverend Thomas Malthus, who believed that unless restraints were shown, population would soon outstrip subsistence), to **conscious generation, voluntary motherhood**, and **prevenception**. She and her colleagues finally narrowed the choices down to **race control** and **birth-rate control**. After much heated discussion they agreed on the latter. It was only after a sharp drop in the rate of conversation that we were left with just **birth control**.

When you said **birth control** to most women of the 1920s and '30s it meant the **diaphragm** (c. 1880, *dia*, "through"; *phragm*, "fence") and **cervical caps**, known as either **Dutch caps** or

Malthus caps (late 19th–early 20thC). Some paid their respects to the **diaphragm** as a **womb veil**; while those pitching woo used it as a **catcher's mitt** (1950s), without which no ballgame could be properly played. More recently, they've been **ladies' saucers**, a metaphor reinforced by an old *Realist* cartoon which identified flying saucers as **diaphragms** dropped by nuns on their ascent to heaven.[1]

The **diaphragm** was followed by the **intrauterine device**, invented in the '20s, but not perfected until the '60s. By 1966 it had already been reduced to an **IUD** to help some inarticulate S.O.B. deal with a potential IOU. The **IUD**, however, proved as fleeting as its nickname, the **pussy butterfly** (1950s). Its successor, the **birth-control pill**, was introduced in the late '50s and in five years realized such popularity that it came to be simply called **The Pill**, and everyone—well almost everyone—knew which pill it was.[2]

The Pill no longer has a monopoly. In 1982, a French pharmaceutical house announced another pill, one which would end pregnancy if taken within seven weeks of conception. It was finally approved by the FDA for sale in United States in 2000. No comforting brand name here; rather a bit of cold science-fiction and a name with which all could identify—**RU-486**. More comforting and more easily remembered is **the morning-after pill**, an emergency **contraceptive** to be taken within 72 hours of unprotected sex to prevent pregnancy. No problem of women forgetting to take this pill, however; few even know of its existence, and those who do are denied unhampered access to it. For anti-abortionists, it's simply too bitter a pill to swallow.

Sins of Emission

Disappointed in the options? Hold everything! There's still **coitus reservatus**.[3] The prophet Mohammed never **ejaculated**, believing that reversal of the flow of **semen** (c. 1398) back into his bloodstream could invigorate his mental powers and "prepare his sensitive brain and nervous system for self-hypnosis and extrasensory perception."

Another major personage who chose not to share with others was Sylvester Graham (1794–1851), a noted health advocate whose major claim to fame lay in promoting the value of whole wheat and the cracker which was named for him.

Graham's research revealed that loss of an ounce of **semen** was equivalent to a loss of several ounces of blood. Every time a man **came** he reduced his life expectancy. The only solution lay in men adopting restraint and self-discipline, rather than wasting their lives away.

No chupa, no shtupa.
No wedding, no bedding.
(Lit., "no marriage canopy, no pushing, or fucking")
　　　　—*Yiddish proverb*

Graham found a large and receptive audience for his ideas. His books (mid 19thC) were translated into several languages and went through dozens of printings. But today Graham's ideas are mocked, and the entire world knows him simply as crackers.

Gimme a Break!

Even with all the precautions, accidents still happen. Our woman friend fell for him in a big way. In what proved an unfortunate twist of fate, she not only **sprained her ankle** (18thC for having been seduced) but **broke her knees** (19th–20thC). The French used to say, "**Elle a mal aux genoux**": "She has sick knees").

"Break a leg!" may be good luck in the theater, but no such luck in this instance. In eighteenth-century England gossip had it that "**She hath broken her leg above the knee**" (Beaumont and Fletcher, Cibber, Grose). For a young lady to **break her knees** or **leg** (c. 1670) meant not only **seduction** and **defloration** but, worse yet, **pregnancy**.

English women still occasionally say, "I **fell**" for "I'm **pregnant**," and there are still parts of the United States where a **broken ankle** announces the blessed event as well as an **abortion**. Either way, it's a fractured romance.

Knock, Knock

That's what happens when you take a **leap in the dark** (18th–20thC)—you get **knocked up** (19th–20thC, from 16th–17thC **knock** for **copulation**, as in **knocking shop and knocking house**, all from **nock** for the **cunt**). In England, it's better they "knock you up" early in the morning, "waking you to help you start your day," than you be caught **knapping** (c. 1820–90). Caught with your guard down, he **boomed the census** (20thC), and you've been **storked** (early 20thC). No laughing matter this. He may have been **kidding** (19th–20thC), but the joke's on you.

Ova Bearing Personalities

When the situation arises, it's best you not make **light** (14thC, **lewd** or **wanton**) of it. For some it hits a particularly sensitive nerve. Witness the seventeenth-century father who cried out, "My faire daughter was **hit on the master vaine** and **gotten with child**" (late 16th–17thC). Any such remarks were sure to leave both father and daughter with an **inside worry** (17thC).

Say what you like but don't say **pregnant** (c. 1545). We've been uncomfortable with the word for several hundred years. As Johnny Carson reminded us, as late as 1964 you still couldn't say it on TV.

Beware what a moment of passion can bring
The girl has a baby, the boy has a fling.
—Anon., 20thC

I have no children myself; but my wife has four, besides one in the basket and two in the grave.
—Captain Bee, 1823

Now that she's **with child**, everyone speaks of **her delicate state of health** (Dickens, c. 1850) or being in a **way** or **condition** described as **certain, delicate,** or **family**; at the very least, it's **interesting** (19thC). When in a **familiar way** (c. 1891), everyone knows she'd **done naughty things, done a lap-clap** (mid 17th–18thC: "got **pregnant**") and been **playing tricks** (20thC). It is, after all, rather **obvious** (c. 1897–1914), she being **awkward** (19th–20thC), **bumpy, lumpy** (c. 1810–1910), **high-bellied** (c. 1850), and **apron up** (19th–20thC). In the best of circumstances, she's a **lady in waiting**, clearly **expecting** (c. 1870) and **infanticipating**. No need to get hot over it, she's fully **heir-conditioned** (c. 1940s).

Rounding Out the Picture

Big as a barn? Consider her **clucky** (c. 1942, Aust.), **in pup** (c. 1860), or **in pig** (c. 1870). Many women, however, didn't particularly like being described this way. Neither did they want to be considered **up the stick** (c. 1920) or suffering from an **ITA**, an **Irish toothache** (c. 1909).

Hoping to lend their state a touch of class, they borrowed "**Je suis enceinte**" from the French. The phrase became extremely popular in the States during the early part of the twentieth century and during the eighties enjoyed a revival among the suburban set. Try as they might, however, there was no escaping the bestial nature of the act. According to Mencken, **enceinte** was also used during the 1920s by Iowa pig farmers, often as **insented**, to describe the condition of their sows. So much for classy foreign expressions.

Enceinte itself derives from the Latin "to gird," and once described the works surrounding a fortified palace. **Pregnant** ladies also once surrounded themselves with a special scent making them **fragrant** (early 20thC). But for that air of finality, most preferred being **gone** (mid 19th–20thC) as in "She's six months **gone**." It was difficult, however, to accept her as **gone**, when she was right there in front of you. And where would she go anyway given the circumstances?

For many, her departure was seen as a matter of sweet justice, a woman's just desserts, often described as **a bellyful of marrow pudding**, qualifying her for **membership in the pudden** or **pudding club** (19th–20thC). Since Restoration days, **pudding** has played a triple role: as **semen virile**, a **penis** (from the **pudden**, a shortened version of the **pudendum**), and as **the act** itself. **Hasty pudding** is an eighteenth-century English term for an **illegitimate child** (c. 1673), settling once and for all the speculation as to the origin of the famous Harvard University club of the same name, or as one "Lampoon" member put it, "We've always known what **bastards** they were."

Babes 'n' Arms

"Son-of-a-gun!" Truly an appropriate comment made by a man discovering he is about to become a father. It fits especially well when speaking of a **bastard** sired by a soldier, though folk etymology provides us with an even more colorful origin.

In nineteenth-century England, it was customary for women to accompany ships' crews on long voyages, providing sorely needed female companionship to help wile away those lonely hours at sea. But, unfortunately, with the inevitable **slip-ups** also came children **born out of wedlock**. Naval vessels were ill prepared for the event, and ships' surgeons often had to improvise when delivering a baby. To insure the requisite privacy, they frequently selected the closed section of the gun deck to perform the operation. As a result, the child literally came into this world "under the gun." Being of uncertain paternity, such a child, when later asked about his father, would simply point to the nearest stationary object, thus making himself into a son-of-a-gun. It's a neat and perfectly logical explanation, though some felt the language misfired by failing to take into account the birth of a daughter.

It serves me right for putting all my eggs in one bastard.

—Dorothy Parker, on going for an abortion

Taking Issue

Remember the woman who was so many months **gone**? Well, apparently she **made a trip** (c. 1823)—for no legitimate reason.

It was really no big deal—only an **incident** (c. 1909), a **by-blow** (late 16th–20thC), but *voilà!* a **love child** (19thC) or **chance child** (c. 1838), **the product of their union, thus merry-begotten** (Grose).

We're not positive about his origins. Most believe he was **born on the wrong side of the blanket** (18th–19thC) or that he simply **came through the side door** (c. 1860). Closer examination, however, shows these to be popular misconceptions. The **bantling** (17thC) began life on the German *bank*, for "bench," while the poor **bastard** (c. 1327) originated with the *bast*, a pack saddle used by mule drivers as a bed on which many an **illegitimate child** (c. 1673) was spawned.

He that get a wench with child and marry her afterwards is as if a man should shit in his hat and then clap it on his head.

—Samuel Pepys, Diary, 1663

Pledging Allegiance

Of one thing you can be sure: the **son-of-a-gun** could easily have been a **misfortune** (19th–20thC). The father, having given her a **green gown** (18thC a **turn in the grass**, referring to the stains), could have left her a **grass widow** (16th–early 19thC), burdened with a **bachelor's baby** (mid 19th–20thC). Fortunately, according to Tobias Smollet, he considered it a **pledge** ("In a few hours, a living **pledge** of my love and indiscretion saw the light"—*The Adventures of Peregrine Pickle*, 1751).

There's talk of force and a **shotgun wedding** (19th–20thC). No idle threat, it's a matter of wife or death. He chooses wisely, **making an honest woman of her** (c. 1506, "proposes marriage to one in such a condition"), to which she enthusiastically responds, "This is so sudden!" (c. 1920).

From Bed to Worse

Marriage often spells the end of **sex** as we know it. It's a time when relationships cease being **meaningful**. But folks do adapt and manage to **carry on** (20thC). These arrangements are now called **extramarital** or **co-marital**. Many make light of them, reducing them to a mere **fling** (a "**penile** thrust," early 16thC; a "brief **relationship**," 19th–20thC), ignoring their complex nature. Such arrangements, however, are anything but simple. An **entanglement** (20thC) often foreshadows dire consequences—an **intrigue**, or a **liaison** (two CIA agents **getting it on** in a telephone booth?). It can also, however, be highly instructive as **extracurricular activities** (mid 20thC).

A Place in the Sun

Much work has gone into making **amours** delicate and discreet, but only with limited success. They were considered innocent and open dalliances during medieval times, but once they added a sexual dimension, around the seventeenth century, they became secret and illicit. They soon lost their innocence and fell from grace, ending up somewhere outside the bounds of propriety and on the other side of good taste. The **amourette** (19thC) was of so trivial a nature as to pass quickly in the night. But the **tryst** (14thC), though it started life as a simple appointment, ended up with its people **getting involved** (mid 20thC). It's now a heavy word conveying images of clandestine meetings in dark alleyways and cheap motels. Two people having a **tryst** sounds like something requiring immediate medical attention.

Mind Your Affairs

With **sex** on its way out it's definitely time we got our **affairs** in order. It's important, though, to distinguish between **affaires d'amour** (those primarily sexual), **affaires de coeur** (those primarily of the heart), and ordinary **affairs** (late 16thC, "the female genitalia"). Current **affairs** fall somewhere between the **one-night stand** and the **relationship**. We also have foreign affairs, in

"What has she got that I haven't?"
"Nothing at all, my dear, but it was available."
　　　　　—*Anon., c. 1930s*

which nations give it to one another, and social affairs such as weddings, bar mitzvahs, and showers. Thinking of throwing an affair? For an affair to remember, it should be catered. Anything less would be considered gauche. "Excuse me, Miss, would you please pass the **peccadillos?**"

That Was No Lady

The first **affair** occurred when man discovered the wifely function was to raise a family and administer the household, but for pure pleasure and excitement he had to look elsewhere.

The Old Testament sanctioned such activity with the **concubine** (from the Latin *concubitus*, "lying together"), who was to serve as a man's **consort** on a regular and exclusive basis. Man later broke the monogamy with his **mistress**,[4] **inamorata**, or **paramour** (14thC, originally two words, *par* and *amour*, hence "being in love through or by sexual love"), though there was a time when it described spiritual love, as in the medieval poem where Mary spoke of Jesus as "myne own dere sonne and **paramour**." On a less lofty plane, she became his **sparerib**, **side dish**, **tackle** (17thC), and **flame**.

Verbally, she always did far better than the wife. The wife was relegated to a **conveniency** (17th–19thC), an **ordinary** (17th–20thC), a **comfortable** (17th–20thC), and, at times, an **impudence** (17th–20thC). It was conceded on occasion that she was a **necessary**, but that term, along with a **convenience**, also referred to a **water closet**, putting her in somewhat less than distinguished company. The **mistress**, though at times deemed **peculiar** (17th–19thC), has always been his **natural** and his pure (both 17th–19thC) and—when counted among the very best—his **purest pure** (17thC).

But it's been downhill ever since. When man started playing for keeps, she became a **kept woman** (18th–20thC) and he, her **keeper**, leaving us with images of a caged female held at bay with chair and whip. Her glory faded further with the appellation, a **wife in watercolors** (c. 1780–1840), "like their enjoyments, easily effaced or dissolved." Her slide continued as the **brazen hussy**, finally hitting rock bottom in the twentieth century as **the other woman** and **a little on the side**.

Faithfully Yours

Conjugal infidelity is not a subject you casually **fool around with** (mid 20thC). To be caught **cheating** (20thC) is unspeakable and a topic of **criminal conversation** (19thC). Some even dare

call it **treason** (17thC), **fleshly treason**, or **smock treason**.

Most adults prefer practicing **adultery**, but even with practice it's still hardly adult behavior—in fact, it's not even adolescent. "Adult" and "adolescent" both derive from the Latin *ad* and *alere*, "to nourish or raise toward maturity." **Adultery**, on the other hand, comes from *ad* and *alterare*, "to change into something else," as to corrupt another, or from *ad* and *alterum*, "to turn to another."

Currently, **adultery** itself has been badly corrupted. It began when Mencken dubbed it "democracy applied to love," culminating in today's **swingers** and what some call **open marriage** (c. 1970s).[5]

So too with the word **adult**. We label more and more of our contemporary activities **adult**, though they have become increasing puerile. It's enough to drive one to **an adult-entertainment zone** for some **adult reading matter**.

The Horse of Another Color

The impulse for such activity often occurs around middle age, a time for prancing about and indulging in fantasies of playing the **stud**, aka the **stallion**.

It's the colt, in particular, a horse four years old or under known for its frisky nature, with whom most males identify. They especially enjoy **showing their colt's tooth** (late 14th–19thC), "imagining they have a notion to taste a fancy bit which as often turns out mere vanity and vexation of spirit." So too with the female of the species. **Having a colt's tooth in her head** "is also said of a woman of years who retains the **lechery** of youth" (Bee). Some think it best we put them both out to pasture.

Sugar 'n' Spice

The **colt's tooth** in the male was a sweet tooth, one favoring **sugar** and **sweet brown sugar** (c. 1930, U.S. black), "any attractive young black woman, a **bit of jam** (c. 1850), "any pretty and **accessible** female," or a some **jelly**, "a **buxom**, good-looking girl"—named perhaps for the manner in which she shook.

To have a bit of jam (c. 1897) was to partake of the sweets of sexual pleasure. **Jam** by itself served both as the female **pudenda** and as a sweetheart or a **mistress**; a broadside ballad once having proclaimed, "He made this young girl feel queer when he called me his **jam**, his **pet**, and his **lamb**" (c. 1880). **Real raspberry jam** (c. 1883–1915) was that of exceptional quality and **elderly jam** (c. 1880–1915), stuff long past its prime.

When we were boys the world was good
But that is long ago;
Now all the wisest folks are lewd,
for adultery's the go
The go, the go,
Adultery's the go.
—Victorian ditty

"Thou play'st the stallion every where thou comest....No man's bed's secure, no woman's unattempted by thee.
—George Chapman, All Fooles, 1605

Showtime

Alas, he's also past his prime, but doesn't know it. Still struggling to awaken memories of past glory, he awards himself a memento of previous competition. Placed not a shelf or in a display case, but about his arm, it accompanies him wherever he goes. It is called a **trophy wife**.[6]

He suffers now from the **Jennifer syndrome** (both 1990s)—a disorder in which the aging male displays his virility primarily through displays of macho acquisitiveness, assisted by the **trophy wife**, egging him on to new visions of material grandeur.

The Meanest Cut

Long described as "suffering from bed and boredom," wives also look outside for romance. It's easy enough to **take a slice** (mid 18th–mid 19thC), it being unlikely that anyone would ever miss a piece from an already cut loaf. As Shakespeare said,

> Easy it is of a cut loaf
> to steal a shive, we know.
>
> —*Titus Andronicus*

Just make sure, however, that you don't get caught **in flagrante delicto** ("in the act," Latin, "while the crime is blazing") with **your rem in her re** (c. 1860, "a thing in a thing"); that could prove nasty, no matter how you cut it.

Birds of a Feather

The mere thought of wifely infidelity was enough to drive a husband cuckoo. The cuckoo is a bird noted for laying its eggs in the nests of other birds. Dr. Johnson tells us that townspeople used to alert an unsuspecting husband to the presence of an **adulterer** by calling "cuckoo" after him. Over time, the cry became identified with the husband instead. He was now said to be **cuckolded** or to have been **made a cuckold of** (13th–20thC). To **cuckold the parson** (late 18th–late 19thC) was to put one over on the local minister, i.e., to "sleep with your wife before she is" (Grose). **Sharing a mistress** was an activity considered somewhat less cuckoo, the partners being known as **brothers starling** (17th–19thC) for having built in the same nest.

Horns of the Dilemma

Once she flew the nest, the wife was free to express her previously suppressed **horniness**. She was now **selling horns** (17th–mid 19thC); the husband was **wearing them**, leaving him

horned or **hornified** (17th–18thC)—expressions which originated with stags in the rutting season who, when they lost a female in a contest to another, also lost the respect and association of their colleagues. People further certified this condition by making a **V**, the sign of the horn, at him, with the first and second fingers forked out.

It was hardly the proudest moment in a man's life. **Giving or getting a bull's feather** (17th–19thC—Fr., *planter des plumes de boeuf*) was considered anything but a feather in his cap.

It's somewhat curious, though, that given such a surfeit of old terms to describe the injured husband, we have no contemporary expressions to draw upon.

And fear of horne more
grief of heart hath bred
Than wearing horns hath
caused an aching head.
*   —Song, "Good Susan be as*
*   Secret as You Can," 17thC*

Barking Up the Wrong Tree

Men have always vacillated on the subject of the **unfaithful** wife. The definitive stand on the subject was taken by King Boleslaw II of Poland during his war with Russia. Concerned about the rapidly increasing incidence of **infidelity** on the home front and its impact upon troop morale, he introduced some rather unusual measures. Boleslaw legislated that children born of such **trysts** be taken to the woods and allowed to die and the offending women be obligated to nurse puppies in their stead. The women were further required to take these dogs wherever they went, often appearing publicly with them on their laps. Boleslaw, however, would have been surprised at the results of his edict. The practice proved so commonplace and ultimately so popular that it also became quite fashionable, giving birth to the notion of the lap dog.

Try and Try Again

With **adultery**'s work completed, there's little left to do. The torrent of sexual activity is reduced to a dribble. Man now **sleeps like a cow,** "with a **cunt** at his **arse.**"

'Tis only reality—not **sex**—which now rears its ugly head. He's all mixed up, as are his metaphors. How can we put it? **Dominie-do-little** (mid 18th–early 19thC), there's **no money in his purse** (19th–20thC), **no toothpaste in the tube** (1990s), and **the flute has fallen silent** (18th–19thC). He looks to be **impotent** (literally "powerless"), what one seventeenth-century punster called **impudent**—and he's that too. Some thought him a **nincompoop** of sorts, an interesting composite of **no income pooping, poop** (17th–18thC.) being an old term for to **copulate,** as in the seventeenth-century expression, "I saw them close together at **poop-noddy.**" With luck it'll prove only a simple **genital dysfunction** (c. 1980s) set right by a visit to his friendly neighborhood **sex-surrogate** (c. 1980s).

His rod and its butting head
Limp as a worm.
His spirit that has fled
Blind as a worm.
*   —William Butler Yeats,*
*   The Chambermaid's Second Song,*
*   early 20thC*

Twenty to thirty, night and morning
Thirty to forty, night or morning
Forty to fifty, now and then
Fifty to sixty, God knows when.
*   —Anon.*

Stand by Me

On Viagra was old man Muldoon
When he went on his third honeymoon
　Morning coffee was brewin'
　When he started in screwin'
And he finished at twelve o'clock noon
　　　　— Anon., 2001

That didn't do it. Nothing, in fact, seems to help. The situation only worsens, but he's not alone. He is yet another victim of the national epidemic known as **erectile dysfunction,** or **ED** (c.1991). This coincided with the advent of a magic potion whose very name conjured up vigor—the imagery of the power, flow, and grandeur of Niagara Falls—promising to unleash a veritable torrent of desire.[7]

Alas, for most, the fireworks never materialize, for even the smallest sparkler first needs to be lit.[8] For others, it sparks some introspection, causing the more thoughtful to wonder what it's really all about—for which it deserves its title, "wonder drug."

No need to despair, however. Hope always springs eternal.

　　Here lies John Penis
　　Buried in the Mount of Venus;
　　He died in tranquil faith
　　That having vanquished death
　　He shall rise up again
　　And in Joy's Kingdom reign.

　　　　　　—Count Geoffry Potocki de Montalk,
　　　　　　"Here Lies John Penis," 1932

Tips of the Tongue

1. Another drop occurred in 1993 when the so-called "female **condom**," marketed under the name "Reality," won approval from the FDA. Women, however, proved to be out of touch with it, rejecting the device as an alternative to regular male **condoms**. Not so the **gay** community. Though the FDA refused to allow its testing for **anal intercourse** because **sodomy** was illegal in some states, rebellious **gay** men experimented with it during **buttsex**. No big deal; it was only a Reality check of sorts.

2. Referring to it as **The pill** generically has occasionally been confusing. Prince Charles once inquired of a young lady traveling with him on the royal yacht if she had taken her pill. She blushed and stammered, "No...not really." It was simply an innocent mistake. All the Prince was concerned with was her Dramamine. She apparently had another form of C sickness in mind.

3. **Coitus Reservatus** was only one of the three Roman generals standing guard against **pregnancy**; the other two were **Coitus Obstructus**, and **Coitus Interruptus**.

4. **Mistress** has been a title of respect since the fourteenth century and also an honorable term for a sweetheart or lover. She's made a lasting contribution to the language as the source of both "Miss" and "Mrs." "Miss" is her first syllable, and "Mrs." a contraction of the word ("mis'ess"). According to Pope, it was common during the reign of George II to refer to a single lady as Mrs. so and so. "Mrs." as a married label came only much later. The **Miss** became most closely identified with a **paramour** during the seventeenth century, as when speaking of Charles II's **Misses**. Since that time, whenever we speak of a **mistress** we also think of her in those terms.

    "Ms.," of course, our most recent invention, was a product of the women's liberation movement of the seventies, which sought to break with past practice. The first issue of *Ms. Magazine* in 1972 stated that the term Ms. "is being adopted as a standard form of address by women who want to be recognized as individuals, rather than being identified by their relationship with a man."

5. Looking for a new angle on infidelity? Just brush up on your plane geometry. Where we once had only a **love triangle** (early–mid 20thC), we now have the ever-widening **circle of love** (Helen Gurley-Brown)—transforming all its critics into squares. "I love my wife, but oh Euclid!"

6. The **trophy wife** is formally defined as, "a stunning second wife, twenty years younger than her predecessor, who has

exchanged a modeling career for that of teaching her new charge how to dress, where to eat, which proper charities to favor, and the fine points of holding a backyard party for 300." (David Olive, *Business Babble, 1990*)

7. The truth is that the name **viagra** was not the product of any such linguistic imagination. Slidenafil citrate is a chemical compound originally created for treating heart problems. There being nothing closer to a man's heart than his **penis**, it invariably proved successful in increasing the bloodflow therein. When they were ready to bring it to market, the name was chosen not for what it was, but for what it wasn't. According to the team leader at Pfizer, "It had to be simple, easy to pronounce, and have no special or unusual meaning in any foreign language." It was not to be an English word nor one which might cause any confusion or embarrassment. To insure this it went through a series of linguistic, legal, and trademark screens. The name has nothing whatsoever to do with either "vigor" or "Niagara." According to members of the team, the primary reason for selecting **viagra**, was because it was innocuous.

8. One man saw fireworks, but wasn't pleased by them. Joseph A. Moran, a car dealer from Camden, New Jersey, sued Pfizer for 110 million dollars for having crashed his car into two parked cars after taking **Viagra**, alleging "It caused me to see blue lightening coming from my finger tips, at which point I blacked out."

The Last Word

s this the end? Is **sex** dead? **Necrophiliacs** argue that it is. The rest of us are hardly prepared to agree. "Not over my dead body!" we say. There is, however, a consensus that **sex** is a deadly serious business. As W.C. Fields reminded us," Sex isn't necessary. You don't die without it, but you can die having it."

Most favor the **mort douce** ("sweet death"), also known as **dying in the saddle** or **with one's boots on**. It has claimed many a prominent figure, who found it quite a way to go. When the producers of TV's "Hill Street Blues" had to explain the death of Sergeant Esterhause (1983–84, coinciding with the real death of actor Michael Conrad) they had him die in the arms of his **paramour**. Others allegedly exiting in this fashion included a former Vice President of the United States and a French Archbishop locked in a **conjugal embrace** in a **house of ill repute**. Speaking of his father's death under similar circumstances, comedian Richard Pryor noted how "he **came** and went at the same time."

However, it also happens under more traditional circumstances. Death has frequently been used as a metaphor to describe the **sexual spasm**. As Benedick promised Beatrice (in *Much Ado About Nothing*), "I will live in thy heart, **die** in thy **lap** and be buried in thy eyes." But no need to mourn. Samuel Butler reminded us, "O 'tis a happy and heav'nly death when a man **dy's** above and a woman beneath" ("From Love," mid 17thC).

Never Say Die

Others also consider **sex** a dying activity. The scientific news magazine, *Discover*, in a 1984 article entitled, "Why **Sex**?" discovered that **sex** is an inefficient way for an organism to reproduce itself. For the first time in recent memory, **sex** faces tough competition from an alternative lifestyle. The word is out about "the new **celibacy**" (from the Latin *caelebs*, "unmarried," which originally referred to a state of living alone and only later to **sexual abstinence** and

Take your course, use your force
Kill me, Kill me, if you please;
Nay. I'll die willingly
In this sweet death, I find such ease.
    —Anon., Roxburghe Ballads, *1871*

I will die bravely like a smug bridegroom.
    —*Shakespeare,* King Lear

renunciation of marriage), a practice which has recently generated a small but loyal following.

The Catholic Encyclopedia defines **celibacy** as "the renunciation of marriage …for the more perfect observance of **chastity**," which is really the end game here. If you want to do it right, just cut to the **chaste** (from the Latin *casta*, "morally pure"). Germaine Greer, who campaigned for female equality and sexual freedom in the 1970s, later came out in favor of **chastity**, and recent surveys show jogging to be a more popular form of recreation than **sex**.

Though **sex** appears to be in a decline, let us not be too hasty in writing it off. Reports of its demise may well be premature. Agreed, it's no longer in the full flush of youth, but neither is it ready for interment. Perhaps it's best we think of it as being in the intensive-care unit. And desperately in need of your support.

But **if you can't say it, you can't do it** (mid 20thC teenage aphorism). And that could be the death of us all. Now is the time for all good men (and women) to come to the aid of the life force. Isn't it time you also did your part and finally agreed to give a...

FUCK

We may eventually come to realize that chastity is no more a virtue than malnutrition.
—*Alex Comfort*

God grant me the strength to be chaste, just not yet.
—*St. Augustine*

HASTE AND WASTE:
THE BOOK OF THE TOILETTE

Yet More Words to the Wise

he U.S. Supreme Court first confronted the issue of indecent speech in the 1971 case of Cohen v. California. Paul Cohen was convicted and sentenced to 30 days in jail for wearing in a courthouse corridor a jacket which on its back said "FUCK THE DRAFT!" The court reversed Cohen's conviction, finding his speech protected by the First Amendment. Writing for the court, Justice Harlan noted that "One man's vulgarity is another man's lyric," suggesting that the First amendment protects not just the intellectual content of speech but the emotive content as well. In 1978, the Court refined its ruling further:

> WASHINGTON (UPI)—The Supreme Court Monday upheld, 5-4, a ban against airing seven "filthy" words when children might be listening. The broadcast industry called it "a harsh blow to freedom of expression of every person in this country." Justice John Paul Stevens' opinion rested on the unique characteristics of broadcasting: Society's right to protect children from "inappropriate speech" and the right of unwilling adults not to be assaulted with offensive speech. Justices Potter Stewart, William Brennan, Byron White and Thurgood Marshall dissented on the ground that Congress intended to prohibit obscene speech—not words deemed merely "indecent." The words involved were cocksucker, cunt, fuck, motherfucker, piss, shit, and tit. (July 3, 1978)

When people read the story of the Supreme Court decision in their newspapers, they found something missing—the words. Most editors apparently were terrified of putting them into print.

The *Portland* (Maine) *Press Herald* hit upon a somewhat ingenious compromise, offering to mail a list of the seven "dirty" words to anyone who requested them and enclosed a self-addressed envelope. After a story about the *Press Herald's* offer was carried by the Associated Press, about sixty requests were received at the paper, mostly from out-of-state residents from as far away as British Columbia and West Germany. The correspondents included such notables as the author of *Bawdy Language*. On September 7, 1978, *Rolling Stone* tried to put things into perspective:

> Maybe words really are as dangerous as sticks and stones, more dangerous than ideas, in fact, because the Supreme Court will fight like a motherfucker to protect our ideas; they just want to ban some of the words our ideas are made of.

That was more than twenty years ago. George Carlin immediately immortalized them as his famous seven words, and they have since caught on like never before. Today, the airwaves are awash with them, even when children might be listening. They're the staple of Sports talk radio, "shock-jocks," and certain high-profile personalities who, having little else to say, thrive on them.

Some even consider their use a patriotic duty and an affirmation of our democratic ideals. As noted by Adam Carolla in a conversation with Jon Stewart on the *Daily Show*, "If you can't say 'douche bag' (on the air) in the good ole U S of A, then the terrorists have won." The only thing holding them back is the force of political correctness. Joe King, a.k.a. Joe Queer, head of the punk group The Queers strenuously defended their song "Homo" against those who were offended by its title (though the song itself was highly sympathetic and supportive of **gays**).[1]

The FCC, for the most part, has adopted a policy of benign neglect. Fines have been levied ($7,000 an incident) but only on those stations which have crossed the line between indecent speech and that of an obscene nature, prosecuting those who do so "in a blatant appeal to prurient interest as defined by applying contemporary standards." Most times their other two criteria don't even come into play: that the material must depict or describe, in a patently offensive way, sexual conduct specifically defined by applicable law; and the material taken as a whole, must lack serious literary, artistic, political, or scientific value. Cable channels and the film industry continue to push the envelope even further. Alas, though the words now appear to be fully liberated, few know how to use them properly.

In polite society, however, they continue to be shunned. Fortunately, those currently engaged in the struggle against the onslaught of verbal filth can now turn for assistance to high technology in the form of "TV Guardian,"—the foul language filter that plugs directly into your TV, electronically (via a sophisticated

Teachers in Charlotte, North Carolina, are forbidden to say in class the words abortion, bisexual, gay, homosexual, lesbian, masturbation, orgasm, transsexual, and transvestite. Below grade 8, they are also forbidden to use the words birth control, condom and contraception. The theory behind these prohibitions seems to be that hearing these words will encourage students to have sexual intercourse, masturbate or to become homosexuals.

—Censorship News, Winter 1966, No. 4.

algorithm) intercepting more than 150 "objectionable" words and phrases, muting them totally or substituting profanity-free phrases in their stead in the closed caption text.[2]

What they hope most to exorcise are the **four-letter words**, a term that, according to Eric Partridge, originated in 1928 with the publication of *Lady Chatterley's Lover*, as well as with a parallel phrase, **the four-letter man**, a term of derision—a roundabout way of calling someone a **shit**. As a rule, **four-letter words** can contain more or less than four letters (one referred to in the Supreme Court decision contains twelve), but they invariably deal with the taboo topics of either **sex** or the toilet. *The Erotic Tongue* didn't give a **shit** about the latter. As a result, a large and colorful vocabulary was passed over.

Many consider these words truly obscene, "disgusting and foul," from the Latin *obs-*, "onto" and *c(a)enum*, "filth." These are the verbal outcasts, the untouchables, residing in the farthermost regions of bawdy language. But they cry out to be heard. They are not for everyone. They are certainly not for the squeamish or the faint of heart.

For the truly intrepid wordsmith, we now turn to "Haste and Waste, The Book of the Toilette." In the immortal words of other pioneers, "To seek out bold new adventures. To boldly go where no man has gone before." To ease the transition, we segue gently from *The Erotic Tongue*, beginning with sexual matters which also straddle the Toilette.

Tell me a word
that you've often heard
Yet it makes you squint
If you see it in print
—D.H. Lawrence

Detritus

1. In the words of Joe Queer himself, "To me it's like the same mentality of people who want to ban *Huckleberry Finn* and *Tom Sawyer* from school libraries. You have to consider the reasons why that language, specifically, is being used. I can understand how it could be uncomfortable to read words you don't like, but there's more to it than the words themselves. There's also the message that the person's trying to get across."

   So spoke this champion of free speech, whose band conveys such meaningful messages in classics such as "Ursula finally has tits," "I'm OK, You're Fucked," "I want Cunt," and "I Can't Stop Farting."

2. The manufacturers of device further inform us that one can choose between two different modes, one even filtering out exclamatory uses of the name of God, Jesus and Christ; the other allowing for God's name just in case you're watching a program with religious content. Examples of its overall effectiveness are included on its website (www.tvguardian.com):

Without TV Guardian	With TV Guardian
It's a !%& #!%n shame!	It's a shame!
Move your #&s!	Move your tail!
She's such a #%&#h!	She's such a nag!
That's b#%*!#%@#!	That's baloney!
Did you two have &#x?	Did you two have hugs?
J#%&s, you scared me!	You scared me!
#%!@ you, @&s#%!#!	Go away, jerk!
Oh, &#!t!	Oh, crud!

Ragtime

ot tonight dear. It's that **certain time**. How can I put it? I'm **ill**, **unwell**, **so**, **so-so**, (mid 19th–20thC), and **indisposed**. What's wrong? Why, I **fell off the roof today** (sometimes **out of a tree**). I'm suffering from the **domestic afflictions** (the **DAs**, 19th–20thC). If you're thinking about the **little house under the hill**, forget it! There'll be no **interior decorating** today; I'm **having the painter in** (early 20thC).

From the masculine perspective, the **gentlemen's pleasure garden is out of business**, **the gate is locked and the key is lost** (19thC). In case you still haven't gotten the message, there's **no roadmaking today**, **Leather-Lane and Main Avenue are in a state of no thoroughfare**, and the **road is up for repairs** (mid 19thC). Or as only men could put it, in their usual deft and subtle way, **her cherry is in sherry** (Swing musicians, 20thC), and her **snatch-box is decorated with roses** (US Navy, WWII). Computer geeks consider her **not user-friendly** (1990s).

A Moon for the Misbegotten

We're talking **menstruation** (c. 1382) here, a simple word meaning both "month" and "moon-change," the two being virtually synonymous. Americans once even spoke of **mooning** and **moontime** in that context . In France it's still **le moment de la lune**. Similar associations also exist in many non-western cultures. On the remote islands off the Northern tip of Australia, the natives believe that **menstruation** is caused by the moon, who came down to earth in the form of a man to seduce pubescent girls. In New Guinea, they refer to that time of month as **mun i killim**, "the moon of injury."[1]

The lunar cycle is the source of dozens of expression, one of the more obvious characteristics of **menstruation** being that it returns every thirty or so days.[2] In tribute to its punctuality, The French call the time, **les règles**, "the rules." This made for **the monthly**

"There is nothing funny about the menstrual period...these are not suitable topics."
— *Jackie Gleason (on Norman Lear's decision to treat the issue in* All in the Family*)*

Women complain about premenstrual syndrome, but I think of it as the only time of the month I can be myself.
— *Roseanne Barr*

215

Curses! Foiled again!
    —Anon

time, **the time**, **her time of month**, and **the monthlies**, variations of which appear in virtually every Western language, as in Belgium where it is **mijn maandstonden**, "my monthly moment."

Leave it to the Germans to make the most of their time, referring to it as **monatliche botshaft** ("monthly message"), **monatliche Blüte** ("monthly flower"), **monatlicher Zoll** ("monthly tax"), **monatliche Reinigung** ("monthly cleaning"), and **monatliche Blödigkeit** ("monthly stupidity").

I am Woman.

Especially stupid is the lack of words or phrases in our culture for the auspicious occasion when a girl becomes a woman. All we have is the sterile **menarche** (1895–1910, from the Greek *men*, "month," and *arché*, "beginning"). Worse yet is the question asked of young girls in Puerto Rico concerning the onset of the **menses: "Te cantó el gallo?"** ("Did the Rooster sing to you?"). Her coming of age is reduced to a signal of her availability. No one asks about the hen or how she experiences the moment. Her interests are secondary.

There are cultures, however, which honor the occasion. In Japan, they speak of **the cleavage of the melon**; in Ancient India, **the flower growing in the house of the Lord of love**. Anne Frank wrote in her diary of her coming of age, "I have the feeling that in spite of all the pain, unpleasantness, and nastiness, I have **a sweet secret**."

If men had periods, menstruation would be a sacrament.

    —Anon., 1990s

Say it with Flowers

Once it becomes a regular occurrence, flowers are always in order, long having been a standard euphemism for the condition. There are numerous references to it in the Old Testament. The French speak of **les fleurs**, the Indians, of **a time of flowers**. In 19th century America, women had **a case of the monthly flowers**. As noted in "Act One" of *The Erotic Tongue* ("Breaking Faith"), flowers fall from Persephone's apron when Hades seizes her and carries her away to the underworld, symbolizing not only defloration, but you-know-what else.

Though it's known for putting women through their changes, men like to think of those flowers as condolences for themselves, taking the most elementary and obvious aspect of womanhood and treating it as a personal nuisance. Perhaps it's time they also got into the flow of things.

The Old Menstrual Show

Most men see only red when it comes to the **menstruating** woman. In many pre-modern cultures, they segregated her from the normal flow of village activity, fearing she'd contaminate everything in sight. In contemporary society, women are still considered unreliable and unstable beings during **that time of month.**

Sex with a woman during that time (described as **three-quarter jazz time, one quarter ragtime** during the 1920s) has always been a definite no-no, a closed matter, **period** (early 19thC–20thC), end of discussion. The Old Testament warned, "If any man lie with her at all and her flower is upon him, he shall be unclean seven days." (Leviticus 15:24).

In some societies, such activity was considered sacrilegious, leading to the most devastating consequences—everything from vomiting, wasted flesh, soft bones, and discoloration of the skin to lost vital juices and **VD.** As a taboo activity, it's up there at the top.

Seed which are touched by her become sterile, grafts wither away, garden plants are parched up, and the fruit will fall from the tree beneath which she sits...a swarm of bees, if looked upon by her, will die immediately. Brass and iron will immediately become rusty. Dogs tasting the blood will go mad.
—Pliny

Scream Bloody Murder

Also taboo is matricide and patricide. In June of 1893, Lizzie Borden of Fall River, Massachusetts, was put on trial for the ax murder of her wealthy father and her stepmother. It was one of the most discussed events of the Gay Nineties and among the most notorious crimes in American history. The most damning piece of evidence against Lizzie was the bloodstain on her skirt. When asked to explain it, she answered, "**I have fleas,**" a weird euphemism of that time for **menstruation.** Rather than bugging her further, and knowing little of the heavy-duty monthly protection which was then the mode (precluding such leakage), the all male jury bought her explanation, acquitting her of the charges. Another school of thought attributes her acquittal to the jurors writing the murders off as a form of temporary insanity attributable to her condition (How those fleas do bite!). Contemporary students of the case remain convinced of her guilt, labeling her "America's **menstrual murderess.**"[3]

Lizzie Borden took an ax
And gave her mother forty whacks
When she saw what she had done,
She gave her father forty one!
—Doggerel of the time

That Grand Old Flag

Has man been properly warned? **Abso-bloody-lutely!** If he had been paying attention, he'd have seen that **the flag is up** (c.1850). Employed in rural areas, the flag lets you know that **there's a letter in the post office** (male-box, late 19thC). After all, how else would you know it's a **red-letter day?** In the Navy, when the **flag was flying**, it was **flying Baker** (B), a red flag used during target drills indicating a dangerous condition, such as ammunition being loaded. The message was clear, "Beware, keep off!"

In the Army they also made the connection, referring to the red flag on the firing line as **Maggie's Drawers.**[4] The women's armed services during WWII came up with their own: **I've got the rat, I'm Blood Mary today** (both WACS), and the **machine is kaput**

(Signal Corps). But even with all the warnings, there was always some sucker who would **mount the red flag** anyway. Intrepid sailors were said to **do a Moses** and **part the red C**, an act considered by many as a miracle of sorts.

With Friends Like That

Some men took it personally, treating the onset of the event as a hostile incursion. The French used to say, **Les Anglais sont débarqués** ("The English have landed"); Americans referred to **Paul Revere's ride** ("The British are coming!"), reviving memories of an old enemy clad in red-coats—"the damned **bloody** English!" Americans, always obsessed with subversion from the bottom, later identified the invaders as the **dirty reds**, noting how **the chick is communist!** (part of the Cold War rhetoric of 1940s and 50s), though the original **reds** describing the condition date as far back as the sixteenth century.

More benign visitors include both royalty and common folk: **Der rote König (The Red King**, 20thC) from Germany for whom we rolled out the **red carpet** (20thC) as well as **Jacques, François**, and **Martin** from France. In the United States, the **Captain was at home** (18th–19thC), unless of course, the lady of the house was **entertaining the General.**

More than likely, she was simply loaded down with a house full of relatives. Her favorite aunts and cousins are **paying a visit**, or **are** simply **here.** Aunts include **Sally, Tilly, Jane, Susie**, and **Ruby**, as in "red." In Canada, she receives a **visit from Aunt Flo from Red River**, the perfect double-entendre for the occasion. In Germany, **Tante Rosa kommt aus Amerika** ("Aunt Rose comes from America").

Cousins come from all over, often prefaced by **red-headed**, as in **my red-headed cousin from Virginia.** There's also plain old **cousin Tom**, an acronym for "Time of Month." Rounding out the household, we have: **my Grandma, the woman's home companion, my (little) (red-headed) friend** (19th–20thC)—all making for the ultimate in togetherness. When things get too crowded, women simply pack their bags and go elsewhere—to see **Sophia** or to **visit her relatives at Mont Rouge** ("Red Mountain").

You Know What You Can Do With 'Em

The accoutrements of the condition began as a simple **rag** (also **jamrag** and **being on the rag**, all 20thC). But modern chemistry wove its magic, transforming it into a **sanitary napkin** (20thC) and—God help us—a **sanitary towel** (19th–20thC). In a more colorful vein, it's been the **gentlemen's pleasure garden padlock**, a **window blind, a curtain** (all 19thC), and a **man-hole cover**

When does a missed period become a question mark?

—Adolescent Humor, 1950s

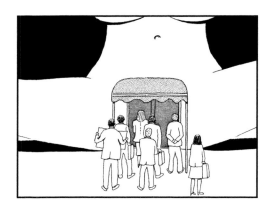

(20thC). Would you believe a **mickey-mouse mattress** (c. 1940s)?

In simpler times, in ancient Japan, women used about a dozen paper tampons collectively called **kama**, a "pony." It reappeared in that same form during the forties in this country when a woman **riding the rag** was also said to be **riding the white horse** or **the cotton pony**. Only later, did she step up to the **cotton bicycle**. Today's multitasking woman couldn't care less about her **menstrual cycle**, preferring a revved up Suzuki or four-on-the-floor.

And why not? There's little to worry about with so many options to pick from, manufacturers having always been quick to jump into the breach. It began big-time with **Kotex** (1921), the brand name that's now almost generic. Others quickly followed suit. Soon the menstruating woman could **cover the waterfront** (20thC) with a multitude of brands, including New Freedom, once the domestic political program of President Woodrow Wilson. She could ward off all advances with **Shields**, and size up the situation, using either **Minis** or **Maxis**.[5]

The 1930s saw the introduction of the **tampon**, a word derived from *tampion*, "a plug or stopper placed in the muzzle of a weapon." It proved a bang under such trade names as **Fax**, **Fibs**, and **Wix**, though **Tampax** (late 1930s) took the lead in name recognition.

The twenty-first century opened with a host of additional products: **Gladrags**, **Lunapads**, **Daisy Fresh**, and **Pandora Pads**, as well as new technology in the form of the **Instead Cup** and the **Keeper**—all of which anxiously await their moment to assume a more permanent place in the language. Women are happier than ever with their choices, business is booming, and everyone is bullish on the industry. A truly amazing phenomenon! How else can one describe it but as a rags-to-riches story?

Have you heard the one about the two vampires sitting around just chewing the rag?
—Teenage Humor, 1950s

BE COMFORTABLE

Detritus

1. As noted by the authors of *The Curse*, the definitive study on the topic, many poets have linked the blood and moon together, forging powerful and dramatic images.

    > It was night, and the rain fell; and falling it was not rain, but having fallen, it was blood. And I stood in the morass among the tall lilies, and the rain fell upon my head—and the lilies sighed one unto the other in the solemnity of their desolation. And all at once, the moon rose through the then ghastly mist, and was crimson in color.
    >
    > —Edgar Allan Poe (Untitled Prose Poem)

2. The association between moon and tides is there as well, with talk of **surfing the crimson tide** and being at **high tide** (Laurie Anderson, 1990s). There have even been isolated efforts at making **lunar** synonymous with that time. Perhaps it's now

appropriate to disassociate from our lunacy—"being driven mad by the phases of the moon," reclaiming moon phraseology once and for all as an all-purpose physical, emotional, and spiritual description.

3. Many consider the Borden verdict a **bloody** shame. **Bloody** was, after all, once a perfectly acceptable intensifier. It was "bloody hot" for Jonathan Swift while taking a walk in 1711, and Samuel Richardson felt "bloody passionate" in 1742.

    During Victorian times, however, the term became associated with the argot of the lower strata. As the social and economic gap between classes widened, so did the linguistic distance. There was no clearer marker of class membership than the word **bloody**, which, because of its association with the poor, was deemed thoroughly offensive.

    Today's Brit, however, is your **bloody** typical cell phone user, but the adjective's as mild as "damn" and "hell," with "ruddy" and "blooming" the preferred options. Even Prince Charles complained in 1969 how "English...is taught so **bloody** badly."

    The one exception to all this, of course, is the land down under, where **bloody** is still considered "the great Australian adjective" (see the poem of the same name by W.T. Goodge). There are lots of theories as to the word's origins. Some, of course, put the blame on **menstruation**, the "bloody flux." Others say that it's a possible reference to a "blood," an aristocratic young roisterer who was always **bloody** drunk.

    Some single out an old Irish word, *bloidhe*, meaning "rather," as its root. Others find its roots in an old term for dysentery.

    Could it be a slurring of "by our lady," an invocation of the Virgin Mary? Shakespeare himself used "by'rlady." Not **bloody** likely! It leaves unanswered how phonetically it made the transition to **bloody**. The OED opts for "S'blood!" an ancient oath shortened from "God's Blood."

    But it probably all boils down to the sight of blood itself being so vivid and distressing. The Germans had *blutig*, the Dutch *bloedig*, the French *sanglant*. At the risk of sounding overly sanguine, it's really all that **bloody** simple.

4. Artist Judy Chicago also raised the issue in 1971 with her painting, "The Red Flag," depicting a woman removing a **tampon**.

5. The origin of Kotex? An indignant woman suggested that the name is Polish for **pussy**. Research by the manufacturer, Kimberly Clark, however, revealed that the closest word in Polish is *kotek* or *kociak*, meaning "kitten." Its real roots are somewhat more innocuous, the product being likened by the manufacturer to Co (tten) + Tex (ture).

We're Number One

oing with the flow brings us to our very next topic—**pissing** (17thC). **Pissing** (17thC) derives from the French **pisser** via Old French and vulgar Latin. It was Standard English until around 1760, as in "He would not once turn one for a kisse. Every night he riseth for to **pisse**" (Hazlitt). About the same time it became a popular expression in the United States, a nation with few "pe-ons" and a highly energetic pioneer stock **full of piss and vinegar.**

Pissing has been received differently depending on the culture. It was anything but **number one** (nursery term, 19thC) to the followers of Mohammed, who were so repelled by it they chose to squat in the act rather than let a single drop fall on their person. The Hottentots, on the other hand, couldn't seem to get enough of it. The high point of their marriage ceremony came when the priest **urinated** (c. 1599) upon the bride and the groom.

Here in the West we are generally more **pissed off** than **pissed upon.** When you **piss people off**, you get them angry. President Lyndon Johnson was one who got **pissed off** frequently. But even he could be selective about it. Queried once as to the reason he retained the difficult J. Edgar Hoover as Director of the Federal Bureau of Investigation, he explained: "I'd much rather have that fellow inside my tent *pissing* out than outside my tent **pissing** in."

There have, however, been a few exceptions where **piss** has been welcome. In the seventeenth century we used **piss** as a facial cleanser and to remove birthmarks and freckles. Today, it's the critical ingredient in the kinky activity known as **water sports.**[1]

Though **pissing** is a universal phenomenon, not everyone can **piss** well. Some people are notoriously **piss-poor.** Clemenceau, the French Prime Minister during World War I, **pissed and moaned** about his prostate, lamenting enviously of Lloyd George, his British counterpart, "Ah, si je pouvais pisser comme il parle." ("If only I could **piss** like he can talk.")

When Nature is calling, plain speaking is out
When ladies, God bless 'em, are milling about,
You make water, wee-wee, or empty the glass;
You can powder your nose; "Excuse me" may pass;
Shake the dew off the lily; see a man 'bout a dog;
Or when everyone's soused, it's condensing the fog.
But be pleased to consider and remember just this—
That only in Shakespeare do characters piss!
  —"Ode to Those Four-Letter Words"

The Receiving End

For some, the problem is **not having a pot to piss in**, the ultimate impoverishment. The **piss-pot** (15thC) or **chamber-pot** (c. 1570) has long been the vessel on the receiving end, and was once an essential household item. Being without one often was sure to leave you up **shit creek**. The Scots heard the plea for assistance through the **rogue with one ear** (late 17th–early 18thC), offering up the **master can** (18thC).

To Kings and Queens we humbly bend the knee
But Queens themselves are forced to stoop to thee
—Anon., "Ode on a Chamberpot," 17thC.

Others graced the vessel with their name. Ending up on the bottom of the **po** (19thC), however, has often been more than just pot-luck. It's also been a political and social statement. There was **Oliver's Skull** (late 17th–early 19thC), so named by Royalists to whom Oliver Cromwell's name "fairly stank," as well as **Sacheverell**, after a British clerical foe of the Whigs "famous for blowing the coals of dissention."[2]

So too with the **Twiss**, after a Richard Twiss (1747–1821), who after making a tour of Ireland published some rather uncomplimentary remarks about the country. In retaliation, the Irish painted his portrait on the bottom of **chamber-pots**, together with the refrain, "Let everyone **piss** on lying Dick Twiss." Twiss was reportedly philosophical about the entire incident, letting things fall where they may.

Labeling the item thus was not without repercussions. In 1885, William Randolph Hearst was expelled from Harvard for sending each of his teachers a chamber-pot with their picture on the bottom, thereby ending his tenure as a student while launching his career in yellow journalism.[3]

Piddling Matters

The **chamber pot** was not alone in bailing us out of our predicament. The **urinal** has also played a major role since the thirteenth century, though originally intended to only receive specimens for medical examinations. Today it receives cigarette butts, gum wrappers, used **condoms**, and other assorted flotsam. The **urinal of the planets** was a seventeenth-century British nickname for Ireland, an allusion to the frequent rain there, as well as the regard with which it was held.[4]

There's no need to ever be **piss poor** with a **urinal** nearby. When you **piss on ice** (c.1950), you're living well, making you remarkably successful or happy. It derives from the chemical cakes resembling ice which lie in the **urinals**. Now everywhere, they were once restricted to only the most posh eating establishments.

The comfort of interior facilities not withstanding, real men prefer **pissing** outdoors, for which a wall is considered de rigueur. It was a practice, however, which The Old Testament looked on unfavorably: "Therefore behold I will bring evil upon the house of Jereboam him that **pisseth** against a wall." (I Kings, chapter 4).[5] Experience indicates yet further caution. **Pissing in the wind** is generally "a waste of time and effort," as futile as **a pisshole in the snow**; while **pissing up a storm** (all 20thC) is sure to "create a great fuss."[6] Few **pissed up a storm** more than comedian Lenny Bruce, whose fantasy was getting up at a giant Jehovah's Witness rally and crying out: " Is there one other sinner out there who has ever **pissed** in the sink?"

"Urology Department; could you please hold."
—Jocular phone response, 2001

Water, Water, Everywhere

Unlike **shit**, which has numerous associations with the animal world, **piss** has but a few. One of the rare literary allusions to it can be found in Shakespeare, when, in act 4 scene 1 of *The Tempest*, Trinculo the jester notes, "I do smell all **horse-piss**; at which my nose is in great indiscretion."

For more one has to go further down the animal ladder. A "pismire" is an ant whose name derives from the smell of **urine** associated with anthills and the formic acid therein. One of the earliest references to it can be found in "The Summoner's Tale" in Chaucer's *The Canterbury Tales*. It, in turn, begot the **pissant**, whose original meaning was also an "ant." Its previous association with the odor of **urine** then gave us its current meaning as "an insignificant wretch or thing of no value."

No matter how you shake or dance
The last few drops find your pants.
No matter how you jiggle and squeeze
The last drop dribbles down your knees.
—Anon., 1950s

There's certainly little value attached to being inebriated. When **thoroughly pissed**, you're quite drunk. In England, you can **be pissed as a coot, a rat**, or **a parrot**. The favorite by far among those frequenting a pub is being **pissed as a newt**. Raconteur Nigel Rees legitimately asks, "Why a newt?" British lexicographer Eric Partridge theorized that the original expression was "tight as a newt," simply because it had a pleasant sound to it. Not wanting to get into a **pissing contest**, a strenuous argument, with his old mentor, Rees gently dissented: "The great thing about newts is the characteristic they share with fishes **arse'oles**: they are watertight. And you can't get any tighter than that!"

Opening the Floodgates

When it comes to **pissing**, most folks are somewhat stand-offish. They seldom make it past the first letter, leaving most **p'ing** or **pee-ing**, a highly popular form of the act since the eighteenth century. Some say it twice for added emphasis, making **pee-pee (p.p.,** late 19thC), though once was enough in the late 1940s for the highly popular underground text, "The Yellow Stream, by I. P. Daley."

Others **piss** with great enthusiasm, working actively to become part of the larger mainstream. Little kids **make** or do **a wee-wee** or **a pee-pee** (late 19thC), **do a dickey-diddle** (20thC, Cockney), **a puddle**, or **make a sissy**—batteries not included.[6]

Men often view their body as a holy vessel, but when **piss** comes to shove, they've proven none too sturdy. They **leak** (c. 1590), **do** or **have a leak** (mid 19thC), and **take a leak** (20thC). Under the most adverse circumstances, they've **had a run-out** (20thC) and even have had to **pump ship** (18thC) so as to **pass water** (c. 1860). Waxing metaphoric, they like to say, "Ain't it **a (real) pisser!**" connoting either a very difficult task or a truly remarkable person or thing.

Making Waves

DOWN-RIGHT COCK.

No. 34

There are many ways to **piss**. You can be **pissy**, **pissy-ass**, or **piss elegant** (20thC), acting overly proud or pretentious or affecting refinement. The actual act of **pissing**, however, is pretty basic. There's nothing to it.[7] That's why we say **piss easy** (20thC.) to describe anything real simple to do. **Back teeth afloat?** (20thC)— just **let 'er flicker!** (19thC). Start by **shaking hands with an old friend** (c. 1880) or **with your wife's best friend** (WWII) or, in the army, **with the bloke who enlisted** (British, WWII). Terrified of **wringing the rattlesnake** (20thC) or **siphoning the python** (Australian, 20thC)? Why not simply **wring your sock out** instead?

For the ladies, it's a break from that everyday routine—**tea-time**. It's best perhaps that someone else pour; she has to **squeeze the lemon** (both late 19thC). M'lady's disappeared? Look to the garden. She's probably gone to **plant a sweet p(ea), pick a daisy, shake the dew off the lily**, or **water the old petunia** (all early 20thC).

It's not always as placid as that, however. **Going to the bathroom** can also be an adventure of sorts. During the latter nineteenth century she was faced with the rather daunting choice of **watering the dragon** or **shooting the lion**. The challenge has long since passed, but women still never go unaccompanied when **attending to their ablutions** (19thC).

Today, some females reach back to their nursery days to express their needs, preparing to **tinkle** (20thC), **piddle** (late 18thC–20thC), from the blend of **piss** and "puddle," and **whiz** (mid 20thC), as in "golly, gee!"

As you can see, there's been many a classy expression for **making water** (c. 1375), from the formal **urination** (14thC) and **micturition** (mid 19thC) to the functional **draining of one's radiator** (20thC) and the poetical **wringing the dew off the branch**. Few, however, put it more poignantly than the soldier in Brendan Behan's *The Hostage* who had to **shed a tear for Nelson**. Brush back the tears, lad! Granted he was a great naval hero; that's still no reason to be **p.o.'d** about his passing.

Detritus

1. The net currently overfloweth with **watersports**, featuring such stellar sites as peelover.com and goldenporn.com. Theurinearchives.com promotes itself as the most comprehensive, "including but not limited to pictures and movies of acts of desperation, panty, underwear clothing, and diaper wetting, **pee** and **piss** drinking, solo and group **urination**, **golden showers** and acts, medical and gyn fetishes, **pissing** orgies, hidden cameras, voyeur **pee**, indoor and outdoor **peeing**, infantilism, and **pee** containment."

   Precedents for this may be found in the Old Testament (Book of Isaiah, Chapter 36): "Hath he not sent me to the men that sit upon the wall, that they may eat the dung and drink their own piss with you?" Shakespeare later encouraged us with "Graze on my lips; and if those hills be dry/Stray lower, where the pleasant fountains lie."

2. Women were also the subject of **po** nomenclature. The Duchess of Fontange, Louis XIV's beautiful red-headed mistress, was best known for her magnificent hairpieces two or more feet high, adorned with bows, feathers, jewels, ribbons, and so forth, a style so closely associated with her it was given her name. But it proved such a nuisance that it was declared execrable in England, causing her name and reputation to go to pot.

3. We have long since moved beyond portraiture into what is now called **piss art**, a term coined by Christopher Chapman who in 1997 curated an exhibit on the topic in South Australia. Its foremost practitioners include Jackson Pollock and Andy Warhol. Pollock warmed to the mode by his frequent and public **urinating**, the most famous incident occurring when he **pissed** into Peggy Guggenheim's fireplace. Pollock's technique, dripping paint on to flat canvases, also invoked the idea of his painting being a metaphor for **pissing** and the **penis** as a tool to draw with.

   Warhol made his first **piss painting** in 1961 as homage to Pollock, and in the 1970s produced a group of "oxidation paintings," so called because they were created by **pissing** onto the canvasses prepared with copper paint, the resulting patterns being the effects of the oxidation. Warhol engaged his friends in the process, watching as young men **pissed** on them to create them. The story goes that their eligibility for participation required only that they drink a particular Mexican beer in order to provide the effect he most liked.

Since then we have also been graced by Annie Sprinkle's post-porn modernist performance art during which she **pisses** on stage and Robert Mapplethorpe's efforts which managed to successfully **piss off** both the N.EA. and a large segment of the U.S. Congress.

4.   **Urine** and **urinals** are less than popular words; while **urinalysis** (c.1885-90) conjures up images of thousands marching zombie-like about with paper cups in hand. *Urinetown,* however, is highly acclaimed Broadway musical, the recipient of rave reviews and many awards. The title of the work, though, was the subject of much soul searching prior to its adoption, the producers fearing more conservative theatergoers would be put off by it. They even tried to change the name prior to the musical's debut, but sponsors of the festival in which it was to appear refused. The rest is history. The show and the title both proved to be a real **pisser**, "something special." As one reviewer noted, "It was a kind of combination of a badge of honor and thumb in the eye." Or it could have been, as noted by the star of the show, that theatergoers took the title as a warm welcome to the Big Apple, hearing only "You're in Town,"

5.   This is further underscored in chapter 16: "He left him not one that **pisseth** against a wall, neither of his kinfolks, nor of his friends." Further admonitions may be found in chapter 21, as well as twice in the I Samuel.

6.   Such are the risks of **pissing** outdoors. Most men make light of it however. In some countries, in fact, it's taken for granted as described in a late nineteenth-century anecdote. The tourist asks of the gendarme, "Où peux-je aller pisser?" To which the policeman, with a gesture that takes in all 207,076 miles of that fair country, replies, ""Mais Monsier, vous avez toute Le France."

7.   It's all done through what is called the **pisshole**, a.k.a. the **urethra;** the **external opening of the urethra, the external urinary meatus, meatus uranarius, the pee-hole, pee-pee hole, pisser, urethral meatus, the urethral opening, the urethral orifice** and the **piss slit**—whether as a function of gender or professionalism of vocabulary.

Falling Behind

 -H-I-T. It is probably the most popular word in the English language and responsible for some of our most expressive sentiments. We've a **shit-load** of expressions that capture perfectly the nature of the human condition. Add a simple exclamation point and what better way to register disgust, disappointment, or frustration? It can mean very little—nothing, or the least quality as "This ain't worth **shit.**" or represent the very best, as in top quality street drugs: "This is some **good shit!**"

It's everywhere. You'll find it in the most exotic places—in your pants, alongside a shave, shower, shine, and shampoo, **on a stick,** and **in a handbag** (all 20thC). Most people are **full of it;** those who aren't simply act **shitty.** We start the day telling others, "I feel like **shit,**" eliciting the remark, "You do seem flushed." Dispassionate observers reinforce the sentiment, noting how **you look like shit** or **like ten pounds of shit in a five pound bag** (both 20thC). We pretend not to notice the resemblance.

Down and Dirty

We have **shit** for brains, and allow **shit-heads** with bogus credentials (BS—"**bullshit,**" MS—"more **shit,**" and PhD—"piled high and deep") to run our institutions. Such is society's fate. Individually, some **shit in high cotton,** enjoying prosperity, living high off the hog, "high cotton" being equated with wealth. The rest of the population, however, is simply **shit out of luck.**

But we're anything but grateful for it. We're repelled by its presence. We approach it cautiously, deal with it reluctantly, and treat it like—well—**shit.** We **kick, beat,** and **stomp the shit** out of people. We trivialize it as **diddlyshit,** which explains why it has traditionally been **number two** (19thC). As the Penguin (Danny De Vito) in *Batman Returns* (1992) reminisced about his parents who threw him in the sewers as a child, "I was their number one son, and they treated me like **number two.**"

When you speak of a movement, or sit on a seat,
Have a passage, or stool, or simple excrete;
Or say to the others, "I'm going out back,"
Then groan in pure joy in that smelly old shack.
You can go lay a cable, or do number two,
Or sit on the toidy and make a do-do,
But ladies and men who are socially fit,
Under no provocation will go take a shit!
　　—*"Ode to Those Four-Letter Words"*

Boys, I may not know much, but I do know the
difference between chicken shit and chicken salad.
　　—*Colonel Sanders*

227

Shit or **shite** has been around a long time—since the four-teenth century as a verb and the sixteenth century as a noun. Between the fourteenth and eighteenth centuries, it was widely used and considered neither dirty nor disreputable. Around 1795, it disappeared from the lexicon, not to surface again for another hundred years.[1]

Though people are in touch with it daily, they're pretty ignorant on the subject. They don't know **frog shit from pea soup** or **shit from Shinola** (both 20thC), leaving our luncheons in a state of confusion and our shoes with a terrible luster. Others **don't know sheepshit from cherry seed**, and **can't tell owl-shit from putty without a map** (both early 20thC, rural U.S.). Clearly, they need to brush up on their **scatology**, the study of same, from the Greek *skatos*, **shit**. If you **don't know shit**, it's time you learned.

A Matter of Give and Take

Shit is a deep subject, one with profound philosophical meaning. Whether to **give a shit** or **take a shit** is a matter of great debate. Much serious academic discourse has turned on that question. Some people don't **give a shit**. When asked why, they usually respond, "I gave at the office."

Taking a shit leaves us all in a quandary. Really, now, why would anyone **take a shit**? Yet people do it all the time. Right at this very moment, someone, somewhere is **taking a shit**. Graffiti on the wall of a bathroom at the City University of New York posed the question in somewhat dramatic terms: "If you **took a shit**, please return it. No questions will be asked."

There are many types of **shit**—**hot**, **silly**, **tough** (abbreviated as **TS**), **funny**, **simple**, and **regular**—just to name a few. When someone calls you a **real shit**, stand proud! Let's also not forget the non-secular variety. After all, some do it religiously, in which case it's **holy**. Apparently, theirs doesn't stink.

There are times when **the shit hits the fan**; a terrible crisis ensues and things turn nasty. You show fear by being **shit-scared**, **scared shitless**, **having the shit scared out of you**, or by simply **shitting in your pants**. When very afraid, magical things happen, and you might find yourself **shitting blue lights** or **rows of houses**. When registering alarm, shock, or anger, you might also **shit green**, or **little blue apples**. Those gifted with an exceptional constitution **shit a brick** (in Britain it's a **top-block**). This condition is known in medical circles as **constipation**, from the Latin *con*, together, and *stipare*, "crammed full." Doctors and medical professionals prefer **feces** (*faeces*, c. 1639) or **stool** (16thC). The **stool** originally described the piece of furniture on which one **shat**. Over time it came to be a verb, to **stool**, and today, a noun synonymous with the end product itself. The next time your doctor

On the night of June 25th, Colonel R.S. Henderson sat here, after eating a fine fish dinner, and deposited a soft tan stool.

      —*Colonel R.S. Henderson*
       Graffiti (1935), Maledicta

requests a **stool**, ask if he wouldn't prefer a winged-back chair instead.

Down to Earth

The animal kingdom is much more forthcoming, offering us **shit up gooch**, i.e., "a plenitude," of references, a **shit list** of sorts. The true **shit list** is a fancied or real accounting of those you hate or distrust. President Richard Nixon's seemingly endless **shit list** was one of the more prominent of the genre. This one is somewhat shorter. It features **rat shit**, "dislikable or disgusting"; **bat shit**, "crazy"; and **chicken shit**, "of little worth."[2] But when looking to register enthusiasm or excitement, there is only one way to go and that is **ape shit** (or just plain **ape**), though it can also make you irrational and drive you berserk. Looking to describe the depths to which another might sink? Liken their actions to **shark shit** (Australian) or **whale shit**, there theoretically being nothing lower at the bottom of the ocean.

Most popular of all, however, are **horse shit** (many times preceded by **happy**) and **bullshit** (often shortened to **bull**), used to describe nonsense or pretentious talk, a form of personal expression perfected by the **bullshit shooter** or **bullshit artist. Bullshit** is the sine qua non of politics. The word, however, is shunned in print. As reported by the press: "Treasury Secretary Paul O'Neill used a **barnyard epithet** during an interview to dismiss any claim by anyone able to predict the course of the economy or the state of the budget 10 years in advance."

My contribution was the witticisms; yours the shitticisms.
  —Robert Frost to Ezra Pound,
    correspondence, 1936

Shitticism: A scatological figure of speech.
  —OED

Getting the Drop On

Animals, however, show no such restraint. They are in fact quite generous, freely leaving their **calling** or **visiting cards** (19thC), gracing the landscape with a surfeit of **road-apples** (20thC), **horse-chestnuts** (20thC), **buffalo-chips** (19th–20thC), **meadow-muffins**, and **pasture-paddies** (all 20thC).

Circuses and zoos attach value to it, requiring that visitors pay for packaged **pachyderm poop** and **dromedary doody** (both 20thC) to energize their suburban lawns. For this they are quite grateful. But city-dwellers can live without **dog-doo**. Alas, pet-owners don't give a **shit**, but their pets do. Their only hope rests with a renewed sense of civic responsibility and an appliance known as the **super-dooper-pooper-scooper-picker-upper** (1970s).

Animal **shit** is usually referred to as **dung**. It's a word that's been with us since before the year 1000 and the answer to the riddle posed by Monty Python, "What is brown and sounds like a bell?"

Dropping By

Our fine feathered friends also do their part. **Guano** is a natural fertilizer made from bird droppings, a prized commodity during the nineteenth century and traded by Europeans and Americans. It helped build countries like Peru, expanded empires such as the United States, and made companies and individuals involved extremely rich. Yet people consider it of dubious value. Don't tell that to the birds however. In the days of the horse and carriage, things were **shit for the birds** (early 20thC), referring to the horse droppings from which they extracted the seeds. We later shortened the expression—meaning things worthless—to "for the birds."

After the Fall

Farmers know it more commonly as **manure** (16thC), an abbreviated form of *manoeuvre*, Old French for "to work with one's hands." Its original meaning was "to cultivate the land" and later "to fertilize" it, before finally becoming the fertilizer itself. To President Harry Truman, the word was synonymous with both politics and farming, "**manure, manure**, and more **manure**." Hearing the President extol its virtues thus caused a staid spectator to comment to Truman's wife, "You should teach Harry to say 'fertilizer,' not **manure**." To which Bess responded, "You don't know how long it took me to get him to say **manure**."

Much has been written of the pleasure of sexual intercourse; as for me, give me a solid movement of the bowel.

—Samuel Johnson

Down in the Dumps

The only true synonyms we have for the human variety are **crap, feces, ordure,** and **excrement. Excrement** stands for a host of things given off from the body.[3] Finding the list too all-encompassing, we simply reduced it to **just so much shit.**

   Ordure (c.1380) comes from the Old French *ordure*, "filth," from the Latin *horridus*, "dreadful," leaving us feeling "horrid." **Crap**'s our most common word (18thC), derived from the Middle English *crappe*, for "rubbish," or the Dutch **krappe**, for **excrement.** People once **did** or **had a crap** (19thC), before finally learning how to **take one** (20thC).

   Bringing up the rear is the **turd,** an old-timer dating back to the tenth century with the notable distinction of being the only word for **shit** that can be used in the singular. For other expressions, we turn to the nursery. There you'll find some **cradle-custard** (20thC), otherwise known as **cack** (19thC) or **caca,** from the Latin *cacare*, "to **defecate**," as well as some **do-do**—the cry of the toilet-training mother: "Do, please do!"

A Royal Mess

Caca is even in the history books. The first public act of the son of Louis XIV, the Dauphin, was to answer a call of nature before a court of dignitaries, who dutifully and enthusiastically applauded its appearance. It was only a matter of days before the textile makers of Paris started producing and marketing cloth with a fashionable brown hue, promoted as "**Caca**-Dauphin." Critics might **poo-poo** all the above (from the 19thC **po-pou**, for a **chamber-pot**) or simply say "**Poppy-cock!**" (from the Indo-European **pap** and **kak**, for soft and sticky **shit**), in which case they'd be perfectly correct.

Foreign Bawdies

English has no monopoly in such matters. There are also folks screaming "**Merde!**" running madly to the facilities to effect a simple act of **defecation**. They're in serious trouble, **in deep shit**, or as the French say, "On est dans la **merde**."[4] In Modern German, the vulgar noun for **shit** is *scheisse*, and the verb is *scheissen*. In English, it contributed to the construction of all those shyster lawyers hounding us as well as providing us with a proper response to them: "Erzähl mir nicht solche **scheisse**," "Don't tell me such **shit**."

Medieval German is also a good source for **shitty** words. Many went on to become an integral part of Yiddish, later finding a home in the American slanguage. Their roster includes **dreck**, used in such remarks as "You shtick (piece of) **dreck**, you!" and "This book is nothing but **dreck**!" It also provided the verb *kacken*, "to **shit**," which helped make things **farkackt**, "**shitty**" or completely "**fucked up**," as well as creating the **kacker** or "**shithead**." It also left us with what the male of our species is destined to become— an **alter kacker** (aka A.K.), literally an "old **crapper**," a crotchety, fidgety, old man.

Eating One's Words

Though most of us are full of **it**, we still get upset when someone tells us to "Eat **shit**!" The classic rejoinder to this request is, "And what shall I do with your clothes?" The act, however, is not without historical precedent. Those in the American armed services during WWII remember eating **shit on a shingle**, creamed chicken or creamed or chipped beef on toast, while British recruits dined on **shit on a raft**, beans on toast. Sergeants also constantly reminded them to wipe that **shit-eating** grin off their face. How **shit eating** leads to gloating or an expression of satisfaction, however, shall forever remain a mystery.

W. A. Mozart

Andante
Lick my sweet ass

Andante
Lick my ass grand- ly

Allegro ma non troppo
Oh dear- est friend I beg— of—
you Do lick me quick- ly quick- ly in the
ass Oh lick Oh lick— Do lick me quick- ly
quick- ly in the ass

May cause intestinal cramping and anal leakage
—Olestra warning on potato chip bag,
1998

There are only two reasons to sit in the back of an airplane. Either you have diarrhea or you're anxious to meet people who do.
—Henry Kissinger

Eating **shit** is called **coprophagy**, from *kopros*, Greek for **dung**. The sixteenth-century alchemist Paracelsus suggested it as an aphrodisiac for one's intended love. Others picked up on the idea, preparing special cakes of **dung**, the dough of which was rolled with the bare buttocks. The idea, however, never caught on, most considering it a half-baked, if not **half-assed**, notion. Bloom in *Ulysses* and Mozart and Hitler in real life had an appetite for such stuff. Larry Bird of the Boston Celtics once proclaimed publicly that Moses Malone of the Houston Rockets also partook, causing a considerable uproar in NBA circles. Generally speaking, however, **coprophagy** is not considered to be in good taste.

At Loose Ends

Uh-uh! It seems you're coming down with the **whiffle-waffles** (19thC), the **gripes** (17thC), the **colly-wobbles** (19thC) or the **mulligrubs** (16th–20thC). There's a queasiness in the stomach, rumblings of **flatulency**, or as they liked to say in eighteenth-century England, "You've got a **rumpus in yer chittlins.**" What can you say when life's got you on the **runs** (19th–20thC)? There's the **squitters**, the **scoots** (20thC), or the **thorough-go-nimbles** (c. 1694). If you're feeling adventurous, a **bad case of the wild squirts** or the **screaming shits** ("Ai-i-i-e-e-e!"). In a lighter mood, trip the light fantastic with a nimble **quickstep** (early 20thC), **the back-door trot** (the **BDT**), the **trots** (c. 1870), or the **Aztec Two Step** (20thC). Formally speaking, you've got **diarrhea**, from the Greek *diam*, through," and *rheim*, "to flow." More crudely, you're now **up shit creek without a paddle** or, more eruditely, **up a fecal estuary without any means of locomotion**, "facing some pretty serious difficulty." Plans for your trip abroad apparently have failed to firm up. You've encountered **Montezuma's revenge**, **the touristas** (both mid 20thC), the **GIs** (either from "Gastro-Intestinal" or "Government Issue" or a combination of both, WWII), and **Delhi-belly** (20thC). Alas, there's no time to speak of **diarrhea** (14thC), never mind spell it properly.

John Locke, the great eighteenth-century philosopher, believed that our thought processes accurately reflect our bowel habits. Firm **turds** mean firm reasoning ability, solid analysis, and coherency of thought. Loose **stools** equal loose ideas and sloppy logic. Apparently, it's time we all **got our shit together** (1960s).

As you can see, there's no escaping it. Whether traveling on **Hershey Bar Road** or up **Dirt Alley**, you're always on **Shit Street**.

Enough! Let's **cut the shit** already. Given that **fuck** and **shit** are our two most popular obscenities, there's no more powerful form of dismissal than screaming "**Fuck this shit!**" and moving on.

Good Riddance

Disposing of our subject matter is quite another matter. The great myth of our culture is that **shit happens**, a belief the populace proudly proclaims from the bumpers of their cars. The harsh truth, however, is that it is an act of conscious and deliberate will. You **defecate** (c. 1864), **excrete** (c. 1668), take an **Irish shave** (early 20thC), **squat and grunt, do** or **take a dump** (20thC), or **make potty** (a **potty** being a children's **chamber-pot**, one in which you make **iddie-biddie-diddies**). You can also **bury a quaker** (not from the religious sect but from the shivering and shaking required), or **chuck a turd** (both 19thC). The challenge, though, is not only to **do your job** (late 19thC) but to do it diplomatically. "Excuse me I have to...

Obey the call of nature (c. 1747)

Water my horse (18thC)

See a man about a dog (19thC)

Dance my dance (17thC)

Pluck a rose (18thC)

Pick a daisy (c. 1860)

Post a letter (20thC)

See my Auntie (c. 1850)

Go and sing sweet violets (19thC)

Powder my nose or puff

Wash my hands

Dispatch my cargo

Go to the bank and make a deposit

Cash a check

Look at the crops

Feed the goldfish

Pay my doctor's bill

Retreat to my sanctum sanctorum (all late 19th–
early 20thC unless otherwise noted)

Give a Chinaman (or ethnic person of your choice)

a music lesson

Write a Jew (or ethnic person of your choice) **a letter**
(both early 20thC and both now politically incorrect).

However quaint these sentiments, they fail to meet the needs of the current generation. Up-dating them a bit, politicians could be **issuing press-releases**, Generals **doing a body-count**, race car drivers **making a pit-stop**, and writers **banging out a story**. Street people, of course, could just be **doing their thing**. Computer geeks? **Developing new software**. What else?

Doctors have to _____   Policemen have to _____

Plumbers have to _____   Actors have to _____

Carpenters have to _____   Lawyers have to _____

A favorite activity of Kinky Friedman, Western singer and mystery writer extraordinaire, is to **take a Nixon**. Feel free to introduce your own favorite politician or newsmaker into the mix. Submit your entry now. **Dump your Enron stock? Evacuate a Taliban?** What have you? Skeptics should simply **relieve themselves of their doubts. Void** (15th–16thC) where prohibited by law.

Your Patriotic Doody

Be that as it may, it's no cause for complacency. These are, after all, perilous times which call for action. During the 1952 campaign when Ike was indecisive about including Richard Nixon on the ticket, Nixon told him, "There comes a time in matters like this when you've either got **to shit or get off the pot.**"

If you gotta go, you gotta go. Do not pass go. Do not collect your two hundred dollars. This is a national emergency. It's time to mobilize the troops and **go to siege** (c. 1400). And this means you! You may not know **squat**, the position ultimately naming the end product itself. But everyone has to **do their duty** (also **doody**, 19thC). Women and children will have to **evacuate** (c. 1667) or have a **clear-out** (c. 1923). Young or old, we all have **obligations to discharge** (19thC). It's time to truly **give a shit**, "to show that you care, really care."[5]

National security's a messy job—especially when handled by the FBI and the CIA. The authors of *End Product*, the definitive study of **shit**, recalled an incident they heard recounted during a Senate investigation of civil rights violations by the two agencies.

A bulldog veteran of J. Edgar's days was washing his hands at a sink in the Senate Building during a hearing recess. A dapper man stepped out of one of the stalls, and looking with distaste at the FBI agent, moved directly to the door. The agent at the sink spoke into the mirror at the retreating gent: "In the FBI they always taught us to wash our hands after we **did a job**." The man at the door turned, pointed a sheaf of sworn statements at the bulldog and replied, "In the CIA they taught us not to get **shit** on our fingers."

Detritus

1.   Its origins can be found in the Indo-European *skei-*, "to divide," a variant of *se*, "to cut" or "cutoff," as in "sect," "bisect," and "scissors." In fact, it began life in the Old English verb *scitan*, "to divide from the body," later appearing as *bescitan*, "to befoul" (beshat). The *c* functioned as a *k* in Old English, but altered to the sound *sh* before vowels *e* and *i* in passage to Middle English, giving us *shitten*, "to shit."

      The *c* retained the *k* sound, however, in passing into Scottish and other dialects such as Erse, the most common forms being *skate, skite,* and *scut,* all which in addition to referring to anything in the vicinity of the **anus** or any "expulsion of the **anus**" also carried the meaning of "dirty," "cheap," or "low." Hence an old Scottish remark, "He played me daughter Kate a fearful skite," translates as "He played a **shitty** trick on her."

It was left to John Ciardi, poet and linguist, to further fill in the dots, making the connection to a **cheapskate** (a cheap shit, i.e., "the lowest of the low"), a **blatherskite** or **bletherskate**, "a noisy shit," and the **scut** of a rabbit or deer, its "tail," the part nearest the **anus** as well as the scut of a boat, an old term for the stern, i.e., "the rear of the ship." This also made for **scut** work, that which is unpleasant, drudging, and dirty, such as that which is done in hospitals where chores such as **urinalysis**, collecting **stool** samples, and other "dirty" jobs are often recorded in what is called a "scut book." Pretty **deep shit**, you say? You can always discount the above, writing it off as so much **scuttlebutt**.

2. There is nothing more **chickenshit** than the press. On April 11, 1997, the "Drudge Report" summarized how various editors handled the reporting on an exchange of words a day earlier on the House floor between House Majority Whip Tom DeLay (R-Texas) and Rep. David Obey (D-Wisconsin): *Boston Globe*: During a debate on campaign finance, DeLay "erupted" as Obey displayed "an article from two years ago alleging that lobbyists had written legislation in DeLay's office." DeLay: "That's **chicken shit**." *Washington Times*: Obey raced over to DeLay and "poked a finger at him." DeLay then "shoved him back with both hands and could be heard in the gallery saying 'gutless **chickenshit**'." *Roll Call*: Quotes Obey, who says DeLay "poked me in the chest and called me a lying **chicken-shit**." *Los Angeles Times*: DeLay "directed a profanity." *New York Times*: "chicken droppings." *Philadelphia Inquirer*: "chicken s-t." *Wall Street Journal*: "chicken (expletive)!" *USA Today*: "chicken-." *Washington Post*: The two "engaged in animated discussion." The *Milwaukee Journal Sentinel* quoted Obey: "He put his finger firmly in my chest — twice — and said, 'You're a gutless chicken (expletive).' "

3. Technically speaking, excrement includes blackheads, breastmilk, dandruff, earwax, feces, fingernails (when cut), hair (when cut), menstrual effluvium, nasal phlegm, pus, saliva, scabs, semen, squamous cells (when shed), sweat, tears, urine, and vomitus.

4. In 1966 *The Realist* magazine reported that the name for the new Rolls Royce was to be the *Silver Mist,* but that was before someone noticed that *mist* was German slang for **shit**. After

throwing a brief **shit-fit**, the marketing people **shit-canned** the idea, transforming the vehicle into the *Silver Shadow*.

5.   **Shit** is now right up there with **fuck** and **cocksucker** as the most daunting of words to get by network censors. But, as they say, **shit** happens. And what better place than in the rough and tumble world of professional sports? The ABC network is the first known network to have aired the word when during a Monday Night Football game Al Michaels said it quite bluntly to Dennis Miller.

     The record for the greatest number of **shits**, however, rests with Comedy Central's "South Park"—162 times in a single episode, validated by a counter in the corner of the screen. It happened when the fictional police show "Cop Drama" aired **shit**, causing the once taboo word to become commonplace, people now using it in virtually every situation. This coincides with a mysterious plague that begins to befall the world. Hoping to better understand what's going on, the children do some research and learn that the reason cursewords are called that is because if they are misused, a curse is brought down upon its users. Meanwhile, use of the word continues to spiral out of control. The network commits to "Must **Shit** TV," demonstrating the lengths to which its executives will go for ratings. Fearful of the consequences, Chef and the children go to the network to try to get them to stop. The network refuses. The network head says **shit** enough times to evoke a beast from hell, which appears in the studio. Chef and the boys, however, come to the rescue, joining forces with the 14th-century knights of standards and practices and a magical rune stone to defeat the monster. The forces of good prevail. The network agrees to follow the guidance of the knights of standards and practices, and the kids end the show with a plea to everyone to begin watching what they say, using **shit** only in extreme circumstances.

     The most interesting reaction to the episode came from the Los Angeles based Parents Television Council (PTC), which declaired that the show "obliterates any television decency standards." As an example, they cited the conversation between two of the kids, Stan and Cartman:

> Stan: Now that shit's out, it isn't fun to say it anymore.
> Cartman: Yeah, they've taken all the fun out of shit.
> We're gonna have to start saying other words like
> (bleeped) cock and (bleeped) fuck.

     Taking it literally, PTC responded, "If someone doesn't take a stand, this endless crusade on the part of the creative community to constantly push the envelope of taste and decency will continue until there are no standards left." No **shit**, guys, maybe next time you'll even consider watching the show.

Using Your Head

I t's obviously time to ask for **the facilities**, the **lavatory** (or the abbreviated **lav**)—an old nineteenth-century word from the Latin *lavatorium*, "a place for washing." Hoping to disguise your mission, you might request **the place where you cough** (c. 1920). Speaking more directly, the **shithouse** (19thC), the **can** (c. 1900), or the **head**. Why the **head**, when "tail" is more appropriate? It could be from the manner with which many relate to authority—a political statement of sorts. Or, as is more likely, from the location of the ship's **facilities**—in the "bulkhead."

When all is said and done, most Americans need room to do it. Today's favorites include **wash-rooms** (c. 1878), **bath-rooms** (c. 1850s), from a time when the necessary fixtures joined the bath, and **powder-rooms**.[1] **The little girl's room** (c. 1940s) is still with us today, though its counterpart, **the little boy's room**, is seldom referred to. Dual-room names continue to dominate the landscape of restaurants nationwide: **His 'n' Hers**, **Gents and Ladies**, **Gulls and Buoys**, **Lads and Lassies**, and **Braves and Squaws** (Ugh!).

Many prefer the **restroom**. But if you asked for it in England, your hosts would likely point out the cloak-room or show you to the bedroom. Perhaps you thought yourself couth by not asking for the **toilet** (c. 1820s–30s), or one of its mutant off-spring the **toidy** or **toy-toy** (20thC), but the **toilet** still works fine there among the working-class. The **toilet** derives from the French **toilette**, the diminutive of **toile**, the cloth once covering the table on which sat one's preparations, making it all very acceptable.

Drop Everything

The British middle-class, however, prefers the **loo** (early 20thC), though its origins remain somewhat of a mystery. Some think it derives from the cry "Gardez l'eau!" "Mind the water!"—a warning to look out below, supposedly from the days before modern plumbing when emptying chamber pots from upper-story buildings was a

Stand clear, it's shorter than you think.

Ladies will please remove their hats during the performance.

—Wit and Wisdom from the W.C.

Behold the Coward and the Brave
The haughty Prince, the humble Slave
Physician, Lawyer, and Divine
All make oblations at this Shrine
                    —*Jonathan Swift*

Pushes.

No. 1141.

commonplace occurrence. Others suggest it is a misreading of room number 100, supposedly a common European **toilet** designation. Alas, the most popular designation there is "00" (zero, zero).

A more exotic theory traces it to Bourdaloue, a long-winded eighteenth-century Jesuit who ended up naming a china **urine** receptacle to be slipped between a woman's legs. So proper was the **loue** (the shortened version, popular during the 18th and 19thC) that it could even be used in public when the lady was wearing full skirts.

Have all these possible derivations only further muddied the waters? In lieu ("the place" and yet another possibility) of the **loo**, there's always the **water-closet** (**les water** in France) dating from around 1755 when it first moved into the house from outside, most commonly referred to today as the **WC** (19thC).

House Calls

Early on, we sounded the alarm with the **gong** (c. 1000) as recorded in Chaucer's "The Parson's Tale," the **gong-house** being a much-visited place until passing into obsolescence around 1800. In a more contemporary vein, we had *The Gong Show* (TV, c. 1970s), noted for its high ratings and low humor. Though it had no direct ties to **the gong**, it's now apparent where the show's host, Chuck Barris, got most of his material.

The **gong** was followed by the **privy** (c. 1375, a "private place"), your basic **out-house**, later called a **siege** (c. 1400), a **siege-house** (c. 1440), or a **siege-hole** (c. 1447), this at the time when man had difficulty distinguishing his **ass** from a hole in the ground. When inclement weather struck or a certain urgency was felt, things often went to **pot** indoors.

For comfort sake, we added a **stool** or **stool-of-ease** in which we enclosed a **chamber-pot**, giving us **a close(d) stool** (all 16thC). Oft-times you couldn't tell it from another fine piece of furniture so well was it disguised. Two centuries later we topped it with the fancy name, **commode**.

As late as the seventeenth century, however, things continued to be bogged down, what with the **boggards**, or the **bog-houses**, dotting the landscape. But we also had the **latrine** (c. 1642, army use), a shortened form of the Latin **lavatrina**, "washbasin," whose basic item was the bucket.

During WWI, British soldiers called it the **furphy** after its manufacturer, **Furphy** and Co. Its simplest incarnation, the **honey-bucket**, was never to be confused with m'lady's **honey-pot** (early 18thC) from *The Erotic Tongue*. If it didn't suit you, you could always fall back on the **master can** (18thC).

Throughout all of this, we never lost sight of our purpose, placing our treasures in **a (necessary) vault** (c. 1609), a **necessary**

house or a **necessary place**. By the eighteenth century it had become just **necessary**; a hundred years later, a **convenience**.

Classier designations soon followed, including the **chapel**, **the house** or **place of ease**, **The House of Commons**, **the throne**, and **where the Queen goes on foot** (all 19thC and all very British). The English always enjoyed mixing metaphors of waste and politics. Unfortunately American have not been so inclined. Perhaps it's time to reconsider, given all the **shit** that goes down in Washington.

What's in a Name?

For that personal touch, we also associated the receptacle with real people. President John Quincy Adams laid the foundations of American foreign policy. He also installed the first toilet into the White House, making **Quincy** (early 19thC) a household word.

The most popular name, some claim, was derived from the developer of the modern flush toilet, Thomas Crapper, who during the 1870s was issued patent number 4,990 for his "Crapper Valveless Water Waste Preventer."[2]

The **crapper** is now coin of the realm. But in the 1890s, women spoke of having to **spend a penny**. To meet her needs and those of men as well, we developed the public **washroom** (c. 1878) and the **public comfort station** (first appearing in print in 1904 in *The New York Evening Post*)—what the British called a **public convenience** and the French, according to Mencken, a **Vespasienne** (c. 1920s). Vespasian was the Roman Emperor who forced his citizens to pay to use the city **latrines**, thus introducing the first **pay-toilet** (20thC) to the civilized world. How soon they forget!

You Name It, It's Yours

First names also had their moment. The first indoor **privy** with flushing arrangements was invented in 1596 by Sir John Harrington, a godson of Queen Elizabeth. He announced his invention to the world in a volume punningly entitled "A New Discourse on the Stale Subject called the Metamorphosis of Ajax." Ajax was a famous Greek warrior, but as employed in England of the time he was pronounced "age-aches."

On a more familiar level, it translated into a **Jakes** (c. 1530), **Jake's place** (mid 18thC), and the **Jacques** (a cultured **Jakes** perhaps?). We've also had the **jerry-come-tumble**, the **Harry**, **Sir Harry**, the **Joe** (c. 1840–50s, U.S.), and today's favorite, the **John** (18thC), once also known as **cousin John** and **Sir John** (19thC). **John** has a fine old history, dating back to at least 1735, when one of the regulations issued at Harvard stated, "No Freshman shall go into the Fellow's **John**."

DRAWN HALF SIZE

No. 231

Mencken pointed out how **Johnnie** was the vogue for college girls back in the twenties, with **George** and **Fred** having their moments as well. Really now, can Bernie, Melvin, and Sidney be far behind?

Tonight Show host Johnny Carson, however, was not about to take any such **shit**. When the manufacturer of portable **toilets** came out with the new "Here's Johnny" line, Carson responded by suing for 1.1 million dollars in damages, claiming use of the phrase by the **toilet** company constituted a trademark infringement, unfair competition, and a violation of Carson's rights of publicity and privacy. In a landmark decision, the Court ruled in favor of the manufacturer—leaving Johnny open to a lifetime of public abuse. When reporters sought out his reaction, Carson allegedly responded, "It's never fun being dumped on."

Detritus

1. According to H.L. Mencken, "During the days of prohibition, some learned speak-easy proprietor in New York hit upon the happy device of calling his **retiring-room** (c. 1848) for female boozers a **powder-room**."

2. We refer those skeptics who think him a product of this author's warped mind to Crapper's published biography entitled *Flushed with Pride*. One reviewer wrote, "Although this book has the ring of a classic hoax, the author presents ample evidence that this man not only lived but made a lasting contribution to mankind's comfort."

There are those who think it simply coincidental that the receptacle came to be known as the **crapper**, like having a surgeon named "Cutter." The evidence speaks for itself. Though **crap**—as noted earlier—has long been a fine old English word, **crapper** was seldom if ever employed; nor had it been recorded earlier in dictionaries of slang or common usage. It only came into vogue during the nineteen-twenties and only in America.

Its origins are indisputable. Crapper's firm did a lot of work in military hospitals and barracks during WWI. It was clear from the markings on the units that they were manufactured by one T. Crapper of Chelsea; it being commonplace to have the manufacturer's name prominently displayed on their product. The device caught the fancy of American soldiers stationed in England during the war, many of whom were from rural America and knew only of outdoor **privies**. Taken with this new-fangled invention, they then brought the name back home with them, making the **crapper** a distinctly American word.

The Sound and the Fury
(the little f)

n act 3 of *The Comedy of Errors*, Dromio of Ephesus remarks to Dromio of Syracuse, "A man may break a word with you, sir, and words are but wind, Aye, and break it in your face, so he break it not behind." **Breaking wind** (c. 1852) is a task of herculean dimensions; **farting** is so simple even a child can do it. Yet most folks would rather die than **fart**.

> If death must come as often as breath departs
> Then he must die, who often farts;
> And if to die be to lose one's breath
> Then death's a fart; and so a fart is death.
>
> —*The Erotic Muse* (1735)

There are those who consider it one of the most offensive and repugnant words in the English language. Some think it may even give the **Big F** a run for its money. Closer study, however, reveals that the fear of the **fart** is blown far out of proportion. Admittedly not the most genteel of words, it does have a playful dimension. Though hard to imagine, it also has legitimate roots. They can be found in the old Sanskrit word *pardate*, "he **breaks the wind**." There is also a clear line from the Old English *feortan* to the Middle English *farten* to today's **fart**. The **fart**'s been around for quite a while. According to the OED, its first documented use occurred around 1250. Chaucer used it in 1386 in *The Summoner's Tale* and in his *Miller's Tale*, where he wrote, "He was *somdel squaymous of farting*." He then relates an incident in which Nicholas plays a cruel joke on poor Absolon by **farting** in his face. Not particularly pleased by the act, Absolon retaliates, applying a hot poker to Nicholas' **ass**.

Since Chaucer's time, the word has been a favorite of many English satirists. Ben Jonson and others used it freely. Samuel Johnson's dictionary of 1751 included it, citing a quotation from Jonathan Swift to illustrate its use: "So from my Lord his passion broke. He **farted** first and then he spoke."

> When your dinners are hearty with onions and beans,
> With garlic and claret and bacon and greens
> Your bowels get so busy distilling a gas
> That Nature insists you permit it to pass.
> You are very polite, and you try to exhale
> Without noise or order—you frequently fail—
> Expecting a zephyr, you carefully start
> But even a deaf one would call it a fart!
>
> —"Ode to Those Four-Letter Words"

Gone With the Wind

The **fart**'s fine lineage not withstanding, other reference works have been more standoffish. The esteemed *Oxford English Dictionary* unequivocally declared **fart** "not fit for proper use." Nobody knows why the OED chose to close down this innocuous form of personal expression or how the decision was made. One can only imagine a group of eminent scholars gathered in their ivory tower, deliberating upon the fate of words, having a beer or two, and shooting the breeze.

> "Personally, I favor letting off some rectal steam."
> "No, no! I much prefer an anal escape of wind."
> "Really gentlemen, it's hard to top voiding wind from the bowels."
> "All in favor of the fart..."

Having to give us something to do, they finally agreed to let us **have the vapors** (16thC–19thC), "supposed emanations from internal organs or from substances within the body."

Does the Australian **gurk** sound any better? Yet etymologist Richard Spears, in his classic dictionary of slang and euphemism, organized his synonyms (all 76 of them) for **breaking wind** under that particular obscurity, defining the category as "to release intestinal gas audibly." Anything to avoid giving the **fart** its proper due.

And so the **fart** fell from grace—expelled from polite society and relegated to second-class status. **Farting around** (c. 1900) came to signify purposelessness; anything overly pretentious was **arty-farty**." **Farting off** (c.1968) made you inattentive and neglectful, leading to one blunder after another, causing you to **fart away** (c.1928) or squander your opportunities.

The Random House Dictionary of the English Language defined a **fart** as "an irritating or foolish person." One in his dotage was written off as an **old fart**. Worthless items and activities were **not worth a fart in a windstorm** (both 20thC). And when your mind went blank and you did something incredibly dumb, or experienced an inexplicable aberration in your software program, you had a **brainfart** (c. 1983). "I normally remember my social security number, but I had a **brainfart**."

Even young children eschewed the **fart**, preferring instead to **poop**, from the great all-purpose word for the stern of a ship that through the years has stood for the **rear end** as well as all activity generated therein (**shitting**, 20thC, **farting**, 18th–20thC).

Excessive **farting** is called **flatulence**, from the Latin *flatus*, "a blowing or breaking of wind." Around 1711, it attained figurative status, signifying "vanity" or "pomposity." More recently, the medical profession joined academicians in declaring it a legitimate ailment.[1]

If the OED had hoped by its actions to suppress the **fart**, they failed miserably. A vocal minority continued to **fart** in the face of official opposition; others went so far as to pop off in public. The scholars meanwhile persisted in the belief that they had curbed the practice, when, as everybody knows, they had simply blown it.

Blowhards

The fart, however, continued to remain a matter of deep philosophic speculation. Buried deep in the bowels of the *Phenomenology of Spirit* is a pointed but obscure reference to it. After discussing the differences between the universal and individual consciousness from the point of view of utility, Hegel wrote, "The beyond...hovers over the corpse of the vanished independence of real being...merely as the exhalation of a stale gas, of the vacuous *Etre suprême.*"

Men of letters also paid homage to it, including such disparate spirits as Shakespeare, Robert Burns, Jonathan Swift, D. H. Lawrence, and J. D. Salinger.

> All of a sudden, this guy sitting in the row in front of me, Edgar Marsella, laid this terrific fart. It was a very crude thing to do, in chapel and all, but it was also quite amusing.
>
> —Holden Caulfield, *Catcher in the Rye* (1951)

Ben Franklin, in a scatological masterpiece now in the Library of Congress, underscored the need of mankind to express such "scentiments," calling upon our finest minds to come up with a drug which when mixed with food would "render the **natural discharge of wind** from our bodies not only inoffensive, but agreeable as perfume." Arguing as to how the invention was critical to human happiness, he concluded with the thought that when this discovery was made, the sum total of all the knowledge prior to it in comparison would scarcely be worth a "fart-hing."[2]

It seems remarkable that given the on-going assault on the human body directed by Madison Avenue and the "better living through chemistry" crowd that nobody has taken Dr. Franklin up on his challenge and that such a product is not yet on the market.

One can only imagine what copy editors from the top agencies might come up with, penning such lines as "for the **fart** who has everything" and "the **fart** beautiful." and product names such as "Wind-X," "X-scent," or "Scentimentally yours." Dreams aside, we do have **Beano** (1990s), a few drops of which promise to still those carbohydrate-eating bacteria and "sotto voce" most **musical fruits**. Alas, the odor remains as challenging as ever.

That Certain Something in the Air

Farts come in all sizes and shapes. They range from the simple **whiffle** (18thC, a small whiff?) to the real **gasser** (20thC). Though

It's okay to fart in public as long as you don't giggle.

—Grace Slick of the Jefferson Airplane

their presence is easily detectable, they often come disguised. Germans say "**Er hat einen toten Vogel in der Tasche**," "He has a dead bird in his pocket." English-speakers of the eighteenth century **burnt bad powder**. Most people today **cut the cheese, cut it**, or **cut one** (all 20thC). And we don't mean cheddar. But care is indicated: if you cut things too close, you're could also **cut your finger** (20thC). More cautious types, hoping to avoid injury may simply **lay one**, conveying a gentler and less violent connotation.

The London Blitz

The British reduced the **fart** to basics, what with the **bip, biff, framp, parp**, and **poot**, but **trumped** (18th–20thC) all others with their animal references. "**There goes a mouse on a bicycle!**" they call out (the Irish prefer, "**There goes another seagull!**"), alerting us also to other potential hazards such as **low flying ducks, stepping on a toad, shootin' bunnies**, and **barking spiders**. Often it's put in the form of a question: "**Who stepped on the duck?**" or "**Who let fluffy out?**" The answer? "Oops! **I let fluffy off the leash.**"

Bring it up again, and let's vote on it.
—Adolescent Humor, 1950s

Bombs Away

All **farts** fall into the category of **back-talk** (20thC). Some are soft-spoken (**SBD, silent but deadly**, mid 20thC), others **silent but violent** (**SBV**, 20thC). One can barely hear anyone **dropping a rose** (20thC), which by any other name would still not smell sweet.

Many, though, are of a more explosive character. Beware of lovers who greet the day with some **morning thunder** (20thC). Hold on to your hat when your neighbor has **a blow-off** or **lets fly a rouser** (sometimes a **fat-one** or a **fat 'un**, 19thC), also known as a **hinderblast** (mid 16thC), a **razzer**, or a **rattler**. It's MAYDAY when he lowers the **sonic boom** (20thC). Take cover from approaching **scud missiles** (1980s).

Shake, Rattle, and Roll

Such **farts** carry with them major life lessons. They alert us to danger lest one be "hoisted on (or with) one's own **petard**." The **petard** derives from the Latin **pedare**, "to fart," related to the French, **péter**, with that same meaning. As a weapon of war, it was an ancient short-fused time bomb or grenade often used to blast a hole in castle walls. It was deployed with great risk. If the soldier placing the charge didn't get away soon enough or if the fuse was faulty, he could be severely wounded or even killed by the exploding **petard**. The phrase then came down to us metaphorically, alerting us to situations which must be handled with care—those times when we might be caught in our own trap or when a plan of our own making might backfire on us.

> Let it work;
> For 'tis the sport to have the engineer
> Hoist with his own petard; and't shall go hard
> But I will delve one yard below their mines,
> And blow them at the moon...
> ——Shakespeare, *Hamlet*

More recently, Neil Simon, in his play *Biloxi Blues*, suggested that one of the soldiers could **pass** enough **gas** to blow up the world in a barracks discussion of what one might do with their last week on earth. Thankfully, some explosive charges just fizzle out. In the eighteenth and nineteenth centuries, a **fizzle** was an inaudible **fart**, derived from *fist*, "to break wind," from the Middle-English word *fisten*. *Fisten* originally meant "to **fart** quietly," allowing one to exit with a whimper rather than a bang.

Facing the Music

Not to fear. This too shall pass. Sit back, relax, and enjoy a unique musical interlude as a close friend **winds up his horn** (18th–mid 19thC) or sounds the **back-door trumpet** (mid 19thC). Occasionally the **bum-fiddle hits a sour note** (late 17th–early 19thC); for the most part, though, it's quite entertaining. **Honk** (20thC) if you love **ars musica** (late 18th–19thC).

Whereby hangs a tail, sir?
...By many a wind-instrument that I know.
—Shakespeare, Othello

Ars musica, a.k.a. **anal audio** (20thC), made its cinematic debut in Mel Brooks' *Blazing Saddles* (1974). In a ground-breaking scene, the cow-pokes are gathered about the campfire eating beans when they suddenly break into a unique musical medley. Beans have traditionally inspired **Ars Musica**; accordingly, they are known as **musical fruit** and **whistle berries** (20thC). Alas, commercial TV was not so inspired. When the film was first edited for home use, the censors experienced a major sense of misdirection, depicting the men as belching rather than **farting**.

Farting had established itself as an art form long before Mel Brooks. Joseph Pujol (1857–1945) was a **fartist** extraordinaire. As a young man, he realized he could do what few others could. He was able to take enough air into his rectal orifice to produce sounds through his **anus** that would last ten or fifteen seconds, producing a strong note ten or twelve times running—sans odor. Hoping to go public with his unique talent, he searched long and hard for a stage name.

> Open the dictionary and what do you read? Péteur (farter), "someone who has the habit of farting." Should he call himself le péteux? Insulting expression—to go like a péteux (coward) is to leave without dignity...It would have to be

something else. Then he had an inspiration of genius; he would call himself Le Pétomane. The new title would offend no susceptibilities and could be announced in any drawing room. Words have their own dignity.[3]

—*Le Pétomane*

Performing at the Moulin Rouge and other major night clubs in Europe, Le Pétomane became the greatest stage attraction of the Gay Nineties and the toast of the continent. Playing his instrument to perfection, he produced a variety of noises and sounds for his audience's pleasure—favorite tunes of the day, musical instruments such as the violin, the bass, and the trombone, and weaponry such as machine guns and cannons. After smoking a cigarette thus, he capped the evening with his pièce de résistance—blowing out a candle thus from a foot away. Each night he brought the house down, receiving—what else but—a thunderous ovation.[4] What a unique talent was Pujol's! How ironic that he had to toot his own horn when his accomplishments spoke so eloquently for themselves.

All my life I shall never forget the first time I ever saw him or the second time I heard Him...astonishing...marvelous...sublime! Never had I been carried so high into the Ether of art...never, never, never...

—Anonymous comedian, quoted in *Le Pétomane*

The great one is now only a dim memory. Mel Brooks paid homage to him by naming the Governor in *Blazing Saddles*, William J. Le Pétomane. Others picked up the challenge. Pujol's legacy today lives on in the person of one, Mr. Methane (after one of the key components of the **fart**) who claims to be the world's only performing **flatulist**. You can check out his credentials at www.mrmethane.com.

Let My People Go!

Farts are a repressed minority. The mouth gets to say all kinds of things, but the other place is supposed to keep quiet. But maybe our lower colons have something interesting to say.
—*Mel Brooks, 1974*

Farting is not just light entertainment. It has its serious side as well. Since the days of ancient Greece, it's been a source of fresh ideas and the enemy of tyrants and dictators. French essayist Montaigne wrote in chapter XII of his Essays, *Apology for Raimond Sebond*,

Metrocles broke wind a little carelessly while disputing in the presence of his school and hid himself in his house for shame, until Crates came to visit him, and, adding to his consolation and arguments the example of his own freedom starting to break wind in rivalry with him, relieved him of that scruple; and besides, drew him to his own Stoical sect, which was freer, from the more polite Peripatetics, whom he had followed till then.

As a mode of personal expression, constitutionalists consider it a form of free speech under the protection of the First Amendment.

Some, however, draw the line at inciting social revolution. There is no right to yell "**fart!**" in a crowded theater. In Spain, when you **fart**, you "**free the prisoner.**" Why fight it? If you don't let him go, he's likely to escape anyway. Once released, you'll find him an articulate spokesman for his cause: when **brother round-mouth talks** (18thC) people listen. You there! **Silence in the court, my bum's about to speak** (British, 20thC).

Concluding our study of *Bawdy Language*, we end on a high note with "Gute Fahrt!"—which is not what you think but only the German way of saying "bon voyage." Better yet, with the title of a work by Chicago poet, Shéree Anne Slaughter— *May the Fart Be With You.*

Detritus

1. Thanks to medical science we learn that the normal person **farts** 14 times daily on average. A 1976 paper entitled "Studies of a **Flatulent** Patient" described a record setting 34 **events** in 24 hours. The least **Vesuvian** person remains officially undetected.

2. Franklin was not alone. Mark Twain's *1601* (written between *Tom Sawyer* and *Huckleberry Finn*) features a meeting between Queen Elizabeth, several literary dignitaries, and members of the court. The story centers around a monstrous **flatulence** cut loose during the course of the session, as described by one William Shaxpur: "Heaven's artillery hath shook ye globe in admiration of it." Described as "an exciting and exceeding mightie and distressful stink," the Queen adds, "Verily in mine eight and sixty yeres have I not heard the fellow to this **fart.**"

   She asks who produced it. Raleigh admits to it and apologizes profusely. "Then delivered he himself of such a godless and rock-shivering blast that all were fain to stop their ears, and following it did come so dense and foul a stink that which went before did seem a poor and trifling thing beside it."

   Another literary figure enamored with the power of the **fart** was François Rabelais who immortalized the one cut by Pantagruel in *The Histories of Gargantua and Pantagruel*: "… with the fart he blew, the earth trembled for twenty-seven miles round, and with the fetid air of it he engendered more than fifty-three thousand little men, misshapen dwarfs; and with a poop, which he made, he engendered as many little bowed women, such as you see in various places, and who grow, except downwards like cows' tails, or in circumference, like Limousin turnips. 'What now,' exclaimed Panurge. 'Are your farts so fruitful? By God, here are fine clumpish men, fine stinking women. Only let them be married together, and they'll breed horse-flies.' So Pantagruel did, and called them pygmies."

3.   Pujol's discounted choices included a *péteur* (fem. *péteuse*) a "sorry person;" a *péteux*, a "coward," and a *pétesec*, a "stiff, unkind fellow"—all unhealthy character traits traced to a simple act. The **fart** itself is **le pet**, lending a whole new meaning to a "pet peeve."

4.   His was, however, a somewhat rocky career. According to *Le Petit Journal*, in 1894 he had, on a lark, performed independently at the gingerbread stall in the outdoor market, unknowingly breaching his contract with his employer.

> When the Director of the Moulin Rouge heard of this escapade, he had the idea of going after him and bringing him back with some well placed kicks...in his musical area; but on reflection and not wishing to damage the instrument, he has preferred the law to stick its nose in the affair, and is claiming the 3,000 francs fine, stipulated in the agreement.

Pujol lost his court case and had to pay up. Legal precedent had been established precluding this man's right to **fart** in public. He was further challenged by imposters, primarily a woman billing herself as "the Female *Pétomane*." A quick enquiry, however, showed her to be a fraud, working with a pair of bellows hidden beneath her skirt. Disgraceful!

Afterword

n Medieval times, the Lord in power frequently issued edicts called **bans** for a variety of purposes, the most important of which was to conscript men for battle. All called were expected to comply. One shirking his duty was considered outside the **ban**. This made for the French *bannir*, "to proclaim," labeling him an outlaw, leading to his **banishment** and making him a **bandit**, from the Italian *bandito*.

Over time, the **ban** evolved from a proclamation to a prohibition. In our culture we primarily **ban** ideas. Words such as those which make up the body of this book are often the subject for **banning**, making writers outlaws of sorts.

The lord's **banal** rights also gave him exclusive control of everything on his estate: the ovens, mills, storage facilities etc., and the right to decree who used them—conditions set forth in the **bans**. There were **bans** for everything, even for formal notice of intended marriage, as when they posted the **banns**. Covering so many situations, and issued with such frequency, the **ban** came to be considered commonplace or trite. Yet another **ban**...ho-hum. This explains how those working to **ban** ideas and works of art today would merely substitute their own **banal** stuff in its stead.

Equally **banal** is the senseless bombardment of these words and their cheap exploitation. Knights once raised the flag of their sovereign lord in tribute to him. It was called a **banner**. The word is now considered a symbol of principles, making for **banner** headlines and **banner** years—proclaiming things "leading" or "foremost." These are **banner** years for dirty words. Never before have they had it so good. The French gave us *mettre à bandon*, "to put under another's control," hence to give it up. **Abandon** the principle of freedom of expression to the self-styled lords of morality? **Banish** the thought. But let us also raise high the **banner** of taste and creative use of language for all words, bar none.

That anyone should pass up the well established colloquial words of the language and have recourse to the Latin,
"defecate," "urinate," and "have sexual intercourse," is indicative of grave mental health.
                                                    —Allen Waker Read

Bibliography

Ammer, Christine. Editor. *The American Heritage Dictionary of Idioms*. Boston: Houghton Mifflin, 1997.

Angier, Natalie. *Woman: An Intimate Geography*. New York: Houghton Mifflin, 1999.

Arango, Ariel. *Dirty Words: The Expressive Power of Taboo*. Northvale, NJ: Jason Aronson, 1989.

Asimov, Isaac and John Ciardi, eds. *Limericks: Too Gross*. New York: W.W, Norton, 1978.

Badcock, Jon (Jon Bee). *Dictionary*. 1823.

Bailey, N. *The Universal Etymological English Dictionary*. London: J.J. & P Knapton (et al), 1721, reprinted by George Olms Verlage, 1969.

Barnhart, Robert, editor. *The Barnhart Concise Dictionary of Etymology*. New York: Harper Collins, 1995.

Baring-Gould, William S. *The Lure of the Limerick*. New York: Clarkson N. Potter Inc., 1967

Barrère, Albert and Charles G. Leland. *A Dictionary of Slang, Jargon, and Cant*. Two volumes. London: The Ballantyne Press, 1889–90.

Bartlett, John. *The Shorter Bartlett's Familiar Quotations*. Edited by Kathleen Sproul. New York: Pocket Books, 1953.

Berrey, Lester V. and Melvin Van den Bark. *The American Thesaurus of Slang*. New York: Thomas Y. Crowell, 1953.

Bloomfield, Leonard. *Language*. New York: Rinehart and Winston, 1961.

Boyer, Paul S. *Purity in Print*. New York: Charles Scribner's Sons, 1968.

Brasch, R. *How Did Sex Begin?* New York: David McKay, 1973.

Brenton, Myron. *Sex Talk*. New York: Allison and Busby, 1973.

Brooks, Mel. *Blazing Saddles*. Los Angeles: Warner Bros., 1974.

Bruce, Lenny. *The Essential Lenny Bruce*. Complied and edited by John Cohen. New York: Ballantine, 1967.

Brusendorff, Ove and Paul Henningsen. *A History of Eroticism (Victorianism)*. New York: Lyle Stuart, 1966.

Bryson, Bill. *Made in America: An Informal History of the English Language in the United States*. New York: William Morrow and Co., 1994.

Bryson, Bill. *The Mother Tongue*. New York: William Morrow, 1990.

Burke, W.J. *The Literature of Slang*. New York: N.Y. Public Library, 1939.

Burns, Robert. *The Complete Poetical Works of Burns*. Boston: Houghton Mifflin, 1897.

_____. *The Complete Works of Robert Burns*. Boston: Phillips, Sampson, 1857.

Burroughs, William S. *Naked Lunch*. New York: Grove Press, 1966.

Cary, Henry N. *The Slang of Venery and its Analogues*. Chicago: Privately Published, 1916. 3 vol. (vol. iii being entitled *Synonyms of the Slang of Venery*).

Carlin, George. "Seven Dirty Words You Can't Say on TV." Comedy monologue from *Class Clown*, New York: Little David: 1973.

Carlin, George. *Napalm and Silly Putty*. New York: Hyperion, 2001.

Cassidy, Frederic G., editor, *Dictionary of American*

Regional English, Vol.1. Cambridge: Harvard University Press, 1985.

Chapman, Robert L., editor, *New Dictionary of American Slang*, New York: Harper &Row, 1986.

——. *Roget's International Thesaurus*, Fifth Edition. New York: Harper Collins, 1992

Ciardi, John. *A Browser's Dictionary*. New York: Harper & Row, 1980.

——. *A Second Browser's Dictionary*. New York: Harper & Row, 1983.

——. *Good Words to You*. New York: Harper and Row, 1987.

Claire, Elizabeth. *Dangerous English*. New York: Eardley, 1980.

Coffin, Tristam Potter. *A Proper Book of Sexual Folklore*. New York: Seabury Press, 1978.

Cole, William. *Erotic Poetry: The Lyrics, Ballads, Idylls, and Epics of Love*. New York: Random House, 1963.

Colman, E.A.M. *The Dramatic Use of Bawdy in Shakespeare*. White Plains, NY: Longman, 1974.

Comfort, Alex. *The Joy of Sex*. New York: Crown, 1972.

Cragie, Sir William and James R. Hurlburt, editors. *A Dictionary of American English on Historical Principles* (four volumes). Chicago: University of Chicago, 1938–44.

Cray, Ed. *The Erotic Muse*. New York: Oak Publications, 1968.

Crotty, Jim. *How to Talk American*. Boston: Mariner Books, 1997.

Dawson, Jim. *Who Cut the Cheese: A Cultural History of the Fart*. Berkeley: Ten Speed Press, 1999.

DeBeauvoir, Simone. *The Second Sex*. New York: Bantam, 1967.

Delaney, Janice, Mary Jane Lupton, and Emily Toth. *The Curse: A Cultural history of Menstruation*. New York: E.P. Dutton & Co., 1976.

deRopp, Robert S. *Sex Energy*. New York: Dell, 1969.

DeVere, M. Schele. *Americanisms: The English of the New World*. New York: 1872.

Dickson, Paul. *Slang!* New York: Pocket Books, 1990.

Dillard, J. L. *Black English: Its History and Usage in the United States*. New York: Random House, 1975.

——. *American Talk: Where Our Words Come From*. New York, Vintage Books, 1977.

Dunbar, William. *The Poems of William Dunbar*. Edited by James Kinsley. New York: Clarendon Press, 1979.

Edwardes, Allen. *The Jewel in the Lotus*. New York: Julian Press, 1959.

——. *Erotica Judaica: A Sexual History of the Jews*. New York: Julian, 1967.

—— and Masters, R.E.L. *The Cradle of Erotica*. New York: Bantam, 1977.

Eisiminger, S. "Colorful Language," *Verbatim*, 4:1, 1979.

Ellis, Havelock. *On Life and Sex*. New York: Garden City Publishing, 1937.

Ellis, Jeremy R. *Talking Dirty: Slang, Expletives, and Curses From Around the world*. Secaucus, NJ: Carol, 1996.

Evans, Ivor H., editor. *Brewer's Dictionary of Phrase and Fable*. Cassell, 1981.

Farmer, J.S. and W.E. Henley. *Slang and Its Analogues Past and Present*. Seven volumes, 1890–1904. London: Reprinted by Kraus Reprint Co., 1974.

Farmer, John S. *Vocabularia Amatoria*. 1896. Reprinted. New York: University Books, 1966.

Feiffer, Jules. *Carnal Knowledge*. Avco Embassy Pictures Corp., 1971.

Ferraro, Susan. *Sweet Talk: The Language of Love*. Simon and Schuster, 1995.

Fessler, Jeff and Karen Rauch. *When Drag is Not a Car Race: An Irreverent Dictionary of Over 400 Gay and Lesbian Words and Phrases*. New York: Fireside, 1997.

Finley, Harry. *Museum of Menstrual History and Women's Health*. March 2002. http://www.mum.org.

Flexner, Stuart Berg. *I Hear America Talking: An Illustrated History of American Words and Phrases*. Simon and Schuster, 1976.

——. *Listening to America: An Illustrated History of Words and Phrases from Our Lively and Splendid Past*. New York: Simon and Schuster, 1982.

——. *Speaking Freely: A Guided Tour of American English from Plymouth Rock to Silicon Valley*.

(with Anne H. Soukhanov) New York: Oxford University Press, 1997.

Forget, Carl, *Sex-Lexis*, March 2002. http://www.sex-lexis.com.

Foucault, Michael. *The History of Sexuality*, Vol. 1 Pantheon, 1978.

Franklyn, Julian. *A Dictionary of Rhyming Slang*. London: Routledge & Kegan Paul, 1981.

Freud, Sigmund. *The Complete Psychological Works*. New York: Norton, 1976.

Freyer, Peter. *Mrs. Grundy: Studies in English Prudery*. New York: Corgi, 1965.

Friedman, David. *A Mind of Its Own: A Cultural History of the Penis*. New York: The Free Press, 2001.

Friedman, Kinky. *Steppin' On A Rainbow*. New York: Simon and Schuster, 2001.

Genevieve. *Merde: The Real French You Were Never Taught in School*. New York: Fireside Books, 1998.

Gerber, Albert. *The Book of Sex Lists*. New York: Ballantine, 1984.

Ginzburg, Ralph. *An Unhurried View of Erotica*. New York: Grove, 1958.

Goldenson, Robert and Kenneth Anderson. *Sex A to Z*. New York: World Almanac, 1989.

Goldman, Albert, from the journalism of Lawrence Schiller. *Ladies and Gentlemen—Lenny Bruce!!* New York: Penguin Books, 1991.

Goldstein, Al. *The Classic Book of Dirty Jokes: Anecdota Americana*. New York: Bell Publishing, 1981.

Gover, Robert. *One Hundred Dollar Misunderstanding*. New York: Ballantine Books, 1961.

Graves, Robert. *Lars Potsena or The Future of Swearing and Improper Language*. London: RKP, 1936.

Green, Jonathan. *The Dictionary of Contemporary Slang*. Pan, 1984.

_____. *Slang Through the Ages*. Chicago: NTC, 1997.

Greer, Germaine. *The Female Eunuch*. New York: Bantam, 1970.

Grose, Captain Francis. *A Classical Dictionary of the Vulgar Tongue*. London: 1788. Third edition, edited by Eric Partridge. Reprint, New York: Barnes and Noble, 1963.

Hall, Susan. *Gentlemen of Leisure*. Signet: New York, 1972.

_____. *Ladies of the Night*. New York: Trident, 1973.

Hegeler, Inge and Sten. *An ABZ of Love*. New York: Alexicon, 1967.

Henke, James T. *Courtesans and Cuckolds*. Garland, 1979.

Hoffman, Paul and Matt Friedman. *Dictionary Shmictionary*. New York: Quill, 1983.

Hurwood, Bernhardt. *The Golden Age of Erotica*. New York: Sherbourne, 1965.

Iceberg Slim. *Pimp, the Story of My Life*. Los Angeles: Holloway, 1967.

Joffe, Natalie. "The Vernacular of Menstruation." *Word*, Volume 4, Number 3 (1948).

Johnson, Falk. "The History of Some 'Dirty' Words." *American Mercury*, l. LXXXI, no. 323, pp.538–45. Nov. 1950.

Johnson, Samuel. A *Dictionary of the English Language*. Ayer, 1980.

Joyce, James. *Ulysses*. New York: Random House, 1918.

Kahn, Susan. *The Kahn Report on Sexual Preferences*. New York: Avon, 1981.

Kanner, Leo. "A Philogical Note on Sex Organ Nomenclature." *Psychoanalytic Quarterly*, vol. XIV, no. 2, pp. 228–33. 1945.

Katz, Jonathon Ned. *Gay/Lesbian Almanac*. New York: Harper, 1983.

Keyes, Ralph. *Nice Guys Finish Seventh*. New York: Harper Collins, 1992.

Kiefer, Otto. *Sexual Life in Ancient Rome*. New York: Abbey Library, 1976.

Kimball, Nell (Stephen Langstreet, ed.). *Her Life as an American Madam by Herself*. New York: Grove, 1970.

Kochman, Thomas. *Rappin' and Stylin' Out: Communication in Urban Black America*. Urbana, IL: University of Illinois Press, 1972.

Kronhausen, Eberhard and Phyllis. *Pornography and the Law: The Psychology of Erotic Realism and Pornography*. New York: Grove, 1972.

Kunitskaya-Peterson, Christina. *International Dictionary of Obscenities*. Oakland, CA: Scythian Books, 1981.

Lakoff, George, and Mark Johnson. *Metaphors We Live By*. Chicago: University of Chicago Press, 1980.

Landau, Sidney I. "Sexual Intercourse in American College Dictionaries," *Verbatim* 1:1, 1974.

Landy, Eugene E. *The Underground Dictionary*. New York: Simon & Schuster, 1971.

Lawrence, D. H. *Lady Chatterley's Lover*. New York: New American Library, 1959.

Legman, Gershon. *Rationale of the Dirty Joke: An Analysis of Sexual humor*. New York: Bell Publishing Company, 1975.

_____, editor. *The Limerick*. New York: Bell Publishing Company, 1964.

Lewin, Esther and Albert E. Lewin, eds. *The Random House Thesaurus of Slang*. New York: Random House, 1988.

Lewis, C.S. "Four Letter Words." *Critical Quarterly*, vol. III, no. 2, pp. 118–22. Summer 1961.

Lighter, Jonathan Evan, editor. *Random House Historical Dictionary of American Slang, Volume 1, A–G*. New York: Random House, 1994.

_____. *Random House Dictionary of American Slang, Volume II, H–O*. New York: Random House, 1997.

Loth, David. *The Erotic in Literature*. Julian Messner, 1961.

Lukas, J. Anthony. *The Barnyard Epithet and Other Obscenities*. New York: Harper & Row, 1970.

Macdonald, James. *The Wordsworth Dictionary of Obscenity and Taboo*. London: Wordsworth, 1996.

MacDougald, Duncan, Jr. "Language and Sex." Albert Ellis and Albert Arabanel, eds., *The Encyclopedia of Sexual Behavior*. London, 1961, vol. II, pp. 585–98.

Macrone, Michael. *Naughty Shakespeare*. Kansas City: Andrews and McMeel, 1997.

_____. *Wicked Words*. New York: Crown, 1989.

Major, Clarence. *Dictionary of Afro-American Slang*. Chicago: International, 1970.

Maledicta: The International Journal of Verbal Aggression. Maledicta Press, 1977-1982, 1996.

Marks, Lara V. *Sexual Chemistry: A History of the Contraceptive Pill*. New Haven: Yale University Press, 2001.

Marvell, Andrew. *The Poems and Letters of Andrew Marvell*. Edited by H. M. Margoliouth. New York: Clarendon, 1951.

Matthews, Mitford M. *A Dictionary of Americanisms* (two volumes). Chicago: University of Chicago, 1951.

McConville, Brigid, and John Shearlaw. *The Slanguage of Sex*. New York: Futura, 1985.

McDonald, James. *A Dictionary of Obscenity, Taboo, and Euphemism*. New York: Sphere, 1988.

Mencken, H. L. *The American Language*. New York: Knopf, 1977.

_____. *Supplements I and II to The American Language*. New York: Knopf, 1978.

Miller, Casey and Kate Swift. *Words and Women*. New York: Doubleday, 1977.

Miller, Henry. *Tropic of Cancer*. New York: Grove, 1961.

_____. *Tropic of Capricorn*. New York: Grove, 1961.

_____. *The Rosy Crucifixion: Book Two, Plexus*. New York: Grove, 1965.

Mills, Jane. *Womanwords*. New York: Virago, 1991.

Montagu, Ashley. *The Anatomy of Swearing*. New York: Macmillan, 1967.

Neaman, Judith and Carole Silver. *A Dictionary of Euphemisms*. New York: Unwin, 1983.

Noble, Sidney. *A Simple Dictionary for Gay Slang*. November 2001. http://gsa global.net/jargon/.

Nohain, Jean and F. Caradec. *Le Pétomane*. New York: Barnes and Noble Books, 1993.

Olive, David. *Business Babble: A Cynic's Dictionary of Corporate Jargon*. New York: John Wiley and Sons, 1991.

Oxford Dictionary of English Etymology. New York: Oxford University Press, 1966.

Oxford English Dictionary, with new supplements on CD. New York: Oxford University Press, 1994.

Partridge, Eric. *Words, Words, Words!* London: Routledge & Kegan Paul, 1933.

_____. Origins: *A Short Etymological Dictionary of Modern English*. Routledge & Kegan Paul, 1958.

_____. *A Dictionary of Slang and Unconventional English*. Seventh edition. New York: Macmillan, 1970.

_____. *Shakespeare's Bawdy*. London: Routledge & Kegan Paul, 1968.

_____. *Slang Today and Yesterday*. Fourth edition. New York: Barnes and Noble, Inc, 1970.

_____. *Dictionary of Historical Slang*. New York, Penguin, 1972.

_____. *A Dictionary of Catch Phrases*. New York: Stein and Day, 1977.

The Pearl: The Underground Magazine of Victorian England. New York: Grove, 1968.

Pearsall, Ronald. *The Worm in the Bud: The World of Victorian Sexuality*. New York: Penguin, 1983.

Pei, Mario. *Double-Speak in America*. New York: Hawthorne, 1973.

Perrin, Noel. *Dr. Bowdler's Legacy*. New York: Atheneum, 1969.

Phythian, B. A. *A Concise Dictionary of English Slang*. London: Hodder & Stoughton, 1973.

Plath, Sylvia. *The Bell Jar*. New York: Bantam Books, 1971.

Pomery, Sarah B. *Goddesses, Whores, Wives and Slaves: Women in Classical Antiquity*. Philadelphia: Schoken Books, 1975.

Random House Dictionary, Second Unabridged Edition. New York: Random House, 1987.

Randolph, Vance. "Verbal Modesty in the Ozarks," *Dialect Notes*, vol.VI, pt I, pp.57–64. 1928.

Rawson, Hugh. *A Dictionary of Euphemisms and Other Doubletalk*. New York: Crown, 1981.

Read, Allen Walker, "An Obscenity Symbol." *American Speech*, vol. IX, no.4, pp. 264–78. December 1934.

_____. *Classic American Graffiti*. Santa Rosa, CA: Maledicta Press, 1977.

Rees, Nigel. *Phrases and Sayings*. London: Bloomsbury, 1995.

Reisner, Robert. *Graffiti: Two Thousand Years of Wall Writing*. London: Frederick Muller, 1974.

Reisner, Robert. *Great Wall Writing and Button Graffiti*. New York: Canyon Books, 1967.

Reisner, Robert. *Selected Scrawls From Bathroom Walls*. New York: Parallax, 1967.

Reisner, Robert & Wechsler, L. *Encyclopedia of Graffiti*. New York: Macmillan, 1974.

Reyburn, Wallace. Flushed with Pride: The Story of Sir Thomas Crapper. London: Macdonald, 1969.

Richter, Alan. *The Language of Sexuality*. New York: McFarland, 1987.

_____. *Sexual Slang*. New York: Harper Collins, 1993

Rossi, William A. *The Sex Life of the Foot and the Shoe*. New York: Ballantine, 1978.

Rosten, Leo. *Hooray for Yiddish!* New York: Simon and Schuster, 1982.

_____. *The Joys of Yiddish*. New York: McGraw-Hill, 1968.

Sabbath, Dan and Mandel Hall. *End Product: The First Taboo*. New York: Urizen Books, 1977.

Sagarin, Edward. *The Anatomy of Dirty Words*. New York: Lyle Stuart, 1962.

Salinger, J. D. *The Catcher in the Rye*. Boston: Little, Brown, 1959.

Seaver, Richard and Austin Wainhouse. *The Complete Marquis de Sade*. New York: Grove Press, 1965.

Shakespeare, William. *The Annotated Shakespeare*. Edited by A. L. Rowse. New York: C.N. Potter, 1978.

Sheidlower, Jesse, editor. *The F Word*. New York: Random House, 1999.

Sherman, Alan. *A Gift of Laughter*. New York: Atheneum Publishing, 1965.

_____. *The Rape of the A*P*E*: The Official History of the Sexual Revolution*. New York: Playboy Press, 1973.

Shipley, Joseph. *Dictionary of Word Origins*. New York: Barnes and Noble, 1995.

Skeat, Walter W., ed. *The Complete Works of Geoffrey Chaucer*. New York: Clarendon Press, 1915.

_____. A Concise Etymological Dictionary of the English Language. New York: Perigee, 1980.

Smith, Ron. *The Bedside Book of Celebrity Sex Quizzes*. New York: Crown, 1984.

Speaight, George, editor. *Bawdy Songs of the Early Music Hall*. London: Redwood Burn Ltd. Trowbridge & Esher, 1975.

Spears, Richard. *Slang and Euphemism*. Middle Village, New York: Jonathan David, 1991.

Stallworthy, Jon, editor. *A Book of Love Poetry*. New York: Oxford University Press, 1974.

Tabori, Paul. *The Natural Science of Stupidity*. Philadelphia: Chilton, 1959.

_____. *The Art of Folly*. Philadelphia: Chilton, 1961.

_____. *The Humor and Technology of Sex*. New York: Julian, 1969.

Tannahill, Reay. *Sex in History*. New York: Stein & Day, 1982.

Thomas, Donald. *A Long Time Burning: The History of Literary Censorship in England.* London: Frederick A. Praeger, 1969.

Thorne, Tony. *Bloomsbury Dictionary of Contemporary Slang.* London: Bloomsbury, 1990.

Tone, Andrea. *Devices and Desires: A History of Contraceptives in America.* New York: Hill and Wang. 2001.

Tulloch, Sara, editor. *The Oxford Dictionary of New Words.* Oxford University Press, Oxford, 1991.

Twain, Mark. *The Mammoth Cod.* Santa Rosa, CA: Maledicta Press, 1976.

Ullerstam, Lars. *The Erotic Minorities.* New York: Grove Press, 1966.

Urdang, Lawrence, Walter Hunsinger, Nancy La Roche, editors. *Picturesque Expressions: A Thematic Dictionary.* Gale Research, 1985.

Walker, Barbara G. *The Woman's Dictionary of Symbols and Scared Objects.* New York: Harper and Row, 1988.

Walters, Ronald, G. *Primers for Prudery: Sexual Advice to Victorian America.* New Jersey: Prentice-Hall, 1974.

Webster's Ninth Collegiate Dictionary. Springfield, MA: Merriam-Webster, 1983.

Webster's Third New International Dictionary. Springfield, MA: Merriam-Webster, 1976.

Wedeck, Harry E. *Dictionary of Erotic Literature.* New York: Citadel, 1982.

Weekley, Ernest. *The Romance of Words.* London: John Murray, 1917.

Wentworth, Harold, and Stuart Berg Flexner. *Dictionary of American Slang.* New York: Crowell, 1960.

Whitworth, John, editor. *The Faber Book of Blue Verse.* New York: Faber & Faber, 1990.

Wilson, Robert, editor. *Playboy's Book of Forbidden Words.* Chicago: Playboy Press, 1972.

Winnick, Charles and Paul M. Kinsie. *The Lively Commerce: Prostitution in the United States.* New York: Quadrangle, 1971.

Wylie, Phillip. *Generation of Vipers.* New York: Pocket Books, 1959.

Young, Wayland. *Eros Denied.* New York: Corgi, 1968.

Zacks, Richard. *History Laid Bare.* New York: Harper Collins, 1994.

Index: Personages And Works

Index: By Topic

About the Author

Lawrence Paros is a master teacher whose work in alternate education has received national recognition; an amateur neuroscientist who has helped design and market a unique device for the treatment of stress, and a professional writer, and self-described authority on language. His published works include numerous articles and a book on education, two earlier books on language, *The Great American Cliché* (Workman) and *The Erotic Tongue* (Madrona and Holt), and *Smashcaps,* a children's book (Avon). He is also a former op-ed page columnist for the Seattle Post Intelligencer and commentator on KUOW-FM, the NPR affiliate in Seattle.

His website, "A Word with You" (http: // www.wordwithyou.com) has garnered numerous awards and attracted more than a half million visitors since its inception. It has also inspired two self-published volumes *(A Word with You America),* one version of which is soon to be published in China. He is currently working on his magnum opus on education, *The Once and Future School: The Story of the Y. S.H.S.*

Paros is an avid crossword aficionado and lover of language. It can be said of him that he never met a word he didn't like, uncomfortable only with how some are used. He considers as "obscene" only those words uttered by government spokesmen and commercial hucksters. A cantankerous sexagenarian (what else?), he lives quietly on the periphery of Seattle Washington with his two cats and a teenage son to whom he is a constant source of embarrassment.